Ethan Brown

QUEENS REIGNS SUPREME

Ethan Brown writes about pop music, crime, and drug policy for publications such as *Wired, New York, Rolling Stone, The Village Voice,* and *GQ.* This is his first book. He lives in New York.

QUEENS
REIGNS
SUPREME

QUEENS REIGNS SUPREME

Fat Cat, 50 Cent, and the

Rise of the Hip-Hop Hustler

Ethan Brown

ANCHOR BOOKS

A Division of Random House, Inc.

New York

AN ANCHOR BOOKS ORIGINAL, NOVEMBER 2005

Copyright © 2005 by Ethan Brown

Grateful acknowledgment is made to Chaz Williams, on behalf of Black Hand Entertainment, for the use of Amazura Ballroom photos featuring DMX and Jay-Z, etc. Photos provided as a courtesy of Black Hand Entertainment. Other photos used by permission of: Curtis Scoon, for the photo of Curtis Scoon, Darren Ebron, and Bernie Mac; Raheem Tyler, for the photos of the Nichols family and friends; Shane Fells, for the photo of Maxine Peterson and the photo of Shane Fells, "Big Cee," and Gerald "Prince" Miller; and Fred Moore, for the photo of Tupac, Biggie, Fred Moore, and Randy "Stretch" Walker.

Cataloging-in-Publication Data for *Queens Reigns Supreme* is on file at the Library of Congress.

Anchor ISBN-10: 1-4000-9523-9
Anchor ISBN-13: 978-1-4000-9523-0

Author photograph © Kate Scott
Book design by Georgia Küng

www.anchorbooks.com

Printed in the United States of America
10 9 8 7 6 5 4 3 2 1

This book is dedicated to

the Snake Charmer,

southeast Queens'

preeminent street historian

CONTENTS

THE PLAYERS

Randy Allen: Former executive with RUN-DMC DJ Jam Master Jay's record label JMJ Records and member of hip-hop duo Rusty Waters.

Darryl "Homicide" or **"Hommo" Baum**: Stick-up kid murdered in June 2000 allegedly by the notoriously violent Brooklyn drug gang called Cash Money Brothers.

Charles Fisher: Former president of Rushland, a fan club that represented Rush Management artists RUN-DMC and LL Cool J. In the wake of Jam Master Jay's killing in the fall of 2002, Fisher started a tipline to solicit anonymous tips about the crime.

Donald Francois: Former employee of JMJ Records and Rush Management.

Jeff Fludd: High-profile Hollis resident who started a crew called Two-Fifth Down with Jam Master Jay and also road managed RUN-DMC.

Irving Lorenzo aka **Irv Gotti**: Music business entrepreneur born and bred in Hollis who rose from the ranks at record labels such as TVT and Def Jam to become the CEO of his own Def Jam–distributed imprint, Murder Inc. (Currently known as "The Inc.")

Christopher Lorenzo aka **Chris Gotti**: Irving Lorenzo's brother and vice president of The Inc.

Damion "World" Hardy: Ex-boyfriend of rapper Lil' Kim and allegedly the leader of a Brooklyn gang called Cash Money Brothers.

Douglas "Butta Love" Hayes: Highly respected Hollis resident who befriended RUN-DMC's Darryl "DMC" McDaniels and shielded him from neighborhood hustlers.

Curtis Jackson aka **50 Cent**: Small-time crack dealer turned superstar rapper. Sabrina, 50's mother, was a crack dealer and crack addict who worked in the shadows of a drug organization run by Lorenzo "Fat Cat" Nichols on 150th Street and Sutphin Boulevard in the South Jamaica section of southeast Queens.

Rodney Jones aka **Boe Skagz**: Nephew of Jam Master Jay and member of the hip-hop duo Rusty Waters.

Karl "Big D" Jordan: Road manager for RUN-DMC and former vice president at Rush Management. Jordan was also a onetime suspect in the murder of Jam Master Jay.

Karl "Little D" Jordan Jr: Son of "Big D" who was arrested in the May 2003 shooting of Jam Master Jay's nephew Boe Skagz.

Harold "Lovey" Lawson: Childhood friend of Jam Master Jay's who lived on Jay's 203rd Street block.

Randolph and **Lamont Lucas**: A pair of brothers from southeast Queens who killed a parole officer named Brian Rooney in 1985 at the behest of Lorenzo "Fat Cat" Nichols. Randolph also served as an informant in the federal criminal conspiracy case against Jimmy "Henchmen" Rosemond.

Howard "Pappy" Mason: Lieutenant in the drug organization run by Lorenzo "Fat Cat" Nichols who ordered the slaying of rookie cop Edward Byrne. Mason also ran his own drug gang called The Bebos.

Darryl "DMC" McDaniels: Hollis-born RUN-DMC MC and lyricist.

Kenneth "Supreme" McGriff aka 'Preme: The CEO of the crack-dealing crew called the Supreme Team. After his release from prison in 1995, he became a hip-hop entrepreneur who went into business with The Inc.'s Irving Lorenzo on a straight-to-DVD movie called *Crime Partners*.

Thomas "Tony Montana" Mickens: A *Scarface*-obsessed cocaine kingpin from the Springfield/Laurelton section of southeast Queens who amassed an empire of yachts, condos, and luxury cars.

Gerald "Prince" Miller: Nephew of Kenneth "Supreme" McGriff who ran the Supreme Team while McGriff was imprisoned.

Jason Mizell aka **Jam Master Jay**: RUN-DMC DJ from Hollis who was slain in his southeast Queens recording studio on October 30, 2002.

Freddie "Nickels" Moore: Hollis-bred former hustler and onetime manager of Tupac Shakur.

Lorenzo "Fat Cat" Nichols: The most feared and powerful hustler in southeast Queens. The Nichols organization not only netted millions from the sale of crack, cocaine, and heroin but also supplied competing crews such as the Supreme Team with drugs.

Ernesto "Puerto Rican Righteous" Piniella: Supreme Team strongman bred in South Jamaica.

Joseph "Bobo" or "Mike Bone" Rogers: High-ranking lieutenant in the Lorenzo "Fat Cat" Nichols organization.

Jimmy "Henchmen" Rosemond: Brooklyn-bred former hustler turned hip-hop producer and manager who has worked with everyone from Groove Theory to The Game.

Curtis Scoon: Former hustler from Hollis turned screenwriter and onetime suspect in the murder of Jam Master Jay.

Joseph "Run" Simmons: Hollis-born RUN-DMC rapper and lyricist.

Russell Simmons: Brother of Joseph "Run" Simmons and cofounder of the Def Jam record label and Rush Management.

Darnell "Nellie D" Smith: Onetime RUN-DMC DJ and crew member.

Eric "E Money Bags" Smith: Aspiring rapper and sometime hustler from the Lefrak City section of Queens who was murdered near a friend's home in southeast Queens in 1999. Kenneth "Supreme" McGriff allegedly ordered the killing of Smith in retaliation for the murder of Supreme Team associate Colbert "Black Just" Johnson.

Eric "Shake" Smith: Milwaukee, Wisconsin-based real estate broker and longtime friend of Jam Master Jay.

Randy "Stretch" Walker: Hollis-bred rapper and manager who befriended Tupac Shakur in the early 1990s and was killed near his home in southeast Queens during the fall of 1995.

Ronald "Tinard" Washington: Southeast Queens stick-up kid and onetime suspect in the killings of both Walker and Jam Master Jay.

Richard "White Boy Rick" Wershe Jr.: Caucasian cocaine kingpin (hence the "white boy" nickname) from Detroit who allegedly ran a multimillion-dollar auto theft ring with Lorenzo "Fat Cat" Nichols from a Florida prison. Longtime friend of rap-rock super-star Kid Rock.

Chaz "Slim" Williams: Hip-hop entrepreneur born in Harlem but raised in South Jamaica section of southeast Queens who mentored 50 Cent and worked with Kenneth "Supreme" McGriff on the *Black Gangster* soundtrack released in 1999.

Derek "Talib" Yancey: Friend and longtime associate of Curtis Scoon questioned by the feds during their investigation into Irving Lorenzo aka Irv Gotti and Kenneth "Supreme" McGriff.

PROLOGUE:
A Sit-Down with Gotti

Irv "Gotti" Lorenzo is ranting about the government with a ferocity and paranoia that are equal parts Oliver Stone and tinfoil-hat amateur conspiracy theorist. The plump, chipmunk-cheeked CEO of The Inc., the record label that counts Ashanti and Ja Rule among its R&B and hip-hop stars and has sold more than 14 million records, is sitting on an oversize brown leather desk chair in the company's cluttered offices at 440 9th Avenue near 34th Street on Manhattan's West Side. He is in the middle of a long, discursive tirade about the nearly four-year federal investigation into his music business empire.

The allegations against The Inc. (formerly Murder Inc.) include money laundering and drug trafficking, but when we met for a sit-down in late December 2004, an indictment had yet to be filed. It's only a matter of time; the prosecutor, Roslynn R. Mauskopf, is a tenacious U.S. attorney who has brought indictments in high-profile cases against defendants such as the pilot who crashed the Staten Island ferry and killed eleven passengers as well as Bonanno family capos. Despite his persistent protestations of innocence, Lorenzo seems to understand this.

"Let me ask you a question," Irv says, looking up from a desk covered with two-way pagers and cell phones. "This is the government, right? This isn't the NYPD. They killed JFK, the government killed JFK, that's pretty much common knowledge, right? I'm not saying anything crazy by saying that, right?" Before I can correct him, Irv continues: "I'm saying that to give you a parallel that the government can pretty much do anything they want to do. It's pretty safe to say that, right? They can start a war with Iraq or Iran, talk about weapons of mass destruction, take all of their oil, give fuckin' Colin Powell billions of dollars to do reconstruction. Everything I'm saying right now isn't a lie, right? This is factual shit, right?"

Irv pauses to answer a cell phone that rings, incongruously, with the tune of Soft Cell's eighties pop hit "Tainted Love." "I'm doing an interview," Irv barks into the phone and then slams it down. "They"—the government again—"can do whatever they want. They can rig elections. When fucking Gore beat them by the votes they say, 'No, fuck you! *Electorally* Bush won.' In the last election, it was Florida, but this time it's Ohio. We're thinking Orlando is the place but they're like"—Irv pantomimes a Republican operative conspiratorially picking up a phone—" 'Go to Cleveland!' " Irv lets out a loud, hiccupy cackle.

Even in the boastful world of hip-hop, Irv Lorenzo is known for having a monumental ego. After remixing a track for Jennifer Lopez (in which he convinced the Latina movie star and singer to use the word *nigga*, thus causing a huge controversy in the African-American community), Irv taunted Puff Daddy by telling him, "Puff, come listen to the new record I did with your old bitch." Irv's Mafia-inspired nickname—given to him by Jay-Z when the two were touring together in the early nineties—comes not from a reputation for street toughness but from his brassy, ballsy, bossy personality. Today, Irv is even more animated than usual. It's easy to understand why: Just a few weeks before our meeting, The Inc.'s bookkeeper Cynthia Brent and Ja Rule's manager Ron "Gutta" Robinson were indicted on money-laundering charges, the clearest sign yet that law enforcement's noose is tightening around Irv and his brother.

The producer and The Inc. impresario hasn't given any interviews about his legal troubles save a short, guarded Q&A with *The Los Angeles Times* in June of 2003, so to him our conversation may seem a rare opportunity to vent his frustrations with the seemingly unending federal investigation into his hip-hop empire. "I'm trying to paint a picture for you that the government can do whatever they want," Irv continues in a more reserved tone, becoming aware of how unglued his rant is starting to sound. "They've been investigating me for four years. They raided my office after two years. This will be going on—what—year number three, this will be the three-year anniversary of them raiding my offices, right? They've been on me four years and they just arrested . . . the bookkeeper!" He lets out a huge guffaw. "And Ja's manager. Do you think they wanted to arrest the bookkeeper and Ja's manager or do you think they wanted to arrest me?"

I want to tell Irv that federal investigations work very slowly and that the indictments of Brent and Robinson could mean that they will testify against him in exchange for reduced sentences. But before I can respond, Irv starts ranting again. "Skip all of the Cynthia Brent shit," he proclaims, waving his hands dramatically in the air, "the blockbuster shit is me, Irv Gotti walking outta here in handcuffs." This will be the first of many times in our conversation that Irv refers to himself in the third person. "So what I meant to say, after I painted this glorious picture of how the government has all these resources, they have all of these things at their fingertips, and they've been looking at me for four years and I'm still sitting here talking to you, I think that's so crystal clear that I didn't do anything. I think anybody with a small brain would say, 'They didn't lock this guy up yet—maybe this fucking guy didn't do anything?' Because you know what? They have snitches on file that everyone knows about, they have all of this shit and how come they can't find something to put together? This isn't a knock on them. I'm not saying this to antagonize them. I'm just saying this to say: 'Maybe I didn't do anything.' "

Irv leans in toward me, pushing aside everything scattered on his desk. "In a twisted way, I'm happy because now it will come to a fuckin' close," he says. "During this whole time I wanted the government to investigate. Because if this is what they're saying about me, please investigate. Get all of your snitches, get all of your informants, gather all of the information you can. Because I know sitting here once you got all of your information you gonna be like, 'Fuck, he didn't do nothing.' " It's the most conciliatory moment of the interview, but it doesn't last long once our talk turns to the focus of the investigation into The Inc.: Irv's ties to one of the most iconic drug kingpins from southeast Queens, Kenneth "Supreme" McGriff.

Two of the allegations against Irv, made by a special agent in the IRS's criminal investigations division, are that 'Preme provided start-up money for The Inc. in the nineties and that the drug kingpin served as muscle for the label, intimidating rival rappers and music business executives. The charges infuriate Irv, though not because he believes them to be wholly without cause. "It's not preposterous," Irv admits. "I can see what they're thinking." Instead, he seems to be upset that the feds believe a street hustler from the eighties, not Lorenzo himself, is responsible for The Inc.'s string of multiplatinum successes in the nineties and beyond. "Back in the eighties, 'Preme was the legend," Irv proclaims, thumping his desk with his fist loudly for effect, "but guess what? I'm the fucking legend now."

Irv's bravado is often reminiscent of both *Scarface* and *Sunset Boulevard* but there is a great deal of truth to it. During the eighties the crack epidemic brought mountains of cash to drug dealers big and small, thus making hustlers iconic. Though a few eighties-era MCs possessed a street pedigree—rapper Rakim famously rhymed, "I used to be a stick-up kid/So I think of all the devious things I did"— hip-hop and hustling inhabited separate social spheres. Street guys went about their business and ignored the hip-hoppers; they considered rappers soft and not street savvy, while the rap business, which struggled to make money at start-up independent labels such as 4th and Broadway, Tommy Boy, and Def Jam, seemed to them a grind with no real payday in sight. Meanwhile, hip-hoppers, particularly those who were teenagers in the eighties like Irv, looked up admiringly at drug dealers. They had the money, the luxury cars, the jewelry, the girls, the respect of the streets, all of the accoutrements that would come to define hip-hop's "bling" lifestyle in the late nineties.

Hip-hop and hustling were worlds apart, but their denizens shared the same neighborhoods and even the same blocks, especially in the place where Irv was raised, southeast Queens. During the eighties, the area was home to hip-hop pioneers such as RUN-DMC and Def Jam founder Russell Simmons, as well as notorious drug kingpins such as 'Preme and his homicidal nephew Gerald "Prince" Miller; Lorenzo "Fat Cat" Nichols and his cop-killing lieutenant Howard "Pappy" Mason; and Thomas "Tony Montana" Mickens. It was one of the most violent epochs in New York history, and the next generation of rappers and hip-hop executives—Irv, his older brother Chris, Curtis Jackson (aka 50 Cent), and Jeffrey Atkins (aka Ja Rule) among them—had a front-row seat to watch the neighborhood's violence and criminality.

When the bottom fell out on hustling at the beginning of the nineties thanks to tough, three-strikes sentencing; a rising body count from the crack wars; and law enforcement innovations such as COMPSTAT (a program that enabled cops to identify neighborhood trouble spots through computer-generated crime statistics and electronic mapping), hustlers looked to start a new life in hip-hop. Rappers, after all, had always been their most sympathetic audience. Hustlers became part of the ever-present hip-hop entourage or took on jobs as assistants, security guards, or managers. Hip-hop might have offered lower pay than hustling, but the risks associated with the streets were no longer worth the gamble.

It was a mutually beneficial relationship. Hip-hoppers needed hustlers to bolster their street cred, especially with the ascent of gangsta rap in the early nineties, which trumpeted values like realness and authenticity. Hip-hoppers inflated their street C.V.s (a stint pitching "nicks," or five-dollar bags of crack, became nearly as important as skills on the mic); assumed the personas of their favorite hustlers (one of The Inc.'s rappers renamed himself "Ronnie Bumps" after a southeast Queens heroin dealer of the same name); or, more often, wrote songs cataloging the misdeeds of eighties street legends.

Hustlers from the crack era—particularly those who reigned in southeast Queens—thus became part of a permanent hip-hop narrative. On 50 Cent's "Ghetto Qu'ran (Forgive Me)" the South Jamaica–bred MC rhymed about nearly every iconic southeast Queens hustler, including 'Preme, Fat Cat, and Tony Montana, and cited historic moments of their heyday such as the Supreme Team's brutal, execution-style slaying of Colombian cocaine distributors for a few kilos. On "Memory Lane (Sittin' in Da Park)," Nas reminisced about how "some fiends scream about Supreme Team, a Jamaica, Queens, thing" while on "The World Is Yours" he rhymed that he was "facin' time like 'Pappy' Mason." That Nas, who is from Queensbridge, not southeast Queens, would pay lofty tribute to hustlers from far outside of his own neighborhood is telling. "They was legends, myths," Irv says of southeast Queens hustlers, "like urban-legend myths."

The meeting of hip-hoppers and hustlers was a combustible one. Survival on the streets requires realistic, unvarnished assessments of hustles (and fellow hustlers), whereas hip-hop thrives on a romantic belief in the outsize urban-legend myths. Irv's naiveté about the legal ramifications of his relationship with 'Preme—which began at a chance meeting on a video shoot in the drug kingpin's former stomping grounds in South Jamaica—ultimately led to his undoing. Though they were both raised in southeast Queens, Irv and 'Preme came from starkly different backgrounds. Irv is, by his own admission, "from a great family with a mother and father, youngest of eight, never been convicted of a crime nor has anyone in my family been convicted of a crime." 'Preme, on the other hand, is an ex-con with numerous drug arrests on his record (including a conviction on a federal continuing criminal enterprise charge) and an extended family deeply immersed in the crack trade. For a while, the pair served each other's needs—Irv burnished his street cred while 'Preme polished his much-faded street rep and made some cash from his new hustle, hip-hop—but before long the feds were bearing down on them.

Even after the risks became clear, Irv never seemed able to separate himself from 'Preme: Just days after our sit-down, Troy Moore (the brother of 'Preme's street associate Tyran "Tah-Tah" Moore) and a low-level southeast Queens stick-up kid named William Clark were shot outside the midtown Manhattan nightclub LQ where The

Inc. hosted an album release party for Ja Rule's album *R.U.L.E.* Both men were shot with bullets from a .40 caliber automatic weapon; Moore survived a bullet wound to his stomach while Clark succumbed to gunshots to his buttocks and chest. Immediately after the shooting, law enforcement speculated that the killer (who still had not been caught as of late 2005) was looking to warn Tyran "Tah-Tah" Moore against testifying in the investigation into The Inc. But Moore had publicly declared his intention never to cooperate with the government even after he was arrested, but never charged, in the shooting of a police officer in August 2003. "It would be stupid to send a message to a man who is not cooperating by hurting a member of his family," Moore's attorney Marvyn Kornberg told the New York *Daily News*. "Something like that is liable to make him want to get even."

On the streets—and even on hip-hop shock-jock Wendy Williams's popular radio program—a more plausible motive surfaced, one that didn't involve Irv or his record label. Moore and Clark were career criminals in their late thirties who, after ambushing hip-hoppers for their jewelry at numerous parties during the fall of 2004, fatally chose a mark who was willing to put up a fight. This theory was given some credence in July 2005 when anonymous law enforcement sources told *The New York Post* that just before the LQ party, Clark had robbed the brother of rapper Foxy Brown. Unfortunately for Ja, however, the *Post* also reported that law enforcement suspected that one of his bodyguards was involved in the shooting and that he, like Irv, could face federal charges, including conspiracy to commit murder.

Justifiably or not, Irv found himself with another 'Preme-related stain, bringing even more unwanted attention to the already beleaguered Inc. camp. Real hustlers are accustomed to such cruel twists of fate, but Irv and Ja held on to a comic-book fantasy of Teflon dons who get away in the end, only to be celebrated by their loyal admirers. The story of southeast Queens and of any inner-city neighborhood is that hustlers almost always end up paying for their dominance on the streets with their lives or with lifelong prison sentences.

The hustlers of southeast Queens made nearly unprecedented sums of cash during their reign in the eighties and became heroes to hip-hop execs like Irv in the nineties, but their lives were far more complex than the one-dimensional portrayal of them by rappers such as 50 Cent, Ja Rule, or Nas. This is the story of the most iconic southeast Queens hustlers—Fat Cat, Supreme, Pappy, Tony Montana, and Prince—and how they came to influence a generation of hip-hoppers. It's not the myth celebrated, Cristal in hand, in hip-hop rhymes, but a true-to-life history of southeast Queens hustlers as they were before they became the stuff of hip-hop lore: savvy CEOs of drug organizations with a lust for violence, drugs, and money that doomed not just them but the lucrative business model they created on the streets.

It is also the story of how many of the most significant events in hip-hop's recent history—the nonfatal shooting of Tupac Shakur at the Quad Studios in New York in 1994, 50 Cent's shooting in southeast Queens in 2000, the murder of Jam Master Jay in Queens in 2002, and 50's high-profile rivalry with both Ja Rule and Los Angeles rapper The Game—have connections to the streets of southeast Queens. What emerges from this tale of hustling and hip-hop is the borough's enormous contribution to the evolution of hip-hop: Bronx DJs like Afrika Bambaataa and Kool Herc may have birthed the music in the seventies, but it is Queens impresarios and supergroups from Russell Simmons to RUN-DMC who commercialized the art form in the eighties and the neighborhood's hustling-obsessed rappers such as 50 Cent who made street credibility the most important ingredient for hip-hop success in the nineties and beyond.

Now, as Irv and Chris Lorenzo face as many as twenty years in prison on money-laundering charges and as 'Preme could be sentenced to death for charges ranging from drug trafficking to murder, the foundation of the hip-hop and hustling partnership is becoming increasingly shaky. The Lorenzo brothers are far from the first in the hip-hop scene to incur the wrath of law enforcement, but their indictment is a potent symbol of increased interest in the hip-hop business from the federal government: In the summer of 2005, rapper Lil' Kim was sentenced to one year in prison on three counts of perjury and one count of conspiracy for lying to a grand jury about a 2001 shooting outside New York radio station Hot 97; Kim's ex-boyfriend Damion "World" Hardy was indicted by U.S. Attorney Mauskopf on drug-trafficking and murder charges, including the killing of Darryl "Hommo" Baum, the Brooklyn stick-up kid responsible for shooting 50 Cent in 2000; and news reports surfaced that the U.S. attorney for the Southern District of New York had begun an investigation into unsolved murders such as those of Tupac Shakur and Jam Master Jay. As rap has become drenched in the slang and style of the eighties drug business—one of the most popular mixtapes of 2005 was Harlem rapper Juelz Santana's *Back Like Cooked Crack 2: More Crack* and one of the year's biggest hits was Cassidy's "I'm a Hustla"—the Lorenzos' case will test the marriage of hip-hop and hustling like never before. It's a relationship that has long driven hip-hop's hit makers from Dr. Dre to The Notorious B.I.G. and helped make the music palatable to suburban whites who vicariously experience dangerous neighborhoods like southeast Queens through the music of their favorite stars. (The fall 2005 release of a video game called "50 Cent: Bulletproof," in which players follow the rapper through New York's underworld, truly fulfills the promise of rap as role-playing.) But it's this long-held desire for street cred that is at last drawing the scrutiny of the federal government; and, obviously, it is the hip-hoppers themselves—not their mostly suburban fan base—who will face the consequences.

Part I:
HUSTLING

1

The Crews Coalesce

Southeast Queens lies at the farthest reaches of the borough, on the Long Island border, a neighborhood so far from Manhattan it might as well be another state. With its wide, almost interstate-like boulevards (Rockaway, Sutphin, Baisley, Guy R. Brewer) and its major parkways (Belt and Grand Central), southeast Queens has little in common with the crowded, narrow streets of Manhattan or even with the remote parts of outer boroughs like the Bronx and Brooklyn.

Though the area is just one small corner of the most middle-class, most immigrant-populated borough, it's not considered a single, unified neighborhood by anyone who lives there. No one says they're from "southeast Queens." This isn't a matter of pride. The area comprises a series of interlocking neighborhoods, each one distinct to its natives. Southeast Queens is home to some of the most sprawling housing projects in all of New York City, most prominently South Jamaica's Baisley Park Houses and the South Jamaica Houses, nicknamed the "40 Projects" because its cluster of tall brick buildings sits beside Public School 40. South Jamaica is composed mostly of public housing though one area, Jamaica Estates, is dominated by the middle class and is the birthplace of Donald Trump. Further to the south are the Springfield Gardens and Laurelton sections of southeast Queens, which are made up of blocks of middle-class housing developments that breed a professional class of doctors, lawyers, and accountants.

Then there is Hollis. Located just east of South Jamaica, the single-family homes of Hollis have for decades been a refuge for lower-middle-class African Americans fleeing the cramped conditions of poor neighborhoods such as the South Bronx and Harlem. Colin Powell's parents bought their first home, a three-bedroom bungalow at 183-68 Elmira Avenue, for $17,500. The neighborhood, Powell wrote in his autobiography *My American Journey*, "carried a certain cachet, a cut above Jamaica, Queens and just below St. Albans, then another gold coast for middle class blacks." Powell's African-American neighbors no doubt shared his lofty sentiments about Hollis; though many of the homes in the area were modest, single-level units, most had ample front and backyards and even basements, a rarity in inner-city neighborhoods, even in the outer boroughs. In Hollis, residents could feel like they were part of a neighborhood but could keep their distance whenever they needed to, just like in the suburbs.

By the mid-seventies, Hollis's luster began to fade: Spurred by the busing of blacks to white schools and the decay of New York City's infrastructure, panic selling of homes by whites became commonplace, while gangs like Black Rain and Seven Crowns and drug distribution networks controlled by Mafia families flooded the neighborhood with heroin. Like many urban neighborhoods in America, Hollis had experienced a spike in cocaine use in the early seventies; heroin, however, was a far more dangerous epidemic, creating thousands of addicts and fattening the bottom line of drug organizations.

As the Mafia maintained a monopoly on heroin importation routes (the drugs originated in southeast Asia, were refined in Italy, and then smuggled to the United States), their profits measured in the billions. With the heroin trade, the Mafia had the best of both worlds: Dealers and middlemen were forced to come to them for product so they could be choosy about which distributors they did business with, thus reducing the risk of being infiltrated by informants. On the other end, because there were no competing grades of heroin, customers didn't complain about heroin that was "stepped on," or cut with substances like baby powder.

Heroin ultimately ravaged the social fabric of southeast Queens.

Addicts were so abundant that senior citizens often shuttered themselves indoors for fear of encountering them. The neighborhood's rapid descent from small-town peace to inner-city mayhem took even law enforcement by surprise. "It used to be that drug dealers crawled out from under a rock and then went right back under that rock," explains former Queens Narcotics Detective Michael McGuinness, "but by the early eighties they weren't going back under the rock anymore." When dopers weren't getting a fix on the streets of southeast Queens they were sticking up bodegas or robbing houses (particularly in Hollis) for whatever they could get their hands on: TVs, household appliances, sneakers, even, ironically, guns tucked away in closets or sock drawers that were meant to protect residents from such intruders. Doped-up burglars with a particularly sick of sense of humor (or an acute lack of shame) would often defecate in the toilets of their victims, leaving the foul mess for the homeowner to find.

Trips to the bank or a check-cashing store became treacherous: Dopers grabbed wallets and pocketbooks from customers the moment they walked out the door. When that breed of victim wised up, heroin addicts turned their sights on easier, but less lucrative marks, mugging Hollis teenagers for their coats or shoes. New York City jails soon became crowded with low-level thugs addicted to heroin.

Addicts who remained on the outside fell victim to predatory business practices from dealers. Success in the heroin business often required killing a few customers with too-pure product; instead of having a deterrent effect, overdoses attracted customers drawn to a potent new product. Heroin was a lucrative hustle, but in the rougher, more competitive sections of southeast Queens, dealing could be just as lethal as using. Most drug dealers would beat or slap around rivals, but heroin dealers famously had no qualms about murdering one another.

For those turned off by the violence, there were hustles far less dangerous than heroin in the seventies. Numbers running was a favorite scheme in southeast Queens; since law enforcement sometimes looked the other way from this seemingly victimless crime in return for bribes, numbers parlors flourished in the neighborhood.

Numbers shops were run by easygoing, affable businessmen with nicknames like "Grumpy" and "Chop," entrepreneurs more dedicated to customer service than most owners of bodegas and supermarkets in the neighborhood. Numbers runners set out doughnuts and coffee for gamblers and kept the floors immaculately clean. Best of all, hitting that winning number—the odds were often set at something like 600:1—provided a high no drug could match. (Indeed, the down payment on Colin Powell's parents' Hollis home came from proceeds from a winning number.) Mafiosi involved in the heroin trade viewed numbers runners as the most trustworthy guys on the streets. They were also highly attuned to the tastes of their clients; since hundreds of customers went in and out of the parlors, numbers runners had a good sense of the underground economy. How many people were into heroin? Coke? The numbers runners knew, and they helped the Mafia.

Unlike in the safer, more sedate world of numbers, steely nerves were a requirement for success in the dope business. No one personified the fearlessness of heroin hustlers better than Hollis native Ronald "Bumps" Bassett. Unlike his fellow dealers, Bumps didn't want adulation or notoriety; he was simply out for the cash. When he left his base on Farmers Boulevard in Hollis to hang out at the open-air drug bazaar of 150th Street in South Jamaica all the young hustlers on the block would excitedly cry out, *"Hey, hey, Ronnie's over here."* "They paid homage to Ronnie Bumps," says one former Hollis hustler, "but he didn't care. He was a man among the boys." Bumps looked the part, too: With his long mane of straightened hair, pale light brown skin, and reddish birthmark just above his mouth he was a dead ringer for Ron O'Neal, the suave actor who played the cocaine kingpin nicknamed "Priest" in the classic 1972 blaxploitation film *Superfly.* Bumps was one of the first real icons of the emerging drug business in southeast Queens, and he would have imitators for decades to come.

The nihilism of the dopers and the flashiness of dealers like Ronnie Bumps served as the inspiration for the generation of hustlers who came of age in southeast Queens in the early eighties.

Without the experience or organizational skills of the street icons of the seventies, the new breed of mostly teenage hustlers started out small. The White Castle hamburger stand on Hollis Avenue and Francis Lewis Boulevard was robbed almost daily, and a depot for Mister Softee ice cream trucks in Queens Village provided another favorite target. Unsurprisingly, bitter feuds broke out among petty hustlers over the most lucrative marks in southeast Queens, battles that in turn led to the formation of organized crews in the neighborhood. "It became a competition," remembers one former hustler raised in South Jamaica's 40 Projects. "You had the guys from Hollis, you had the guys from Southside and then you had the guys from off Linden Boulevard. A lot of dudes from Hollis didn't like guys from over here because we were in the projects. And the guys from the projects didn't like the guys from Hollis because they lived in Hollis. It was just animosity."

The rivalry between Hollis and South Jamaica was typical (in southeast Queens, Hollis is dubbed Northside; South Jamaica, Southside) but it was also based in class. South Jamaica hustlers were mostly poor and uneducated while in Hollis many attended private Catholic schools and went on to college. If Hollis, with its single-family houses and neat lawns, was something of a lower-middle-class paradise, South Jamaica was a lower-class hell of towering brick public housing projects that seemed to block out the sky, abandoned, burnt-out buildings, and desolate stretches of blocks where everyone could feel as though they were alone in the area.

Even among the rough-and-tumble scene of South Jamaica, the hustlers from Linden Boulevard stood out. They were poor—many came from South Jamaica's Baisley Park Houses—and frighteningly tough. They rushed headlong into fights with guns and knives drawn, sending even those with seasoned street pedigrees fleeing for their lives. "They used to come with guns and knives and all we had was our bare fists and a quarter to call somebody," remembers the former 40 Projects hustler. "We got into a dispute with those guys in the cafeteria of Andrew Jackson High School and when the fight started we were quickly outnumbered. We barely escaped with our lives."

There was one more striking difference separating the Linden

Boulevard posse from the rest of southeast Queens: religion. Many claimed affiliation with the Five Percent Nation, a splinter sect of the Nation of Islam (NOI) founded in 1963 by minister Clarence Edward Smith, aka Clarence 13X. Smith, whose followers called him Father Allah, rejected the belief that NOI founder Wallace Fard was God ("the black man is God," he said), and believed that only 5 percent of the world's population is righteous. "Peace, God" was how Five Percenters greeted each other, earning the Linden Boulevard crew the name the Peace Gods. To rival hustlers, their righteous-sounding names, like "Prince G" and "Born Justice," only made them scarier.

One of the most promising young hustlers of the Peace Gods was Kenneth McGriff. Nicknamed "Supreme" or "'Preme" by his fellow Five Percenters (one of the sect's tenets held that blacks were "Supreme Beings"), McGriff cut an outsize figure. Born on September 19, 1959, to transit-worker parents in the Baisley Park Houses, 'Preme carried himself with the swagger of older, more established hustlers in the game, dressing in expensive suits, leaving his crisp white shirt open to reveal a muscled chest. He also had a wide, easy smile, a manicured goatee that made him look like a movie star (or, as many in southeast Queens joked, like a porno actor), and most memorably, piercing green eyes. Behind the ghetto glitz was a seriousness about hustling that elevated 'Preme above his many peers on the streets. He carefully studied the work of older, more experienced southeast Queens hustlers like Ronnie "Bumps" Bassett and even offered to take on some of the most dangerous and thankless tasks for his bosses, such as guarding drugs and cash at southeast Queens stash houses. 'Preme was no street fighter, but he could turn to the Peace Gods, who like him embraced Five Percenter ideology less as a religion and more as a rebellious pose, for muscle. Rivals were well aware that crossing 'Preme invited an attack from the much-feared Peace Gods, giving 'Preme an air of invincibility on the streets of southeast Queens.

In 1981, 'Preme and a group of friends from the Baisley Park Houses formed a crew called the Supreme Team. The grandiose-sounding name was typical Five Percenter hyperbole, and in another nod to Five Percenter ideology the first members of the crew even called themselves the Original Seed. Yet 'Preme and his tight-knit crew did little more than sell small amounts of cocaine and heroin through hand-to-hand sales on the street. The Supreme Team, however, did undertake an important innovation: the merging of Latino and African-American hustlers into one unified crew. 'Preme appointed Ernesto "Puerto Rican Righteous" Piniella one of his top lieutenants, thus ensuring the future participation of Latinos in the Supreme Team, and more importantly, gaining a foothold in the Latino-dominated world of cocaine distribution. A Latino face in the Supreme Team could bring access to the Colombians who moved real weight and to the wholesale pricing that inevitably came along with big drug purchases. Piniella was also genuinely fearless. While Supreme Team members Chauncey "God B" Milliner and Nathan "Green Eyed Born" May often caved in to law enforcement pressure when they landed in jail, Piniella would serve his time without even placing a call for help. He was unafraid, too, to get his hands dirty on the streets, executing rivals and dumping the bodies in the outlying wooded areas of southeast Queens that were dubbed the "burial grounds."

If the Peace Gods represented hustling at its most violent, Thomas Mickens's crew—who plied their trade in the upper-middle-class neighborhoods of Laurelton and Springfield Gardens—were the drug game's most professional players. Mickens inherited his street smarts from his father, Thomas "Lucky" Harris, one of southeast Queens' most storied numbers runners. Though Mickens took his mother's last name, the young hustler claimed to have received two separate inheritances from his father, one when he turned 18 and the other when he turned 21. Harris taught the young Mickens—a high school dropout who so lusted after the high life that he gave himself the nickname "Tony Montana" after Al Pacino's character in *Scarface*—to abhor violence as bad for business.

He also instructed Mickens to keep the circle of hustlers around him tight, as small crews limited one's exposure to informants. When Mickens began his hustling career in the early eighties when in his late teens, he heeded his father's advice, selling cocaine in the vicinity of Merrick Boulevard and 226th Street, backed by fellow hustlers Norvell "Flakes" Young and Anthony Jacobs. At home, girl-friend Shelby Kearney managed Mickens's finances and adjusted his tax returns to ward off IRS audits, claiming that Mickens held a job at an auto shop called Five Towns Auto and made most of his income from gambling.

There were other crews competing with Mickens and 'Preme; the most formidable was undoubtedly the Corley Family. Operating out of South Jamaica's 40 Projects, the Corleys combined the business savvy of Mickens with the brawn of the Peace Gods. Indeed, like Mickens, the young hustlers of the Corley Family—brothers Peter Corley, Donald "Duckie" Corley, and James "Wall" Corley— came from a solidly middle-class background. Their parents owned heating-oil trucks, which made for a lucrative business as the neighborhood's single-family homes required substantial amounts of oil to get through the winter.

Like Mickens, the young Corleys inherited their parents' strong business acumen. They sold heroin and cocaine from vacant apartments in the 40 Projects as well as from their nearby base of operations, the Corley Family grocery on 107th Avenue and 160th Street, ensuring a steady stream of customers from the cluster of towering brick high-rises. The Corleys mostly kept a low profile (though Wall was a regular in the southeast Queens nightclub scene) and the teenage hustlers they employed to hawk their product on 107th Avenue didn't usually carry any drugs. After quietly taking a customer's order, the dealers would call up to the second floor of the Corley Family grocery, and workers would drop bags of cocaine and heroin through a barely visible slot in the window. The immense stash of cash and drugs at the grocery was protected by a reinforced steel door as well as young 40 Projects toughs, who strode the area around 160th Street intimidating anyone who might cross their path.

With the rise of the Corleys, the Supreme Team, and the Mickens crew, drug organizations seemed to be sprouting up in every corner of southeast Queens. Rivalries had existed between the loosely organized hustlers of Hollis and South Jamaica but the balance of power had never tipped in any one direction until 1981 when an ex-con and former Seven Crowns gang member named Lorenzo "Fat Cat" Nichols set up shop on 150th Street near 107th Avenue. The block was ideal for drug dealing—it forked off from Sutphin Boulevard, making it easier to conduct deals with a sense of privacy—and Fat Cat's heroin and cocaine business took off almost immediately. The 150th Street and 107th Avenue site was also just ten blocks away from the Corley Family's 40 Projects base; hustlers from every part of southeast Queens were shocked by Fat Cat's boldness. It didn't help that Fat Cat wasn't a local—he was raised in the Ozone Park section of Queens—and that his background was in armed robbery, not drugs. (Just before going into business, Fat Cat had completed a five-year prison term for robbery.)

Born on December 25, 1958, to a mother employed as a nurse's aide and a father who worked as a plumber, Fat Cat was given his nickname because of his linebacker-thick neck, a head so big it nearly blocked out his friends' faces in snapshots, and his rangy beard. Unsurprisingly, he had the brawn to back up his ballsy entrée into the southeast Queens street scene, administering brutal beatings with an icy, almost clinical precision. One story had Fat Cat knocking a man cold with one hand while talking on the phone with the other. "My father had a great knuckle game," says Fat Cat's son Raheem Tyler. "He even liked to box when business was slow." No one in southeast Queens—not even hardened street hustlers—was eager to test him. To his immediate family, however, Fat Cat (whom they nicknamed "Biz" and "Busy") could be a softie vulnerable to the feelings of others. "If you cry, you got him," said one member of the Nichols family. "He'd say, 'Please stop crying, I'll give you whatever you need.' " Fat Cat was also generous with the income he was generating for himself. "He'd hand out money to guys on the street and we'd be like, 'Why are you doin' that, Biz?' " remembers the family member. "And he'd say, 'You never know when you're gonna need someone in your time of need.' "

Although Fat Cat was a relative newcomer to southeast Queens, his reputation was growing to the point where he was becoming a threat to established players. One late summer night in 1981, a small army from the Corley Family surrounded Fat Cat while he was hanging out with friends at the Rollerdome Skating Rink on Jamaica Avenue. Fat Cat kept his cool, drawing his gun before the Corleys could make their first move, and shot Kilo, the Corley Family's most feared enforcer, in the back. As Kilo crumpled to the ground, Fat Cat ran for the exits. A hail of bullets missed him as he swung the door of the Rollerdome open and hit the streets running. The Corley crew followed him out the door, and the shoot-out continued down to the 40 Projects, leaving hundreds of spent bullet casings all along the cracked sidewalks of southeast Queens. "It was like something out of the movies with guys shooting up and down 160th Street," remembers one former Corley Family member. "I had to hide out in one of the buildings in the 40 Projects the whole night." No one else was injured that night besides Kilo, but Fat Cat had managed to change the balance of power. Before his arrival in southeast Queens, no single crew was dominant. Fat Cat was now the preeminent hustler in the area, the boss among many (like 'Preme) who considered themselves bosses. With such unchallenged power came immense responsibility: Fat Cat's crew would soon become an umbrella organization of sorts, doling out weight to smaller crews and even assisting them in acts of violence.

With his street rep solidified, Fat Cat turned his sights toward expanding his drug business. He and his middle-aged mother, Louise Coleman, opened up Big Mac's Deli, a two-story storefront at 106-60 150th Street near Sutphin Boulevard featuring several upstairs apartments, as well as a game room several doors down at 105-06 150th Street. From this pair of locations, Fat Cat moved millions of dollars in cocaine, heroin, and later crack, even supplying weight to rival crews like the Supreme Team. Fat Cat's organization was all family: His mother, Louise Coleman, sold small amounts of coke and heroin from the game room; wife Joanne McClinton "Mousey" Nichols worked as a drug courier; sisters Honey Nichols and Viola moved weight from crew to crew and managed Fat Cat's drug-packaging operation; Viola's husband Marvin "House Cat" House worked as a mid-level distributor; niece Marcia Nichols "Mott" Williams bagged drugs. There was only one real outsider in the hierarchy of Fat Cat's sprawling drug organization: Man Sing Eng aka "John Yee," an Asian heroin distributor whom the Nichols family nicknamed "Chink." Eng was so removed from day-to-day southeast Queens street life—he imported his heroin from Pakistan and only sold weight—that he was deemed trustworthy by Fat Cat.

To outsiders, a family-run drug-dealing business seems unusual, if not completely perverse. To insiders in the drug game, however, keeping business in the family makes perfect sense. Trusting your crew not to snitch or run off with cash and drugs is perhaps the most essential ingredient for success in the narcotics game. Whom can you trust more than your close family? Even the savviest players on the street can be brought down by an informant or see their bottom line take a hit when drugs are stolen by a disloyal crew member. Furthermore, while most are loath to admit it, it's a fact of the street life that parents are just as susceptible to the lure of fast cash as their children. "At first, the parents are horrified," says a former hustler close to the Nichols organization, "but once they see money coming in it's, 'OK, you can do this, just don't do it here.' Then it's, 'OK, I'll help you stash money or drugs.' Before you know it, the parents are part of the organization."

Fat Cat reluctantly allowed younger members of his family to work for him. "Biz had me counting money for him," explains Marcy (not her real name), a close relative of Fat Cat's, "but I think he was paying me so much—at one point I was making $1,500 per week—so I'd just save up my money, get out of the game, and then leave New York." But he seemingly had no problem with sisters, cousins, nieces, and nephews holding important positions within his organization as long as they were adults. So confident was Fat Cat in his family's ability to handle business at Big Mac's Deli, which sat on one of southeast Queens's toughest corners, that he left the store without even basic security precautions even though the game room and the upstairs apartments were always packed with mountains of drugs and cash. "Fat Cat's grocery store was the only one on the block that had no bars on the windows," remembers Mike McGuiness of Queens Narcotics.

While he relied on his family for business, for serious acts of violence Fat Cat turned to longtime friend Howard "Pappy" Mason, a dreadlocked tough from Brooklyn whom he met while imprisoned at a notoriously brutal prison for adolescents in the Bronx called the Spofford Juvenile Center. Pappy was fiercely loyal to Fat Cat, possessed an almost visceral hatred of law enforcement, and seemed perpetually up for a fight—even with cops. "Cat liked to use guys from Brooklyn because it created a big element of surprise for the guys in Queens," remembers a man close to the Nichols organization. "Everybody knew everybody in our neighborhood, so when these outsiders came in it just threw everybody off."

Pappy had a strong mystique surrounding him. Because of his dreadlocks and his use of Jamaican street slang, street guys in Brooklyn and Queens believed he was from Jamaica when in fact he, like Fat Cat, actually hailed from Alabama. (Fat Cat was born there before moving to Ozone Park.) Pappy instilled in his subordinates—whom he dubbed the Bebos—an obsession with Jamaican culture. Like their boss, Bebos members sported dreadlocks and framed orders for everything from cocaine shipments to hits on potential witnesses with the Rastafarian phrase, "One Love." Pappy and the Bebos sold cocaine and heroin in the 40 Projects (just blocks away from Fat Cat's base at 107th Avenue and 150th Street), but Fat Cat nonetheless considered him an ideal lieutenant. Pappy kept his aspirations in check and even structured his organization to resemble Fat Cat's crew. (Pappy's mom, Claudia Mason, worked as a distributor and enforcer.) Indeed, to hustlers in southeast Queens the Bebos seemed like no more than a ragtag version of the Nichols organization.

Fat Cat ran his organization from a familiar business model. Like the heroin hustlers of the seventies, Fat Cat's small army of drug dealers were "grindin' " (street slang for making dozens of small transactions worth $10 to $25 at a time) in poor neighborhoods like South Jamaica. Profits were sizable, but hand-to-hand dealers often had to work fifteen-hour days.

Thomas "Tony Montana" Mickens, on the other hand, was able to turn over his supply over much faster. He sold to upper-middle-class clients in Laurelton and Springfield Gardens; they bought cocaine by the ounce, so he could make thousands of dollars in profit in a single transaction. Mickens even had business cards printed up to impress his upscale clientele: They read TOMMY, ANY TIME with the phone number of his 231st Street home in Queens printed below his customer-friendly slogan. When Mickens wasn't reachable at his house, he was often hustling at his spot at 226th Street and Merrick Boulevard.

Mickens's direct involvement in the drug business soon left him vulnerable to law enforcement scrutiny. An undercover cop who infiltrated Fat Cat's organization might arrest a runner or a lookout; with Mickens, the officer could get the boss himself in handcuffs. Indeed, one of his most consistent customers turned out to be an undercover cop from Queens Narcotics. In November 1982, the officer made his first buy on 226th Street and Merrick Boulevard, purchasing half an ounce of cocaine for $1,250. After completing the transaction, Mickens was eager to set up another deal and handed the cop his business card. Soon after, he met up with the cop on 226th Street for another sale; but this time, Mickens urged his customer not to make a purchase. "I don't have good quality stuff," he explained to the cop. This kind of honesty was rare among most dealers but commonplace for the client-friendly Mickens. "I don't want to buy it if it's not good quality stuff," the cop replied, and the two set a date to meet again.

Their next meeting took place in February 1983, on 226th Street and Merrick Boulevard, as always. This deal, however, ended with the cop handcuffing Mickens and placing him under arrest. Four months later, Mickens was sentenced to a short prison term. His girlfriend Shelby Kearney held on to his significant savings (upward of six figures) and he was released barely one year later in June 1984; almost immediately he hit his old spot on 226th Street again. He moved ounce after ounce of cocaine, and his cash grew larger by the day. Mickens envisioned houses, cars, yachts, everything his hero Tony Montana flaunted in *Scarface*. The arrest and subsequent prison time had taught Mickens that in order to achieve such lofty goals he'd have to be smarter than the average hustler. So he began to fashion elaborate schemes to protect himself from law enforcement scrutiny. In December 1984, an undercover cop purchased coke from Mickens near 226th Street. Believing that he had busted Mickens, the officer ran the license plates on the 1975 blue four-door Chevy Nova only to find that it was registered to a southeast Queens man named Robert Hines. Mickens registered the Nova in the name of his crew member so that a check of the plates by a cop would result in the arrest of Hines (who was more than willing to go to jail for his boss).

The ruse may have left Mickens one crew member short, but in the months after the arrest Mickens was free to focus on his organization's finances, moving the cash he'd socked away into legitimate businesses like real estate and retail. At the close of 1984, just as Mickens was put on parole for his drug arrest a year earlier, he and girlfriend Shelby Kearney closed on the sale of a home at 179 Hilton Avenue in Queens. It was an impressive accomplishment for a dealer barely in his twenties who'd ascended from the streets. The home also presented formidable challenges for Mickens, however, raising eyebrows among law enforcement and the IRS. On his tax returns, Mickens listed his employment as a worker with Five Towns Auto while Kearney claimed she was a word processor, not exactly jobs that would provide enough cash for the down payment on a home. Mickens moved about $20,000 in cash to the bank account of Kearney's parents, who, unaware of how they were being used, wrote a "gift" check to the happy couple. Mickens then deposited about $11,050 of his drug money into Kearney's bank account, which she converted into a $12,000 check to use as a partial down payment on the home. Finally, Mickens gave a friend $5,000 in cash, which Thompson used to write a $5,000 "loan" check to the Mickens family to purchase the home in exchange for a fee. The flurry of checks may seem like an unsophisticated shell game now, particularly after the passing of legislation requiring that cash transactions over $10,000 be reported to the IRS. But in the early eighties, Mickens's moves made him one of the savvier empire builders on the streets of southeast Queens, the rare young gun who saw beyond the limited gains of the street and into a limitless future.

The Cops Move In

Mickens was gaining momentum in Laurelton but back in South Jamaica, both 'Preme and Fat Cat were experiencing turbulence that would lead to the most serious downturns of their careers. By the spring of 1985, Mike McGuinness and several of the more enterprising cops of Queens Narcotics had documented dozens of hand-to-hand buys in front of Big Mac's Deli and had set up wiretaps that recorded conversations between the extended Nichols clan in which they arranged for drug deals and shipments. "Supreme needs two ounces for eighty," one of Fat Cat's associates said during a phone call wiretapped by cops; on another call, Viola Nichols complained that a crew member had gotten "rocked" (arrested) with "five hundred packets."

The wiretaps were just one part of the case McGuinness and Queens Narcotics were building against Fat Cat's empire. Cops also had confidential informants (C.I.s) on the inside, feeding them information about nearly every aspect of Fat Cat's crew, from the enforcers to the baggers. In the wrong hands, leads from C.I.s can result in fruitless searches and wrongful arrests, but McGuiness smartly sifted the good information from the bad. He also ignored trumped-up claims of impending turf wars and focused instead on smaller, more detailed information about specific deals and the whereabouts of Nichols family players.

McGuiness took pride in his instinctual ability to suss out the motives of C.I.s. It was clear to him who was looking to curry favor with the cops, who wanted to get a rival arrested, who was hoping for a reduced prison sentence for themselves. His gut did fail him once, however, when Queens Narcotics was planning a dramatic raid on Big Mac's Deli in late July 1985. McGuinness heeded one piece of advice that would nearly cost him his life. An informant told McGuinness that if he took down the deli he would not encounter Fat Cat himself, who rarely (if ever) spent time in the building. The tip made sense; smart drug kingpins like Fat Cat knew that, in case of a raid, it was best to have lower or mid-level crew members on hand to take the weapons and drug possession charges that would lead to significant jail time. The informant's credibility was bolstered by his warning about Fat Cat's enforcers, who he said would likely be zealously guarding the stash of guns, cash, and drugs in the second-floor apartments above the deli. While the second floor was dangerous, the informant explained, the downstairs area of the deli—particularly its backroom where the Nichols organization accounting books were kept—was likely to be empty and thus easily securable by cops.

On July 29, 1985, the day of the raid, fourteen cops were assigned to the upstairs of Big Mac's Deli while only two (including McGuinness) were assigned to secure the ground floor. When McGuinness arrived and snuck to the backroom on the first floor, he was shocked to find Fat Cat himself sitting calmly behind a desk. Fat Cat was flanked by two female friends and a pair of crew members including one of the crew's most feared enforcers, Chris "Jughead" Williams. McGuinness reacted quickly to the surprise, pulling out a long, double-barreled rifle, a weapon he describes as "scary to look at from either end." Fat Cat's girls cowered and cried in the corner, and Jughead and his fellow enforcer calmly put their hands up against the wall of the deli. As McGuinness trained his rifle on Jughead, he saw from the corner of his eye Fat Cat reaching for his desk. "Don't move!" McGuinness shouted, thrusting his gun so close to Fat Cat's face that the barrel touched his nose. Fat Cat eased his hand away from the desk drawer, moved to the wall next to Jughead, and threw his hands in the air in defeat.

McGuinness was sweating heavily; if he had shot Fat Cat at such close range it would have been "very messy for both us." He frantically searched the rest of the backroom. When he pulled Fat Cat's desk drawer open, expecting to find the sort of small pistol favored by hustlers, like a Derringer, he found an eighteen-shot assault rifle made by Steyr, an Austrian company that manufactures some of the most lethal weaponry in the world. If Fat Cat had managed to get his hands on the Steyr, McGuinness realized, he could have blasted his way out of the deli. As McGuinness continued his search for any remaining weapons he found another yet another automatic weapon under a thick, plush towel in the middle of Fat Cat's desk chair. A further search of the upstairs apartments and the deli's backroom turned up $180,000 in cash and hundreds of bags of cocaine and heroin. The combination of cash, the drugs, and the guns meant that Fat Cat would likely face a long prison sentence, perhaps twenty-five years to life. "Fat Cat reached for that Steyr," McGuinness recalls, "because he knew his time was up."

Outside the deli, a huge, unruly crowd gathered on the sidewalk. News of Fat Cat's arrest had spread quickly through the neighborhood, and those who didn't get word of the takedown could tell something big was happening from the mass of cop cars parked outside, sirens blazing. As McGuinness and his partner frog-marched Fat Cat to a squad car in handcuffs, he couldn't help but savor his luck in making it out of the deli alive. Feeling flush with relief, McGuinness didn't see Pappy Mason, who had hidden himself inside the dense crowd gathered outside the deli. Just as McGuinness and Fat Cat walked past the spot in the crowd where Pappy was hiding, Pappy drew his gun from his side, aiming it squarely at McGuinness. Pappy was ready to take out McGuinness in front of a crowd of onlookers and dozens of uniformed cops and probably get himself killed in the process. But Fat Cat shook his head and mouthed the word *no* to his most trusted lieutenant. Pappy reluctantly put his gun away, watched helplessly as Fat Cat's bulky frame was stuffed into the waiting cop car, and then disappeared again into the crowd.

As Fat Cat sat in prison awaiting trial in the fall of 1985, his lieutenants plotted revenge against the cops. What could they do to send a message to the police that Fat Cat wouldn't be stopped? In early October, they came up with an answer. During a phone call from prison, Fat Cat instructed his top lieutenants, Pappy, Jughead, and Joseph "Bobo" Rogers to hire a hit man to seriously injure his parole officer, Brian Rooney. Because prison phones are often monitored, Fat Cat was purposefully vague in giving the order to his lieutenants, and in order to put a lot of distance between his organization and the hit, he turned to freelancers for the job. If Bobo, Jughead, or Pappy got arrested for such a serious crime, Fat Cat's crew would temporarily—if not permanently—lose its most capable talents. So Fat Cat's men enlisted a pair of unaffiliated hit men from southeast Queens for the job, brothers named Lamont and Randolph Lucas.

Just after 5 PM on October 10, 1985, the Lucas brothers followed Rooney as he left work at the State Division of Parole on his way to his home in South Hempstead, Long Island. When Rooney pulled his 1974 Dodge Dart up to the corner of 119th Avenue and 155th Street in South Jamaica a little more than two hours later, the Lucas brothers opened fire on Rooney, hitting him once in the back and once in the left arm. As Rooney lay dead, his car, which had been put into gear in an attempt to escape the ambush, lurched forward into a passing truck, striking it on its side. When cops were called to the scene of what they believed would be a routine car accident, they found Rooney slumped over the wheel, his .38 caliber Smith and Wesson revolver still stuck firmly in his waistband.

The Rooney hit would set off a chain of targeted assassinations on the streets and in prisons that would last for more a decade, but at the time his death seemed like little more than a random murder in one of the most unforgiving parts of Queens. "Right now, the motive for the murder is a mystery," admitted Deputy Chief Joseph R. Borelli, commander of detectives in Queens, just after the shooting. A small reward—$5,000—was posted by the State Parole Officers Association for information leading to the arrest of the killers, and Deputy Chief Borelli vaguely promised to look "into the possibility that the slaying was job-related." But the significance of Rooney's slaying ultimately eluded the cops, who never suspected that emerging crews like the Supreme Team or the Nichols organization could be responsible for such a bold, heinous crime. Fat Cat had claimed his first law enforcement victim and had gotten away with it; as his lieutenants had boasted after his arrest, there was no stopping him, not even from prison. Fat Cat could issue orders for hits, hire baggers and enforcers, and arrange for purchases of weight, all from his prison cell. It would take more than a single raid from Queens Narcotics to dismantle the organization that Fat Cat had worked so meticulously to build.

As Fat Cat flexed his muscle behind bars, 'Preme was proving his mettle on the streets. 'Preme had worked his way up from a stash house guard for the likes of Ronnie "Bumps" Bassett to the CEO of one of most promising crews in southeast Queens. While 'Preme still received his supply of cocaine and heroin from bigger dealers like Fat Cat, by the fall of 1985 the Supreme Team was finally coming into its own. 'Preme and a fellow crew member nicknamed "Crusher" cruised the area surrounding Baisley Park Houses in a black Mercedes, flashing the muzzles of high-powered automatic weapons and waving thick wads of cash out their car windows to awestruck residents of the Baisley Park Houses. Supreme Team members were issued matching red jackets bearing the word *Supreme,* and one particularly proud hustler nicknamed "Big Just" placed a wooden sign outside of his apartment building on Foch Boulevard reading, BIG JUST 'PREME TEAM.

'Preme was an able manager of the multitiered Supreme Team, but his fiery temper often got in the way of business. When, in September 1985, a Supreme Team stash house at 155-47 116th Avenue was robbed of $80,000 in cash, 'Preme complained loudly of the robbery to his associates and even to rival crews, in hopes that making his dissatisfaction widely known on the streets of southeast

Queens would result in the money being returned to him. But his effort had the opposite effect, steeling the silence of the perpetrators and handing his rivals a juicy tidbit of information to share with cops. One informant told Sergeant Clyde M. Foster of Queens Narcotics of the robbery and of 'Preme's plans to head back to his base at 166-16 231st Street with Supreme Team members to plot their next move—and package massive quantities of drugs for sale the following day. With the addresses of two Supreme Team locations—both of which were sure to be filled with drugs and cash—Sergeant Foster moved quickly.

Early in the morning of September 10, 1985, Foster telephoned Queens Criminal Court Judge Steven Fisher seeking search warrants for both 166-16 231st Street and 155-47 116th Avenue. "I received information that allegedly a location at 231st Street and Linden Boulevard had been robbed of approximately $80,000 in U.S. currency and narcotics and this was property that belonged to Supreme," Foster explained to Judge Fisher, who immediately granted his request. "Be careful," were the judge's last words to Foster before he hung up the phone. Foster knew well enough to heed the judge's warning; as he testified years later in 'Preme's trial on charges of running a continuing criminal enterprise (CCE), "There was an excellent chance that Supreme would be present in the apartment." When Foster approached the Supreme Team base at 166-16 231st Street just after 9 PM on September 10, 1985, he found not only 'Preme himself but a gaggle of his crew members crowded in the apartment. As Queens Narcotics cops descended on the stash house, its doors and windows slammed shut. One Supreme Team member peered out the window, looked into Foster's eyes, and then closed the blinds. Foster later found out that those eyes belonged to 'Preme himself.

"Police!" Foster shouted at the door. There was no response; all he could hear was the locking of doors. "At which point," Foster explained later at 'Preme's trial, "I hit the door with the ram." Once inside, Foster found 'Preme covered with a white powdery substance, which he was attempting to dump into the sink with the water running. Unfortunately for 'Preme, there were more drugs in the apartment than what was on his face. Foster and Queens Narcotics seized six ounces of heroin and four pounds of cocaine, as well as hundreds of small packages waiting to be stuffed with drugs. There were drugs on top of the refrigerator, in a kitchen cabinet, and hidden in a jacket in the closet; nine firearms; $25,000 in cash, and $6,608 on 'Preme himself.

'Preme was arrested on the spot, but his prosecution didn't begin until late 1985, hampered by the same lack of resolve that characterized the investigation of the murder of parole officer Rooney. In Queens court, 'Preme's savvy attorney Robert Simels convinced the judge that the search warrant on 166-16 231st Street was improperly executed. Queens District Attorney John J. Santucci appealed, but a Manhattan judge reaffirmed the original decision and 'Preme was sentenced on minor weapons and drug possession charges. The Supreme Team CEO didn't entirely beat his case, but he wouldn't be gone from his base in South Jamaica for long.

Just before he went to prison in 1985, 'Preme decided that it was time to party. There was more to celebrate than just his last days of freedom; it was also the twenty-second birthday of his nephew Gerald "Prince" Miller. Prince was 'Preme's second in command, having reached this position by nepotism. The less connected members of the Supreme Team had been furious when 'Preme handed over a prime drug-dealing spot to his nephew, and outrage grew when Prince used this favor to begin assembling a suborganization of his own. But they couldn't stop him from gaining power, and by the time 'Preme was sentenced to prison, Prince had a crew ready to take over the Supreme Team.

Like his uncle, Prince recruited Latinos in order to boost his connections to the Colombians moving weight. He hired brothers Peter "Knowledge" Jimenez and Shannon Jimenez as his lieutenants and appointed the fearsome Ernesto "Puerto Rican Righteous" Piniella to be one of his top enforcers. The move to bring Piniella into the Supreme Team fold was shrewd: He was a southeast Queens tough whose lust for violence bordered on the psychotic, and he had a good relationship with Fat Cat, for whom he'd performed numerous freelance jobs.

At Prince's birthday party, the entire Supreme Team came together to toast the aspiring kingpin and say a final good-bye to 'Preme. The party was packed with A-list hustlers like James "Wall" Corley, and photos from that night feature members of southeast Queens' most prominent crews posing with piles of cash. Supreme Team lieutenants Bimmie, Black Just, and Baby Wise all mugged for snapshots, but the most memorable picture to emerge from the party featured Prince holding a thick wad of cash over the head of an adoring child. There was some worry at the beginning of the night that this get-together wouldn't live up to Supreme Team shindigs past, many of which featured hot hip-hop talent booked by 'Preme's pal, Hollis hip-hop impresario Russell Simmons. 'Preme "used to book Run [of RUN-DMC], the Beastie Boys, LL Cool J," Simmons says. "They would have big parties, every rapper played, and he'd give every rapper one thousand dollars." Fortunately, the hustlers who packed Prince's birthday that night, tossing stacks of cash into the air and showing off glistening rocks of cocaine, more than made up for the absence of rappers.

The afterglow from the event didn't last long: In late 1985, Prince was arrested on drugs and weapons charges, forcing another leadership struggle within the Supreme Team. Just before heading off to prison for a sentence of two to five years, Prince enlisted lieutenant Bryan "Fat Pete" Rich for a series of duties including running his drug spot and managing Supreme Team profits. Fat Pete, of course, was to hand back the reins when Prince returned from jail.

When Prince came home in mid-1986, Fat Pete refused to return the Supreme Team assets. Enraged, Prince decided to send a message to Fat Pete, one so overwhelming it would prevent future Supreme Team power struggles. Prince recruited enforcer Ernesto Piniella to kill Fat Pete, but before Piniella could make the hit, Fat Pete was murdered. The killing is still unsolved, and few details are known about it beyond the date on which it occurred: August 3, 1986. A law enforcement wiretap of a conversation between Prince and Supreme Team lieutenant Chauncey "God B" Milliner made soon after Fat Pete was killed indicates that Prince boasted of his former associate's slaying. "Power. Equality. Truth. Equality," Prince proclaimed to Milliner, Five Percenter code for "Pete." With Fat Cat's assassination of parole officer Rooney and Prince's murder of Fat Pete, the crews of southeast Queens proved that they were willing to go far beyond the typical street-level drug dealers, who usually engaged only in chaotic gun battles. Their layered organization worked well in the distribution of drugs, but this complex structure could also be ruthlessly effective in dispatching acts of violence—and, perhaps more importantly, masking the identity of the perpetrators of such acts. Murder victims seemed to vanish from the streets almost daily, and with so many lieutenants within each organization it became difficult for law enforcement to find out who actually committed the crimes.

The ease with which Prince dispatched rivals helped put him in an empire-building mood. Flush with cash, feeling liberated after spending about a year in prison, and ready to assume an even more prominent role in the Supreme Team with 'Preme himself still in prison, Prince created a business called Future Dimensions, Inc. in June 1986. Future Dimensions was to serve as a front for Prince's real estate deals and luxury vehicle purchases, all of which the aspiring kingpin estimated would flourish as he consolidated more power on the streets of southeast Queens. Prince's first move closely mirrored Fat Cat's business plan: He bought a ramshackle building in South Jamaica and transformed the property into the Supreme Superette. Prince lent the transaction an air of legitimacy by hiring a well-known New York attorney to handle the closing. The Supreme Superette, of course, was anything but a legitimate business; Prince put legendary tough guy Ernesto Piniella on the payroll, and soon the store became one part of a network of southeast Queens drug spots that included a pair of towers in the Baisley Park Houses on Foch Boulevard as well as a building at 171st Street and Liberty Avenue in South Jamaica.

By October 1986, the Supreme Team was generating about $30,000 a day in drug income. To keep the profits coming, Prince enlisted Piniella and his fellow roughnecks Shannon and Peter Jimenez and Hobie "Robo Justice" Townsend, as well as a corrupt

New York State parole officer named Ina McGriff (no relation to Kenneth McGriff) who was dating Piniella. At Piniella's request, McGriff would tip off the Supreme Team to impending raids from Queens Narcotics and turn over personal information about the crew's rivals. If, for example, the Supreme Team were looking for the address of an ex-con who had robbed the crew, McGriff would provide it to the organization for a nominal fee. McGriff often demanded additional bonuses for certain jobs, but to Prince it was money well spent as she consistently provided accurate and highly sensitive information. By the fall of 1986, Prince boasted perhaps the most impressive network of any of the southeast Queens crews: He could tap into the Nichols organization for weight on the cheap (so long as he provided Fat Cat with Supreme Team strongmen), and he was able to stay one step ahead of undercover cops thanks to his new law enforcement friend.

Judged against the profound progress made by the Supreme Team under Prince's leadership, the Nichols organization probably looked like it was cratering: Fat Cat had just begun a sentence of twenty-five years to life on state narcotics and weapons charges stemming from his July 29, 1985, arrest, and his top lieutenants (including his sister Viola) were beginning their descent into drug addiction. Worse, Viola was going in and out of jail with the frequency of a low-level hustler because she was bagging and transporting drugs for several organizations at a time including the Corley Family and the Supreme Team—up to ten ounces at a time by her own admission. Despite these problems, Fat Cat kept business humming at Big Mac's Deli, issuing directives from his prison cell and entrusting higher-ups like Pappy Mason to execute them on the streets. Under Fat Cat's guidance, the Nichols organization was becoming the rare crew to deal in weight and retail quantities of drugs, and its profits reflected the breadth of the business. The Nichols organization often pulled in $100,000 per week, sometimes more. Even rival crews stood in awe of Fat Cat's prowess, and low-level members of the Supreme Team were dispatched to carry out his orders with such regularity that southeast Queens residents could often be heard remarking, "Cat's letting out the wolves again."

The sheer size of the crew, however, was becoming a cause for concern for Fat Cat. Pappy's suborganization—the Bebos—was challenging established crews like the Supreme Team, and Pappy was less restrained than Fat Cat when it came to committing violent acts. A Nichols organization distributor named Brian "Glaze" Gibbs was branching out on his own, too, moving weight to smaller groups and heading up a modestly sized crew that controlled the drug trade in several housing projects in Brooklyn. Gibbs's independence and his showy way of doing business sparked jealousy among Fat Cat's crew.

In 1986, the Nichols organization was more powerful and profitable than ever thanks to a wide-ranging network of suborganizations, but the expansion created new vulnerabilities, namely increased rivalries and exposure to informants. Even Fat Cat, always fearless in the toughest of situations, was worrying about the future. One particular concern was the increasing number of women in the crew—Viola in particular—who were engaging in high-risk activity like grindin' on the block. Fat Cat knew that women caught by the cops were much more likely than men to cooperate with law enforcement in return for reduced sentences. Even from behind bars, Fat Cat exerted tremendous control over his organization, but there was little he could do to prevent his relatives from participating in the riskiest aspects of the family business. With the astonishing ascent of the Nichols organization, each of its players, from the lowliest bagger to the most feared lieutenant, now faced the fate of its imprisoned CEO.

The promising but perilous state of the Nichols organization was mirrored in a powerful new drug, crack. Introduced on the streets of southeast Queens sometime in early 1986, crack instantaneously fattened the bottom lines of the drug organizations; it also created a whole new set of problems, from rampant drug addiction to low-level hustlers suddenly being thrust into the position of street CEOs. "Crack started with the Dominicans who were the retailers between the street guys and the Colombian suppliers," Mike McGuinness remembers. "They were very smart marketers, and crack soon replaced powdered cocaine as the drug of choice." So sudden was crack's arrival that it caught Queens Narcotics cops like McGuinness off-guard. "We'd arrest somebody on the street and say, 'What's this shit?' " McGuinness explains, "and they'd say, 'That's the new shit they're selling: crack.' "

Crack was simple and inexpensive to prepare: Mix two parts cocaine and one part baking soda with a small amount of water, heat that solution until white precipitates form, and then stop the heating when the precipitation stops. Once dried under a lamp, the cocaine flakes into shards; hence the street name "crack." The drug gave its users an enormously powerful high, and its effects peaked soon after the initial rush kicked in. If the turnaround for cocaine and heroin users was measured in hours or days, the turnaround for crack was just minutes.

Crack was a godsend for the low-level, hand-to-hand dealers grindin' on the street; suddenly, an individual hustler could pull in thousands of dollars a day. By lowering the barriers to entry so significantly, crack democratized the drug trade: Newcomers could share in a business that had long been inaccessible thanks to the monopolistic practices of the established crews like the Nichols organization and the Supreme Team. This in turn meant that the streets were swarmed with naïve, inexperienced hustlers. "The privates became generals," remembers one man who was in the life then. "You had guys on the streets who had only experienced the drugs and the easy cash but had never faced any consequences for their behavior. When the cops caught up with them they were shocked. Their new life had come so fast to them that they didn't even stop to think about what might happen next."

At first, established drug business players like Fat Cat resisted the lure of crack. "Biz never wanted to sell crack," remembers Nichols family member Marcy. "He thought it brought way too much heat to the business." Fat Cat's lieutenant Joseph "Bobo" Rogers agreed with his boss's assessment, albeit for a different reason. "We didn't need crack," Rogers says, "because everybody— Corley, Supreme, Fat Cat—was making crack money way before there was even crack. Some weeks, we even had a million in cash stashed up at the deli." Marcy, however, desperately wanted in on the crack game. She saw that crack users were in a perpetual frenzy, locked in a round-the-clock cycle of using and scoring that turned enormous profits for even low-level hustlers. And so she made her case: "I went up to see Biz in prison and begged him to let me sell crack," Marcy recalls, "because I wanted to see that quick crack money." Fat Cat gave his permission, but with one specific condition: She had to sell the drug away from his usual spots. Marcy acquiesced to Fat Cat's request and set up shop on Lakewood Avenue in southeast Queens, far from his operations on 150th Street.

Fat Cat's peers didn't share his sense of restraint about this new phenomenon. Long lines of crackheads soon snaked around street corners near every drug spot in southeast Queens, particularly at the Supreme Team apartments at 116-20 Guy R. Brewer Boulevard. On streets and in apartment-building stairwells all over the neighborhood, crack dealers brazenly shouted instructions to waiting customers—"No dollars, no shorts" (street slang for no single dollar bills, no coming up short on cash)—and those who didn't heed the instructions were either severely beaten or banned from making future purchases. Such scenes played out repeatedly at popular drug spots such as the 40 Projects and the Baisley Park Houses, creating a siegelike atmosphere in neighborhoods that, though hardly unaccustomed to criminal activity, had never seen anything quite like this.

Caught off-guard by the crack explosion, Fat Cat's lieutenants argued that the organization had to get in on the game or lose its market share. "When you gotta compete, you gotta compete," explains Joseph "Bobo" Rogers. "We told Biz, 'Listen, we gotta get in on some of that action.'" The Nichols organization's first attempts in the crack game reflected their latecomer status. "We'd cook the crack too slowly or not cook up enough," Rogers explains, "so by the time we got on out the block there would be one hundred to one hundred twenty-five people waiting in line who would go through our entire supply in an hour." But even when inventory was low Fat Cat's organization reaped enormous profits. "When the block was hot we were making ten to twelve thousand dollars an hour," Rogers says. "We were selling crack faster than we could get it."

With the advent of crack, drug organizations came to resemble small businesses. There were enforcers, lieutenants, cookers, lookouts, dealers, a whole new hierarchy that required serious business skills and the sensitivity of a diplomat to keep everybody happy. Despite the profits, crack's major downside soon became readily apparent. A single experience with crack could make one a user for life, an addictive pull that many a crew member could not resist. The "don't get high on your own supply" dictum was always a myth; drug dealers *did* get high on their own supply, but they were almost always able to moderate their use of drugs such as cocaine and heroin. Crack was an entirely different animal, and even casual experimentation led to full-fledged addiction. Crew members became crackheads, stealing product to support their addiction or making wildly bad judgments, like staging messy murders of drug connections or rival dealers. The crack era is often remembered as highly lucrative, but the truth is that the drug's arrival simply speeded up the demise of a golden age for hustlers.

As crack was enriching everyone from Fat Cat to hand-to-hand dealers, Mickens was riding high on profits from his fast-expanding cocaine business. He kicked off 1986 in high style by purchasing a Ferrari Mondial on January 31. Soon afterward, he began assembling a fleet of cars that included high-end models from Porsche, BMW, Mercedes, Cadillac, and most ostentatiously, Rolls-Royce. Acquiring such high-priced goods without inviting increased law enforcement scrutiny required creative financing. A Mercedes 560 SEC was paid for in cash, $60,300 brought in a brown paper bag to Martin Motorcar, an Atlantic City dealership popular among drug kingpins like Mickens. With the other luxury vehicles, Mickens would put down a large cash down payment ($35,250 toward the Ferrari) which he would then follow up with a blizzard of checks, most in the $900 range. The cars were also registered under a variety of aliases including Thomas Harris, Thomas Harries, and, appropriately for such a Hollywood-obsessed kingpin, James Dean. Others were put in the names of friends of Mickens organization members who were then given a kickback for the service.

Mickens's collection of cars was impressive but it didn't set him apart from his fellow hustlers who, buoyed by the heady profits of the crack game, were snapping up everything from five-figure necklaces with diamond-encrusted pendants bearing their crew's insignia (members of the Nichols organization had a particular affinity for pendants shaped like an anchor) to six-figure Ferraris. Mickens longed to make a purchase that would mark him as southeast Queens' premier hustler, and on February 6, 1986, he bought nearly an entire block of buildings spanning from 226-01 to 226-05 Merrick Boulevard. As he had done in purchasing the fleet of luxury cars, Mickens put together an inventive financing structure to make the home buys. He was careful to write all of the checks in amounts just under $10,000 so he could avoid filing Currency Transaction Reports with the IRS, breaking down the $18,000 deposit required for the properties on Merrick Boulevard into three separate checks for $6,000 each. Mickens was far less cautious in naming the businesses he started in the buildings; each one took the name of his favorite Hollywood drug kingpin, Scarface, aka Tony Montana. In the late eighties, the Mickens/Montana brand—Montana Dry Cleaners, Montana Sporting Goods, and the Montana Grocery— became as recognizable in southeast Queens as national chains like McDonald's. Unsurprisingly though, the brash move of naming his businesses after Scarface and the hive of drug activity around them brought law enforcement scrutiny. "Mickens set up these businesses to show that he had legitimate income," explains Mike McGuinness of Queens Narcotics, "but within a block of these businesses there were people selling cocaine and heroin."

The retail businesses in the Montana name and the fleet of luxury cars were making Mickens a street legend in southeast Queens, but they were also leaving a bread-crumb trail for the feds to scrutinize. Mickens's lust for the luxe life was too great for him to worry about law enforcement, though: By the outset of 1987, as profits from his empire were piling up, he and girlfriend Bettina Jacobs Celifie were hungrily seeking out new acquisitions. The pair would page through yachting magazines and browse newspaper listings for high-priced real estate, but unlike other young couples they weren't merely fantasizing about making these sorts of luxury purchases. On February 3, 1987, Mickens bought a condo at 229-01 Estoril Drive in Diamond Bar, California, a wealthy, conservative, and predominantly white Southern California city that abutted Orange, Riverside, and San Bernardino counties. Diamond Bar wasn't chosen for its wealth or its proximity to three of Southern California's more prominent counties; Mickens selected the unit because it was about a fifteen-minute drive from the home of Celifie's father, Franz, whom he hired to purchase the Estoril Drive condo, according to prosecutors.

On the day of the condo purchase Mickens drove to the sales office in his Mercedes 560 SL which was outfitted with a multi-CD changer and a pair of phones, impossibly luxurious features at the time. Mickens associate Anthony Jacobs, Bettina, and her father took another car to the closing, a convertible red Ferrari that had a gold plate near the stick shift that read SPECIAL DESIGN FOR TOMMY. Despite calling attention to himself with the cars, Mickens insisted on concealing the true owner of the condo. Mickens's girlfriend Celifie issued nearly forty-three checks to the mortgage company to pay the outstanding balance on the Estoril Drive condo, and Mickens signed the sales contract under the name Thomas Harris. This surprised Franz Celifie, who had always known his potential son-in-law's last name as Mickens. To ease Celifie's obvious discomfort about this unusual real estate deal, according to prosecutors, Mickens created an interior design company called Soho West Design for Franz's wife; the first job for the new company was, naturally, Mickens's brand-new condo at Estoril Drive.

The California condo deal completed, Mickens flew back to New York. There was plenty of work to be done with his thriving Tony Montana retail empire and his drug business, but before Mickens got started he made a trip to his favorite luxury dealership, Martin Motorcar in Atlantic City. On February 6, Mickens and Anthony Jacobs hopped into a green Mercedes 560 SL and headed down to Atlantic City, speeding toward their destination on the Garden State Parkway at more than eighty miles an hour. Unfortunately for them, a New Jersey State Police trooper named William Ames clocked their speed at about eighty-two miles per hour (the speed limit was fifty-five), flashed his high beams at the Mercedes, and pulled Mickens over. Ames then radioed for assistance from another trooper, a standard procedure for a pull-over; he hadn't yet realized that he'd stopped one of New York's most powerful hustlers.

Mickens and Jacobs didn't act the part of street guys when Ames approached the Mercedes: they calmly handed over their driver's licenses. But when Mickens opened the glove compartment to retrieve the car registration and insurance, Ames noticed two prescription drug containers sitting near the documents. Curious, Ames asked the pair if he could inspect the bottles, and Mickens, still cool, handed them over. The name on the bottles—J. King—aroused the trooper's suspicion because the names on the pair of driver's licenses were Anthony Jacobs and Thomas Harries. Ames asked whom the drugs belonged to. Mickens said they were his cousin's, but Ames poked his head suspiciously into the Mercedes to see if there might be anything else unusual in the vehicle. He quickly spotted a small yellow bag behind the driver's seat. Catching Ames's eyes, which were now fixated on the bag, Mickens told the state trooper that it contained a small amount of cash which they were going to apply to the purchase of a Mercedes. The Mercedes they were driving in, Mickens explained, was a loaner. By this point, Jacobs had quieted; Mickens was handling things now. The money, Mickens explained, was borrowed from his uncle. Ames asked to inspect the bag and Mickens agreed, adding nonchalantly, "Oh, we got another bag of money in the trunk."

Ames then ordered Mickens and Jacobs out of the Mercedes to open the trunk for him. He gave them a quick pat-down (neither was carrying a weapon), and Mickens opened the trunk, which held yet another small plastic bag. How, Ames asked, had Martin Motorcar allowed Mickens to drive off the lot without paying for the car? Mickens told Ames that his aunt did quite a bit of business with Martin Motorcar so the dealership allowed them to take vehicles with no money down and then pay for them at a later date in cash. The story partially checked out: The Mercedes was registered to his aunt. But the large amount of cash, which Ames was waiting to count until reaching the trooper barracks, still seemed highly suspicious.

Meanwhile, Mickens was starting to lose his cool; he was becoming, Ames said later, "upset, nervous." The officer asked Mickens and Jacobs to follow him back to his headquarters at the Bass River Barracks near Atlantic City; they had no choice and drove there between Ames and his backup vehicle. At the barracks, Ames ran background checks on Mickens and Jacobs and discovered that both had extensive criminal records and that Thomas Harries was actually Thomas Harris Mickens. When Ames discovered a safe-deposit box key after frisking Mickens, he surmised that there could be a lot more cash beyond what was contained in the plastic bags.

Miranda rights were read to Mickens and Jacobs. Mickens angrily protested: He wasn't a criminal, but an upholsterer earning a mere $28,000 a year. Unconvinced, Ames called Daniel Carbone, a U.S. Customs agent with the agency's Organized Crime Drug Enforcement Task Force (OCDETF) to come down and conduct an interview with Mickens. Just a few hours later, Carbone arrived at the barracks with another U.S. Customs agent and a drug-sniffing dog. Fearing that his protestations were harming his case, Mickens stopped talking. But when Jacobs signed a waiver agreeing to an interview with OCDETF, Mickens blurted out that he had $14,695 in cash in the plastic bags. The sudden confession was a shock, Carbone said later. But Mickens didn't stop there: He explained that his uncle would kill him if the money were seized. He then repeated to Carbone the Martin Motorcar story that he'd given to Ames and, inexplicably, unintentionally revealed his own background by claiming that the uncle in question was an entrepreneur who owned a chain of grocery stores in southeast Queens. Carbone, naturally, was unconvinced and he seized the cash Mickens had in his possession ($14,695, the precise amount Mickens had admitted to carrying).

Though Mickens and Jacobs were released from the Bass River Barracks and sent back home, law enforcement would never again take its eyes off their organization. Soon, a massive federal investigation into Mickens and his crew would begin, leading to charges of drug trafficking, money laundering, and tax evasion. Somehow the hubristic Mickens failed to learn the simple lessons of that early February 1987 day, simply dismissing it as an unlucky traffic stop. This carelessness would always infect, and ultimately doom, his organization. Mickens had risen quickly from hand-to-hand dealer to street CEO, but the smarts that had fueled his ascent now seemed to desert him. Indeed, though he was barely in his twenties, Mickens was looking at his last days in the game.

Back in South Jamaica, Prince was just hitting his stride. His drug spots—the Supreme Superette and 116-80 Foch Boulevard in the Baisley Park Houses among them—were thriving. His lieutenants, brothers Shannon and Peter Jimenez and particularly Ernesto Piniella, terrified southeast Queens residents. In the summer of 1987, Prince ably played on his lieutenants' infamy in his quest to become the most notorious street player in the area. The first message was sent to the hustlers who sold weight to the Supreme Team: Refuse a request for drugs and face the grimmest of consequences. When a cocaine distributor from Brooklyn named Anthony "Chink" Carter refused to sell Prince more than a kilo of the drug at a time and then, to add to the humiliation, dated Supreme Superette clerk Laurie Glaspie, Prince turned to Piniella. Piniella was more than willing to assist his boss; he had one of his underlings murder Carter and then he led a crew of enforcers in the kidnapping and killing of Glaspie.

Prince next warned the streets of southeast Queens not to talk trash about his crew. When a South Jamaica man named Kyle Street made an insulting remark about a Supreme Team lieutenant named "Cooley," he was killed by Prince. The Supreme Team's direct competition also found itself in Prince's crosshairs; he ordered the execution of a pair of brothers named Richard and Leroy Stanley who dealt drugs in his South Jamaica territory. Supreme Team enforcers fought bitterly over who would get dibs on the job: Piniella wanted the hit, but a crew of killers led by Peter Jimenez got to the Stanley brothers first. The relentless pace of the killings—Prince's victims were so legion that many still have not been accounted for—gave the Supreme Team leader a psychotic high, but he was fast running out of legitimate targets. So when Prince heard that a cabdriver named Paul Robinson had punched a Supreme Team member, he put a hit out on the man's life even though he wasn't sure that Robinson threw the punch.

Thanks to Prince's campaign of death during the summer of 1987, his stock on the streets of southeast Queens was skyrocketing. Everything about the Supreme Team was becoming outsized: its profits (they netted up to $200,000 per week), its almost pathologically murderous ways, even the cars they drove. At a cost of over $100,000, Prince outfitted a Mercedes with gun ports and the capability to lay down an oil slick and put up a smoke screen. Prince also distributed pricey bulletproof vests to the Supreme Team's eight top lieutenants (at a cost of $1,200 each), who wore the vests proudly *over* their shirts, even in the presence of Queens Narcotics cops. Whether you were a hustler grindin' or a humble nine-to-fiver, the militarization of the Supreme Team sent an unmistakable message: You are fair game.

Under Prince's guidance, the Supreme Team had proven itself capable of nearly every method of murder imaginable. There was one notable exception: They had yet to prove they could reach someone from far outside their neighborhood. For that, Prince turned to the corrupt New York State parole officer Ina McGriff. In the past McGriff had performed mundane tasks like selling the crew fake driver's licenses or altering Prince's file with the parole board to show that he had a legitimate job. But during the summer of 1987 Prince declared that he wanted more from McGriff and he presented her with the formidable task of locating a drug dealer named Isaac Bolden who had robbed one of Fat Cat's girlfriends. Prince was eager to help Fat Cat with the task of locating Bolden because the Nichols organization supplied the Supreme Team with weight and had even forgiven debts 'Preme owed them. "Sometimes Prince and 'Preme would get keys and just not pay for them," remembers Nichols family member Marcy. "Biz didn't mind because he could turn to the Supreme Team for help whenever he wanted to. The Supreme Team was an extension of Biz's crew—but I don't think even 'Preme's workers truly understood that."

McGriff, as usual, came through for Prince: She dug up Isaac Bolden's address in Queens and, as an added bonus, she handed over his brother Henry's contact information in the Bronx, for just $3,000. Prince was enormously appreciative of McGriff's efforts, which had required more than simply looking up a phone number in the New York State Parole Board records. Indeed, McGriff and fellow parole officer Ronnie Younger had broken into a state parole board office in the Bronx while its employees were on a company picnic. Thrilled with his coup, but still respectful of the southeast Queens street hierarchy, Prince gave the Bolden brothers' information to Fat Cat. The next step was Fat Cat's call, but he owed the Supreme Team a debt of gratitude regardless of the outcome.

On August 6, 1987, Fat Cat dispatched a pair of assassins to the Bronx and Queens to take out the Boldens. Henry was shot just once but the job on Isaac was performed with far greater brutality—he was murdered on the spot. Just after 4:45 PM that day, four gunmen in a brown Cadillac strafed Isaac's body with four bullets as he stood in front of his car at 150-66 116th Avenue in South Jamaica, a mere block away from his mother's house (the address Ronnie Younger had shared with the Supreme Team). When McGriff read a newspaper article about Isaac's killing, she angrily confronted Prince. "Is this," she asked incredulously, "the Bolden we gave you information about?" Prince just smirked and said nothing.

While Prince was using his connections on the streets and in law enforcement to create a web of terror that bound together the Supreme Team and the Nichols organization, Thomas Mickens was in a similarly expansive mood despite his encounter with the New Jersey state troopers. He established contact with a cocaine distributor in Atlantic City named Norvell "Flakes" Young, from whom he secured weight on a regular basis. Connecting with a good source for weight is one of the trickiest aspects of the drug business, and with a steady flow of drugs coming from Young's base in Atlantic City, Mickens would be able to maintain his juice on the streets of southeast Queens.

Unbeknownst to Mickens, however, Young was involved in hustles far beyond the drug game: He was one of Atlantic City's biggest pimps, sending cadres of girls out late at night to boardwalk casinos like Harrah's to proposition gamblers working the slots and the tables. It was a far from glamorous trade and Young was a greedy and abusive pimp, taking the majority of his girls' profits and issuing threats of violence when they missed their numbers for the night.

One of Young's best girls was Lucy Latorre, who had worked faithfully for him for more than a decade and even had a son with him. Young allowed Latorre to stay at his house at 2228 Murray Avenue in Atlantic City, even though he disapproved of Latorre's heavy drinking. She had tried and failed at rehab more than half a dozen times, and Young openly mocked her efforts at sobering up, referring to her in front of friends as "the drunk." Just after 11 AM on May 28, 1987, Latorre was lost in one of her many drinking marathons at Harrah's Marina, downing glass after glass of her favorite cocktail, rum and coke, propositioning one potential john after another, even trying her hand at the slots. Latorre had been at Harrah's since nine the previous evening and was inebriated to the point of passing out on the casino's thickly carpeted floor. She was also deeply depressed. Young was beating her, she didn't have a place of her own, and she desperately wanted to get her baby to a better home.

When Latorre spied Detective Craig Hamblin of Atlantic City's Vice Unit sitting near a slot machine she made a desperate decision: She would ask Hamblin, a cop who had arrested her on so many occasions, for help. First, Latorre drunkenly begged Hamblin to loan her $150, the amount she needed to hand over to Norvell Young back home. Hamblin just laughed. "I've arrested you before," he said dismissively. Then Latorre explained that every time she came home with less than $150, Young would beat her. Hamblin turned serious. "Well, if you want to sign a complaint for assault," he said to Latorre, "we can arrest him and get him out of the house." Sensing that this could be her best shot at getting out of a life of prostitution and abuse, Latorre agreed to accompany Hamblin back to the Vice Unit. During the drive, Hamblin radioed Michael Morrison, an investigator with the IRS's criminal division; he was aware of a connection Young had to a big New York drug dealer and wondered if Morrison might know any more.

Morrison couldn't believe his good luck when he got the call from Hamblin. He'd been long investigating Young, and he'd just started an investigation into Mickens after learning of the seizure of cash by the New Jersey State Police in early February. Morrison rushed to meet Hamblin and Latorre at the Vice Unit offices, and when he arrived he found Latorre in a more cooperative mood than he'd imagined. Latorre poured her heart out to Hamblin and Morrison, explaining her long career as a prostitute with Young, his role in Atlantic City's drug and prostitution trades, and more importantly, his connection to Mickens. Hamblin then convinced Latorre to file a criminal complaint against Young, and to support her claim of physical abuse, he photographed several bruises on her body. With Latorre in the backseat, Hamblin and Morrison then drove over to Young's home at 2228 Murray Avenue in Atlantic City. When the trio arrived, they found Young relaxing on his front porch accompanied by one of his girls. "You're under arrest," Hamblin said, to which Young smugly replied, "You didn't listen to the drunk, did you?" Hamblin shot back: "Yes, we did. We have an arrest warrant and you are under arrest."

Hamblin radioed for a car to take Young back to the precinct headquarters. Young had put Latorre's name on the home's deed, so they were free to search the premises with her permission, which she gave. Once inside the house, Latorre handed over insurance paperwork for Young's Mercedes to Hamblin and Morrison. Another one of Young's girls, who was still in the house and had not been arrested, shouted at Latorre, "Are you crazy, or don't you know what you're doing?" Latorre was undeterred, taking Morrison and Hamblin into the bedroom to collect more of Young's paperwork. One car insurance statement provided by Latorre had Mickens's name on it and listed the place of purchase as Martin Motorcar, the dealership that Mickens had been traveling to when he was stopped by the New Jersey State Police. Morrison was elated: He had established Mickens's connection to Young and a fleet of cars. At last, the case against Mickens was taking shape.

The Game Changes

While Mickens's business was being put in jeopardy as a result of mistakes made by a far-flung cocaine connection, Fat Cat was solidifying his power in southeast Queens with violent acts committed by subordinates. The assassination of Isaac Bolden had gone without a hitch—no weapons were recovered at the scene and the police had no suspects—so Fat Cat decided to flex his muscles again from state prison. This time, the target was a girlfriend of Fat Cat's named Myrtle Horsham who had been stealing from the Nichols organization.

Horsham wasn't poaching huge amounts of cash—one of Fat Cat's crew members estimates that she stole only about $20,000—but lieutenant Brian "Glaze" Gibbs argued persuasively to Fat Cat that something needed to be done. "Glaze played on a weak moment with Biz," says Joseph "Bobo" Rogers. "We didn't need to worry about a broad who was stealing only $20,000 when we had niggas out on the block who were stealing $400,000." Horsham wasn't merely one of Fat Cat's girls: She had a five-year-old son with him named TC, nicknamed "Taxi" because Horsham would stuff dollar bills into his tiny hand and send him off in a taxi to relatives or friends. Horsham's thoughtless treatment of TC, along with Gibbs's bloodlust, led Fat Cat to his final decision in the matter: It was time for Horsham to go.

Gibbs quickly rounded up fellow lieutenant Mark "Country"

Garnes and enforcers David McClary and James Troy and headed out in a Cadillac Seville to the apartment complex of a close friend of Horsham's. They sat in the Seville and waited for any sign of Horsham; after several hours they watched her walk into the apartment building and minutes later leave hand-in-hand with TC. McClary and Troy rushed out of the car and hid behind a cluster of bushes near the apartment. Horsham put TC in the backseat of her car and then went back into the apartment. McClary and Troy had the opening they'd been waiting for: They jumped into the car and lay in wait. When Horsham returned and opened the car door on the driver's side, she was shocked to find McClary and Troy crouching in the backseat, holding TC between them.

Horsham shrieked, but McClary and Troy forced her to drive at gunpoint. Gibbs and Garnes, who had parked down the road in the Cadillac Seville, followed close behind. McClary and Troy instructed Horsham to pull into a dead-end southeast Queens street and turn off the engine. Then, either McClary or Troy (it is still not clear who pulled the trigger) shot Horsham seven times in the head, killing her instantly. Cops are also unsure if TC actually witnessed the shooting, but Fat Cat's hired assassins did leave TC unharmed. They loaded him into Gibbs's car, and Gibbs drove TC back to his grandmother's house in southeast Queens. It was the sort of trip "Taxi" had made many times before when Horsham had shuttled him from relative to relative and friend to friend, but this time he was a motherless child, dropped off in his grandmother's front yard by his mom's murderers. Gibbs found a pay phone nearby and called TC's grandmother. "The child is in the front yard," he said coolly. "Come and get him."

It was a cold and calculating hit for the unforgiving streets of southeast Queens. Even Fat Cat's lieutenants were upset with the way the job was handled. "Before I knew what was what, it was too late," says Joseph "Bobo" Rogers of the Horsham killing. "Worse, Glaze always talked a big murder game but never did anything himself. He had these kids do his jobs for him."

Targeted killings had been the stock in trade of southeast Queens crews since the murder of Parole Officer Rooney in 1985.

But the killings committed by Prince and Fat Cat were purposeless, and worse, the jobs were being committed by trigger-happy teens willing to do anything for a buck. (David McClary, for example, was paid only $5,000 and 125 grams of cocaine for the Horsham hit.) This was a sea change brought about by the conscience-loosening crack and the seemingly endless profits the drug brought to the crews. By the close of 1987, even the cautious lieutenants of the Nichols organization were feeling invincible. A disregard for consequences always brings about the beginning of the end for players in the drug business, and the crews of Fat Cat, 'Preme, and Mickens would prove to be no different.

The string of murders committed by the Supreme Team during the summer of 1987 made Prince feared and respected on the streets of southeast Queens, but they also attracted the attention of law enforcement. Queens Narcotics cops like Mike McGuinness and William Tartaglia were now closely monitoring the Supreme Team's activities and recorded numerous drug buys at Supreme Team spots. Late in the summer of 1987, Queens Narcotics even penetrated the crew's inner circle, placing an informant to relay the minutes of the Supreme Team's upper-management meetings directly to Tartaglia.

Just before 'Preme was released from prison in August 1987, an informant told Queens Narcotics that the jailed Supreme Team leader had been busily preparing the crew for his return to the streets. "He wanted to make sure all the members and various locations had their money ready," the informant told Tartaglia. According to the informant, each Supreme Team member was instructed by 'Preme to save a chunk of their profits for the returning CEO himself.

When 'Preme did finally return to southeast Queens in late August 1987, he held a formal Supreme Team sit-down in the Baisley Park Houses. Tartaglia's informant was present at the meeting, and he told the Queens Narcotics cops that 'Preme used the occasion to take a detailed inventory of the crew. 'Preme wanted to "meet new members since his incarceration, and he wanted specifically to know any firepower they had, guns, any muscle, bodyguards, and what locations they had," according to the informant. Satisfied with the Supreme Team's progress over the approximately two years of his incarceration, 'Preme instructed twenty-five or so high-ranking members of the Supreme Team present at the late August meeting to fan out once again at drug spots all over the Baisley Park Houses and redouble their profit-making efforts. In prison, 'Preme had missed the fast money of the streets, and he'd felt a jealous sting as he watched his nephew Prince become a far more potent force on the streets than he'd ever been.

'Preme's meticulous planning for the Supreme Team would go to naught: The feds were working with Queens Narcotics in their investigation of the crew, a move sparked in part by employees of New York's Special Narcotics Prosecutor who were frustrated by the Queens DA's lack of success in prosecuting 'Preme in 1985. In the fall of 1987, all of the major Supreme Team players were being surveilled including Ernesto "Puerto Rican Righteous" Piniella, brothers Shannon and Peter Jimenez, Prince and 'Preme, and even 'Preme's mother. On November 6, a massive force of Queens Narcotics cops and FBI agents raided Supreme Team locations all over the Baisley Park Houses. 'Preme and Piniella were at the movies when a Supreme Team crew member beeped 'Preme about the impending raids. 'Preme then instructed a low-level crew member to dump as much cocaine as possible from the rest of the stash houses. This early warning about the raid allowed the Supreme Team to move nearly eleven kilos of cocaine from one apartment in the Baisley Park Houses. Supreme Team crew members busily dumping the drug from another apartment weren't so lucky; an FBI agent making his way up to a stash house in Baisley Park saw a kilo of cocaine drop from an opened apartment window.

Chaos prevailed that day. Drugs were tossed out of windows and hurriedly flushed down toilets; scales and measures were left covered in cocaine and heroin; jackets bearing the Supreme Team name were left in stash houses. Queens Narcotics cops and FBI agents hit pay dirt: In one Supreme Team apartment there were books with such titles as *The Silencer Handbook, Methods of Disguise, Point Blank Body Armor,* and *Improvised Sabotage Devices,* while in another apartment a police scanner and several scales were seized. In one stash house in the Baisley Park Houses, cops seized copies of the parole information for Isaac Bolden, the drug dealer who had been slain by Supreme Team hit men on Fat Cat's orders.

The raids sent both Prince and 'Preme back to jail once again and shook up the Supreme Team's leadership. Piniella put himself in charge, and he made a savvy, ballsy first move after the disastrous law enforcement crackdown of early November: He simply shut the Supreme Team down. Piniella fired everyone in the crew, closed all of its drug spots, and collected its existing profits (about $300,000), which he then handed over to 'Preme's sister. From his prison cell on Riker's Island, Prince raged at his top lieutenant's disloyalty, but with 'Preme and nearly all of the Supreme Team enforcers imprisoned, he was powerless to stop the liquidation of his crew by Piniella. Restless and angry, Prince thought hard about his next move, which came to him quickly. His connections to cocaine distributors (who were primarily Hispanic) would be useful in prison, which was crowded with Colombian and Mexican hustlers who were serving serious time. The Supreme Team would live on, this time behind bars.

While Prince, 'Preme, and Fat Cat were all imprisoned toward the end of 1987, their legacy was still felt on the streets. But young hustlers were not following the example of the early days of Fat Cat and 'Preme, a time when as Mike McGuinness of Queens Narcotics says, "murders were committed only to preserve power." Instead, the new generation of drug business players in southeast Queens worked from the psychotic playbook of Prince without realizing that his murderous M.O. had contributed in large part to the Supreme Team's demise. Crack was fueling this homicidal new ethos, but the disappearance of wiser hustlers like Fat Cat from the streets played an even greater role. Once, all Fat Cat had to worry about behind bars was family members becoming too deeply involved in the drug business; now, he had to contend with the numerous suborganizations that sprang from his crew, like the Bebos, whose members were more loose cannons than cool CEOs.

A sixty-one-year-old livery driver named Mildred Green would be the first prominent victim of southeast Queens' cruel new street code. Just after 6 PM on September 2, 1987, Green was working at the Big D Car Service at 150-01 Linden Boulevard when a heated argument over a fare broke out between one of the company's drivers, Joel Johnson, and a passenger, Derrick Kornegay. Kornegay believed that Johnson had overcharged him five dollars for a trip, and he and his friend Reynaud Chandler angrily demanded a refund from the bosses at Big D's. When another driver, Jenner Coleman, joined in the debate, Chandler, a dealer who worked in a small, family-run crack crew operating in Fat Cat's territory near 150th Street in South Jamaica, pulled out a .357 Magnum and began firing wildly, hitting himself, Coleman, Kornegay, and Johnson. All four were treated for gunshot wounds at a local hospital and released; Chandler was charged with attempted murder and jailed at Riker's Island. Green was unharmed, but she witnessed the shooting unfold from behind her desk.

The week after the shoot-out at Big D's, Green testified about the incident in front of a grand jury at Queens Criminal Court in Kew Gardens. Her testimony was just one of many affidavits from witnesses, but the hotheaded Chandler was not interested in an honest assessment of Green's importance to the case against him. Just after 10 PM on Friday, October 2, 1987, a threat against Green's life was phoned in to the Big D's office manager, who then called the 113th Precinct in southeast Queens for help. The detective who took the call requested that the desk officer inform cops on patrol to give "special attention" to Big D's, and, as a result, a car drove past the office periodically all night. Big D's office manager also promised to stay with Green until she finished her shift at 7 AM. The night passed without incident, and Green returned to work the following evening unaccompanied by her boss. Believing that the threat had passed, Green didn't bother to call the cops at the 113th Precinct for protection. Early Sunday morning, Waddell Winston

(Reynaud Chandler's thirty-seven-year-old uncle and a member of his nephew's crack-dealing crew) walked into Big D's on Linden Boulevard and killed Green with a single shotgun blast to the head. Her body was discovered at Big D's at around 4:40 AM on October 4, after cops received a call about a disturbance.

During the mid-eighties, southeast Queens had seen countless murders committed by the drug crews, but the slaying of Mildred Green, a grandmother and a Big D's Car Service employee for more than a decade, was an authentic turning point in the history of the neighborhood. Though the Nichols organization, the Supreme Team, and Mickens's crew had received significant attention from law enforcement prior to Green's killing, they were mostly invisible to the world outside of southeast Queens. As hard as it is to imagine in the crime-conscious, post-Giuliani New York of today, the cycle of shootings, slayings, and dramatic police raids that wracked southeast Queens in 1987 barely made an imprint on the city's consciousness. That would soon change, bringing with it an intolerance of the drug business that would doom the crews of southeast Queens.

First, law enforcement would have to come to grips with the mistakes they'd made that led to Green's killing. NYPD Detective Robert Colangelo admitted to *The New York Times* on October 9, 1987, that "the totality of the police response in this situation was insufficient." This was an understatement: The NYPD wasn't simply frustrated with its response to the call to protect Green, they were gripped with a sense of outrage, powerlessness, and, at long last, a resolution to take the streets of southeast Queens more seriously. Thomas Reppetto, president of the Citizens Crime Commission, was much more blunt. "These drug guys are absolutely nuts," he told the *Times*. "They're way worse than the Mafia. They're so young and so violent that they don't have the restraint that the more traditional organized-crime guys have."

Mayor Ed Koch also seemed to sense the importance of Green's slaying, and he offered a $10,000 reward for information leading to the arrest of those responsible. Koch's effort, the first mayoral nod toward the crime wave that was consuming southeast Queens and making boroughs like the Bronx and Brooklyn look tame by comparison, yielded immediate results. On October 9, a team of six police officers and detectives raided Waddell Winston's home at 135-55 232nd Street. When cops burst through the door, Winston ran down to the basement and grabbed a .45 caliber pistol. Before he could squeeze a shot off, he was wrestled to the floor by cops. Winston was arrested and charged in the Green killing and with possessing four ounces of cocaine as well as a cache of weapons, including several 9 millimeter pistols, all of which were seized from his 232nd Street home.

Just a few days after the raid on the Winston home, another member of his crew, eighteen-year-old Tracy Middleton, was also arrested and charged in the Green killing. That both Middleton and Reynaud Chandler were in their teens shocked law enforcement and the media, but it came as no surprise to the streets. In the hothouse atmosphere of the southeast Queens drug scene in 1987, there were likely dozens of small crews just like Winston's. The "new jacks" of the crack era had been making their presence felt in southeast Queens for months.

Law enforcement's worries weren't put to rest by the arrests of Green's killers. The crews were threatening to murder witnesses for testifying even in insignificant cases. One southeast Queens resident, a Guyanese immigrant who went by his last name, Arjune, wasn't dissuaded by the atmosphere of intimidation created by the crews. Arjune lived in a three-story home at 107-05 Inwood Street in South Jamaica that was just blocks from Mom's Deli. By the end of 1987, Arjune's block was so overrun with crackheads and dealers that it resembled an open-air drug bazaar. This stretch of Inwood Street had a storied history in the drug business—Arjune's home had once been a crack house—so when cops performed buy-and-bust operations on the block they weren't sure whether the dealers were part of Fat Cat's crew or a growing cadre of freelancers that one *Newsday* article numbered to be somewhere from thirty-five to forty. Arjune made it a point of pride to call the 103rd Precinct to complain about dealers, users, and lookouts and even fancied himself to be an informant of sorts.

Arjune realized that he would one day incur the wrath of the crews for his close relationship with the cops. On November 10, at around 4:25 AM, shortly after his 911 call resulted in the arrest of a member of the Nichols organization, a pair of low-level enforcers working for Fat Cat's lieutenant Thomas "Mustafa" Godbolt tossed three Molotov cocktails at Arjune's Inwood Street home. The incendiary devices bounced off its slightly decaying wood frame, but the enforcers—seventeen-year-old Robert Webster and twenty-eight-year-old Claude Johnson—refused to stop there. At 6:20 AM, they threw three more Molotov cocktails at Arjune's home; one bounced off the frame, but two others crashed through a window and landed inside one of the rooms. Thanks to strange noises coming from just outside his house all night (scraping sounds against the walls, low, whispered conversations outside) Arjune had been awake for hours by the time the Molotov cocktails hit their mark. Before the fiery homemade bombs could do any serious damage to him or his family, Arjune picked them up and threw them back out of his window. Arjune was only slightly injured, and his home was barely damaged, but the incident frightened him in ways his previous confrontations with the crack crews of southeast Queens had not.

Stung by the criticism about the inaction that had led to the Mildred Green killing, law enforcement took unusually strong action in the wake of the firebombing. Cops were placed on round-the-clock guard outside 107-05 Inwood Street, a move that transformed the Arjune residence into an armed camp. The persistent police presence, however, did little to impede the crews operating nearby, who simply went about their business while steering clear of Arjune's home. It also did nothing to shake the resolve of the still-imprisoned Fat Cat, who had faced down far greater challenges to his empire than a tattletale immigrant. Johnson and Webster were soon arrested for the firebombing, but they were low-level enforcers who could be easily replaced by any number of aspiring street guys. Moreover, enforcers like Johnson and Webster had direct contact only with the crew's lieutenants, making connections to CEOs like Fat Cat difficult for law enforcement to prove. The firebombing of Arjune's home, even with the heat it brought to the streets in the post–Mildred Green era, was a worthwhile expenditure for the

Nichols organization, a potent signal to witnesses and informants of the fate that might await them.

After the attack on Arjune, Fat Cat's crew should have refrained from committing more high-profile acts of violence. Nichols organization lieutenant Pappy Mason and his crew of loyal Bebos followers, however, viewed the firebombing of Arjune's home as just the opening salvo in a wider war on law enforcement and those who cooperated with them.

Pappy's greatest and most intractable flaw was his irrational hatred of cops. There was, of course, no love lost between the police and 'Preme and Fat Cat. But the crew leaders had a grudging respect for the smarter cops like Mike McGuinness of Queens Narcotics. Pappy was different. He'd go on tirades about the cops that stretched on for so long that listeners had little idea what he was talking about when he wound down. Pappy's rage even baffled his Bebos followers, a group hardly inclined to like the police, as they were subjected to daily pat-downs and arrests. Those who knew Pappy say that his adolescence in Alabama—where he was viciously taunted by racist cops—cannot fully explain his antipathy toward law enforcement.

In any case, no one was surprised when, on a freezing winter's day in January 1988, Pappy exploded with rage at a beat cop working near 150th Street and 109th Avenue who instructed him to dump out a beer that was wrapped in a brown paper bag. "Do you know who I am?" Pappy angrily shouted at the officer. "Yeah," the cop retorted, "you're the guy who is gonna pour his beer out." Pappy complied with the officer's request, but as the beer cascaded onto the cold South Jamaica street he shot the officer an icy, homicidal look.

A little more than a month later, on February 24, 1988, Pappy was convicted on a weapons possession charge and given three to seven years in prison. He had been stopped on the street and caught with a tiny pistol. High-ranking members of drug crews accept the fact that police will bring weapons possession charges against them in place of more serious cases, which take time to build. Pappy, however, was furious, and he was embarrassed that he made such a foolish mistake on the streets. Getting shipped out to Riker's Island the next day after his court appearance only intensified his rage. From Riker's, Pappy placed a call to trusted Bebos lieutenant Philip Copeland. "We lose one, *they* lose one," Pappy said, signing off with the Bebos "one love." To a Bebos insider like Copeland this cryptic call was crystal clear: Take out a cop. During a follow-up call, Pappy was more specific, offering Copeland $8,000 for the hit, according to an inmate on Riker's Island who later cooperated with cops. Though Copeland knew he'd have to split the cash with his fellow Bebos (who would serve as lookouts or getaway car drivers) he nonetheless relished the opportunity to serve his boss.

Copeland decided that the perfect mark for Pappy's important job would be a twenty-two-year-old rookie cop named Edward Byrne who regularly sat parked in a squad car outside Arjune's home on 107-05 Inwood Street well into the wee hours of the morning. Despite all the violence raging in southeast Queens and the specific threat to Arjune, the job was nearly as tedious as working at a parking garage. Byrne would spend his shift reading the newspaper or watching a portable television he'd clipped to his rearview mirror. "Dave [McClary, who had assisted in the killing of Fat Cat's girlfriend Myrtle Horsham] knew a cop always sits alone there," Bebos member Scott Cobb said later in a statement given to cops. Copeland found this to be an opportunity he could not resist. He was also drawn to the sheer game-changing nature of murdering a uniformed cop in a marked car. Rival dealers and parole officers had all been slain by the likes of Fat Cat and Prince, but a cop guarding a valuable witness? That had never been done.

On February 25, 1988, Copeland gathered friends Todd Scott, Scott Cobb, and David McClary at apartment 7E at 109-10 160th Street in the South Jamaica Houses. The two-bedroom apartment belonged to Copeland's uncle Roger Phillips, and Copeland usually used the place as a stash house. The crew sat at Phillips's dining room table, which had a porcelain duck centerpiece, and began plotting out the execution of Edward Byrne. Though everyone in the group was no stranger to violence, each was reluctant to take on the triggerman role. So at one point late in the evening, Scott, Cobb, and McClary decided to draw straws from the duck centerpiece; whoever drew the shortest straw would be the killer. Todd Scott drew first and came up with the shortest straw. "It looks like it's you," Copeland said to Scott. "Then we ain't got no time to waste," Scott replied, "Let's get going."

Pappy's hired hands first had to arm themselves. Just after leaving Phillips's apartment, they stopped at the home of Cobb's girlfriend at 108-44 160th Street to pick up a .357 Magnum. They then piled into a clunky two-door 1979 Dodge with tinted windows, which Copeland and Scott had stolen from a heroin addict, and made their way to Arjune's block on Inwood Street, making a final pit stop at 115th Avenue and Sutphin Boulevard to buy bullets from a Jamaican gun dealer. The group then cruised by Arjune's home in the Dodge, sizing up their mark, and continued on to stop for a drink at a nearby bar on Liberty Avenue and Remington Street. After leaving the bar, they again canvassed Inwood Street, this time driving even closer to the slumbering Byrne. "He's sleeping, he's sleeping," Scott blurted out. "That's the one," added McClary. Just after 3 AM, Cobb parked the Dodge about a block away from Arjune's home, at Pine Grove Street and 107th Avenue. Scott then led Copeland and McClary toward Byrne while Cobb remained as a lookout in the idling Dodge.

Suddenly, another police car pulled up beside Byrne's vehicle. McClary jumped into the bushes, but Scott was defiant, not moving from his place on Inwood Street. The cop car shone its high beams on Scott, who then lifted his shirt to show that he wasn't carrying any weapons. "The guy nodded and pulled away," Scott said of the cop. About eight minutes after the cop car turned off Inwood Street, McClary, Scott, and Copeland crept up from behind on Byrne, whose view was blocked by the cage separating the front and backseats. One of the men—it is still not clear who, as they have all implicated one another in the shooting—pumped several bullets into Byrne's head, killing him instantly. Cobb, who named McClary as the triggerman, said that soon after the killing Scott peered inside the window of Byrne's car and burst out laughing. "Todd said the first shot hit the officer, and he seen his brain come out," Cobb said.

"Then Todd said one of the bullets almost hit him because it came through the door. Then David said he told Todd to come on because he was at the car still laughing. David told Todd, 'You could have fucked me up,' because he stay at the car still laughing. Todd was looking in and he's laughing. . . . 'Hee. Hee.' "

With the hit on Byrne a success, Cobb drove his friends home via the Van Wyck Expressway. "We over now," the crew crowed as the Dodge navigated the still-dark streets of southeast Queens. When Cobb arrived at his mother's house at 106-05 159th Street he boasted to his parents that he and his friends had murdered a cop. Adrenaline still pumping, Cobb strode the 40 Projects looking for a confrontation. After a brief dustup with a guy named Derek, Cobb proclaimed, "You gonna hear about me, fuck that!" a former member of the Corley Family says. "Everybody wants to be a ghetto superstar, that's what we figured," the retired Corley hustler recalls. "We didn't know nothing about a cop until the next morning. But when you got a motherfucker with an ego as big as a building ain't no telling what he may do."

When Scott returned home to his uncle's apartment on 160th Street at the South Jamaica Houses—the very place where he planned Byrne's murder—he provided a much more blunt recollection of the night to his uncle. "We rocked that nigger," Scott boasted. "I am the baddest motherfucker around. Nobody can stop me now." Scott's uncle, still drowsy from sleep, shuffled out in his slippers and said listlessly, "You're crazy," and went back to bed. At 7 AM, Copeland came by Scott's apartment to pick him up and then drove to Carmichael's Diner on New York Avenue to plot their next move. They decided to head to Pappy's safe house at 93-08 209th Street in Queens Village. But first they split their down payment from Pappy—$1,100—at Copeland's house at Lincoln Place and Nostrand Avenue in Bedford Stuyvesant.

The cash was providing too great a temptation and they decided shopping would have to come before they went into hiding. Scott bought a hooded parka and a Chicago Bears jersey bearing the number of William "The Refrigerator" Perry from a Brooklyn shop, bragging to the clerk about his hit on Byrne as he paid for the jersey.

The clerk seemed as excited at meeting the high-profile Bebos member Scott as he would meeting an NFL star like Perry. "You guys from Queens are really bad," he said, "killing cops." McClary, who was beginning to see himself as a hustling superstar, humbly accepted the compliment. "The cop was younger than me," McClary explained to the clerk. "He had his gun right on his lap. I could see his blue eyes." The shopping excursion complete, the group went off to their hiding places, McClary and Copeland at safe houses in Brooklyn, Cobb and Scott at a safe house on 209th Street in Queens Village. A pair of prostitutes soon joined Cobb and Scott at 209th Street, a confirmation by their boss of their new status. When they had remarked, "We over now," earlier that night, the exhilaration was tinged with nervousness, but now, safe in one of Pappy's apartments, it felt real.

At 8 AM the morning of February 26, 1988, Queens Narcotics cop Mike McGuinness, who was at home resting from a hurt shoulder, got a call from a fellow officer: "We're all working on that cop killing. Last night they shot a cop." McGuinness had been through a lot— he'd personally collared 'Preme at the corner of Foch Boulevard at Gabreaux Street just months earlier—but news of the Byrne killing floored him. "You kiddin'?" McGuinness burst out. He paused to reflect on the news. "It's gotta be Fat Cat," he explained, "for two reasons: First, the week before, Fat Cat had just been found guilty on state narcotics and weapons charges; second, Pappy had been arrested on a gun charge. The cops picked him up with a Berringer in his shoe. Plus Arjune's house was just a block and a half from Fat Cat's grocery."

The detective on the line with McGuinness seemed skeptical, so McGuinness put down the phone, hopped into his car, and headed to the 103rd Precinct headquarters in southeast Queens. When he arrived at the station house, he immediately understood why the cops had a hard time believing his theory. "Informants were telling them that the killing was done by a group of Jamaicans from Brooklyn who wanted to take over the territory," McGuinness says, "I was like, 'Are you kiddin' me? There's nothing more clear. It's Fat Cat.' "

As McGuinness and the cops of 103rd Precinct hunted down the perpetrators of the Byrne slaying, southeast Queens struggled to come to grips with the fact that the city's streets had almost completely succumbed to lawlessness. This was not news to those who had been exposed to the killings of parole officer Brian Rooney and Mildred Green, to those who had watched the crews take over rundown blocks in southeast Queens and elsewhere with the precision of a Marine unit, to those who had friends and relatives descend into the madness of crack addiction. It wasn't really news to New Yorkers, either, who had long been accustomed to crime and decay, from the arson fires that engulfed the Bronx in the late seventies to the rampant subway crime of the early eighties that culminated in December 1984 with Bernhard Goetz shooting four African-American teenagers who had attacked him on a Manhattan subway car. But the slaying of Byrne was a cataclysmic event in the city's history nonetheless. In a speech immediately following the rookie cop's funeral, Mayor Koch said that Byrne's death was as important a milestone as the passing of Martin Luther King Jr., John F. Kennedy, and Franklin D. Roosevelt. "If drug traffickers have become so emboldened that they can engage in the assassination of a young police officer, then our whole society is at risk and we will have anarchy," Koch said. "That is why his death rivals the others. Not because he is Edward Byrne, but because of what it means to have this police officer assassinated."

Nearly 10,000 cops (including the entire 103rd Precinct) attended Byrne's funeral at St. James Church in Seaford, Long Island, on February 29, 1988. It was the largest turnout for a fallen colleague in the history of the NYPD. Eight cops carried Byrne's coffin, which was draped in the green-and-white flag of the NYPD, into St. James Church as an officer played "When the Battle Is Over" on a bagpipe. The coffin was followed by Byrne's father, Matthew, a former police lieutenant and a close friend of Rudy Giuliani, who was then the U.S. Attorney for the Southern District of New York. Inside the church, as Matthew Byrne clutched a photograph of his son, Reverend Thomas DeVita remarked with sadness upon Byrne's youthfulness as well as the short time he had spent with the NYPD (barely eight months). DeVita also asked the congregation to pray for Byrne's killers. "Eddie's murderers need to be pitied and also prayed for," he said. "They do not know the sanctity of life. They cannot really know or understand what they have done, even though this is such a terrible sin."

This was a charitable assessment of David McClary, Scott Cobb, Todd Scott, and Philip Copeland, one that could only come from a clergyman. As Byrne's family was mourning, Copeland, using an alias, met with Pappy at Riker's Island to accept his boss's praise for carrying out the killing. In the visiting room at Riker's, Pappy embraced his dutiful Bebos lieutenant and slipped a $40,000 gold-and-diamond ring embossed with a map of Africa off his finger and handed it to Copeland.

While Pappy was deeply grateful, Byrne's murder was perceived by Fat Cat as a powerful act of subterfuge that could deliver a death blow to the entire Nichols organization. "The purpose of Edward Byrne's killing was to undermine Fat Cat," explains a man close to Fat Cat and several Nichols organization lieutenants. "Pappy wanted to make sure Fat Cat never came home from prison. He'd tasted power while Fat Cat was away and he never, ever wanted to give it up. And the surest way to do that was to kill a cop and pin it on Fat Cat." Former Nichols organization lieutenant Joseph "Bobo" Rogers believes that Pappy had come to see himself as invincible. "The killing of the cop was more about Pap's ego than anything else," Rogers says. "Cat played the game like a grand wizard. Everything he did was thought through. With Pap, it was the opposite: He acted on feelings regardless of the consequences." A former Corley Family member, however, sees the Byrne slaying differently, as the culmination of one of the most violent eras on the streets of southeast Queens. "I think these guys were living a movie," he explains. "They used to watch *Scarface* and *The Godfather* and they wanted to be that. But the biggest gang in New York is the NYPD so if you hurt one of them you're asking for trouble. That's what the streets got after the killing of Edward Byrne: trouble."

4

Downfall

Byrne's murder brought more than trouble to the streets of southeast Queens: It spurred a national conversation about the failing war on drugs and the rising crime rates in America's major cities. Mayor Koch took out a full-page advertisement in *The New York Times* (paid for with $12,900 from his reelection campaign) headlined OFFICER EDWARD BYRNE WAS MURDERED IN COLD BLOOD. LET'S MAKE CERTAIN HE DIDN'T DIE FOR NOTHING. In the *Times* ad, Koch compared the United States to a banana republic and called for an end to aid to illicit-drug-exporting countries like Mexico and Colombia. More boldly, Koch took aim at President Reagan's anti-drug policies. "We are truly in a war with the drug pushers," Koch said, "but the president is not acting as commander-in-chief. If anything, he's acting as a wimp." Following Koch's lead, *Newsweek* and *Time* ran features about the perilous state of the streets like "Losing the War?" and "Tears of Rage: Americans Lose Patience with Panama and with a Failed Drug Policy."

The attention from media and politicians emboldened the NYPD to take much more aggressive action in southeast Queens. On March 3, 1988, this new approach, which flooded neighborhoods like South Jamaica with cops, bore fruit: Todd Scott and Scott Cobb were arrested and charged with Byrne's murder. The next day, both Philip Copeland and David McClary were arrested on similar charges. The persistence of the cops (nearly three hundred drug dealers had been rounded up in southeast Queens since Byrne's death) and the massive reward for information leading to the arrest of his killers (which had grown to $130,000 thanks to a $25,000 contribution from a group of New York Stock Exchange members) and, of course, the shockingly loose lips of the perpetrators of the crime made this conclusion all but inevitable.

This was just one arrest, however; the streets of southeast Queens—particularly South Jamaica, where most of the crews were based—were going to require a lot more effort to get under control. On March 7, 1988, the NYPD announced the formation of the Tactical Narcotics Team (TNT), a force of more than a hundred cops assigned to tackle the drug problem in South Jamaica. TNT officers would be flanked by city buildings inspectors who would confiscate property from landlords who allowed drug trafficking on their premises. Like the increased police presence in southeast Queens that helped yield Byrne's killers, TNT had an almost immediate effect on the streets. "They watching all the drug spots," Viola Nichols complained during a March 9 phone conversation that was wiretapped by law enforcement. "It's just so hot here ever since that police officer got killed. You know what I'm saying? And, I mean, you know, you can't even make no money." The next day, Nichols again complained about the post–Edward Byrne heat on the streets, this time to Nichols organization lieutenant Brian "Glaze" Gibbs. "He's my man and everything but why did he do that stupid shit," Nichols griped about Pappy Mason during a wiretapped phone call, to which Gibbs responded with evident frustration: "He mad." Nichols then speculated that Pappy had killed Byrne in order to do permanent damage to her brother's organization. "Do you think he did it for the weight to fall back home?" she asked. "Or you think he was a goddamn fool?" Gibbs replied that he was simply sick of the additional scrutiny from the cops: "We're getting tired of taking that shit."

Business at Big Mac's Deli and spots around 150th Street, which had previously run around the clock, was reduced to a few hours a day. "We don't even be allowing the workers to come out until, like, twelve at night," complained Viola Nichols's daughter Monica "Pumpkin" Connally. She lamented to Nichols organization lieutenant Kevin "Gucci" Brown during a wiretapped phone call, "So we don't get no money in the daytime period. . . . They had only made like five hundred that night till the next morning." Sensing the heat about to come down on Fat Cat's organization, Nichols family member Marcy even personally appealed to Fat Cat to let her out of the crew. "I'm scared," Marcy told Fat Cat. "I don't want to be down no more." Fat Cat assured her that the Nichols organization would survive the scrutiny from cops, but Marcy wasn't taking any chances. She moved to a new apartment on Queens Boulevard under an assumed name and spoke to members of the Nichols organization only when she could meet with them in person.

The state of Fat Cat's empire was more perilous than even its leadership imagined. A federal investigation had begun into the Nichols organization at the beginning of March 1988 and the phones of nearly every member were tapped, including the main line at Big Mac's Deli. Spurred by the killing of Edward Byrne, the feds were now closing in on the organization. Fat Cat's bottom line was suffering, but they had no idea that business was about to get much worse.

Thomas Mickens was also under the law enforcement microscope, but unlike the savvier Fat Cat he seemed oblivious to the scrutiny. There was no slaking his thirst for luxury goods even as the feds were arranging cocaine buys near the Montana Grocery. Not long after purchasing the condo in Diamond Bar, Mickens acquired a thirty-eight-foot Bayliner yacht for $110,467.20 in cash. During the transaction, Mickens laid out bundles of bills in front of boat salesman Marc Bechtold, who later said that he spent nearly three hours counting it all.

The acquisitions of the yacht, condo, and luxury cars kept Mickens away from his drug and retail businesses, leaving duties in the hands of lieutenants like Anthony Jacobs. "When Tommy is running, he never ran out," complained a hand-to-hand dealer named George Jenkins, who was working for Mickens, during a wiretapped March 1988 telephone conversation. "I wanted two hundred fifty grams, here comes two hundred fifty more." Jenkins wasn't much more professional than Jacobs: The phone conversation during which he complained about Jacobs's mismanagement of the Mickens organization took place during a cocaine deal with an undercover cop. Indeed, Jenkins was so undisciplined that during the transaction with the undercover he arranged for a separate deal with another customer. Jenkins also had an unfortunate habit of speaking far too freely about Mickens's activities: As he and the undercover cop waited for an associate to deliver the drugs, he bragged about his boss's fleet of cars and his real estate holdings (including a tennis club in Queens). "The feds want him basically for tax evasion," Jenkins explained to the cop. "I don't think they can, you know, like put drugs directly into him." Jenkins then boasted that the feds wouldn't be able to prosecute Mickens as he had shielded himself from law enforcement scrutiny with legitimate investments. "He owns a lot of shit here in Queens," Jenkins said. "He owns half a block here. Merrick and 226th Street. He owns a tennis club over there. . . . He's into a lot, he invests [his money] wisely." To make things worse, Jenkins added, "The guy I work for is on the run."

As it turned out, Mickens wasn't as skilled at hiding his cash as Jenkins believed. His practice of writing checks for just under $10,000 to avoid filing Currency Transaction Reports with the IRS was growing familiar to the feds; indeed, the dozens of checks Mickens would write for a single purchase became a calling card of sorts. Nor was Mickens really on the run; he was splitting his time between Southern California and southeast Queens in order to forestall the moment when cops would finally take him in. "We had lots of buys near the Montana Grocery, lots of people close to Mickens talking about him being the boss," explains Mike McGuinness of Queens Narcotics, "but we came to the conclusion that we weren't gonna get him quickly because he was out in California with that condo and Bayliner."

While it delayed his arrest, living a bicoastal life also meant that Mickens's drug and retail businesses were moving from simply mismanaged to dangerously chaotic. Leslie Banks, the twenty-five-year-old manager of Montana Dry Cleaners, was selling cocaine out of the store, and because her brother worked for the Supreme Team, she was tremendously indiscreet in conducting her business. Banks liked to brag to her customers that her pure, top-shelf product came directly from Mickens himself (which was not true; it came from freelancers) in the hope that the appearance of backing from one of southeast Queens' most feared hustlers would offer her protection on the streets. This assumption was completely wrong, and it would have enormous consequences for both Banks and her boss. "Leslie Banks thought she would be protected by pretending that she was selling Montana's drugs," says a former southeast Queens hustler, "but it had the reverse effect. Instead of being afraid, the hustlers thought there was a payday there."

Word quickly spread through southeast Queens and even the streets of the tougher neighborhoods of Brooklyn: The Montana Dry Cleaners held an enormous stash of drugs thanks to the store's well-connected manager. On May 3, 1988, Brooklyn tough Court-ney Allen and his girlfriend, Hollis resident Cathleen Brown, burst into Montana Dry Cleaners on Hollis Avenue looking for drugs and cash. Brown and Allen were known as a Bonnie and Clyde of the crack era: efficient in the execution of robberies and astoundingly brutal toward their victims. When Banks and coworker Kerry Pow-ell opened the store's safe in the basement for Brown and Allen and no drugs or money were inside, the pair murdered them with gun-shots to the head. A Montana Dry Cleaners employee named Fred-erick Harris tried to prevent Allen and Brown from leaving the store and was shot in the jaw.

The double murder soon brought law enforcement heat that Mickens could no longer ignore. He had to return to Queens before the increasing number of cracks in his empire caused its foundation to crumble. In early May 1988, he returned to New York for Banks's funeral. In order to avoid the cops who were a constant presence near Montana Dry Cleaners since the shooting, Mickens stayed at a lavish $750,000 home he'd purchased in Dix Hills, Long Island, instead of his apartment in Queens. He was growing tired of the cat and mouse game with the feds; buy-and-busts were putting a signif-icant dent in his profits, and he was exhausting the means of hiding his growing number of assets. Indeed, just before his arrival in New York, Mickens filed his first tax return in years, claiming that he'd made $73,710 in 1986, when in fact he'd made in excess of $500,000. Mickens's plan was to lie low on Long Island while lieutenants like George Jenkins and Anthony Jacobs faced the heat from cops in southeast Queens. But it was not to be: A southeast Queens informant immediately relayed the news of Mickens's arrival in New York to Queens Narcotics.

The feds quickly traced Mickens to his manse at 4 Deanna Court in Dix Hills and just after 6 AM on May 10, federal agents and members of the NYPD bearing an arrest warrant raided his home. The raid began with Queens Narcotics Detective William Tartaglia making a call from a public phone near 4 Deanna Court to make sure that Mickens was home. When a male voice answered the phone, agents from the FBI, DEA, and IRS made their move. They were shocked when Mickens himself answered the door. He explained that he had to go to a back bedroom to get a key to open the door, but the agents warned him to step back and then smashed the glass in the door. As the feds rushed through the front door, Detective Tartaglia shattered the sliding glass doors in the rear of Mickens's home. Once inside, Tartaglia let several agents in the house behind him, including FBI Special Agent Nerisa Gay Pilafian, who then performed a protective sweep of the sprawling upstairs area, which boasted a sauna. In Mickens's home office, Pilafian found stationery with the letterhead of Montana Grocery as well as checks bearing one of Mickens's many aliases, "Thomas Harries." As the agents searched his home, Mickens sat quietly in handcuffs in the dining room downstairs. Unlike the more combative Prince or the foolishly sloppy 'Preme, Mickens was not going to put up a pointless fight with law enforcement; nor was he about to give the feds the pleasure of finding narcotics in his Long Island manse.

After years of watching Mickens accumulate a fleet of luxury vehicles and millions of dollars' worth of commercial and residential real estate, the feds had their man. One southeast Queens resident speaking to *Newsday* sounded as though he were eulogizing a great rock star or even a civil rights leader. "Everybody knows Thomas," the man told the *Newsday* reporter on May 11. "If you don't know Thomas, you missed out." Mickens had come to embody, to borrow a phrase from Queens rapper Nas, "'hood movie star." With Mickens's arrest, 'Preme in prison, and Fat Cat's organization under round-the-clock scrutiny from the feds, law enforcement finally had southeast Queens' seemingly invincible triumvirate of hustlers on the ropes.

While Mickens's legacy was being mourned, Fat Cat's organization was under siege, not just from the feds but from rival dealers. A crew of low-level hustlers from Brooklyn seethed with resentment at the success of Fat Cat's lieutenant Brian "Glaze" Gibbs and was looking for any way to take him down. "They all grew up together and the next you thing you know Glaze and his whole crew are eating well in Queens but they're still up in the projects in Brooklyn," explains Fat Cat's son Raheem Tyler. "They were very jealous, and they decided that they could not let that stand." The Brooklyn hustlers began monitoring Glaze's movements, and on May 20, 1988, after overhearing Glaze say, "I'm going to Momma's house," they followed him back home to southeast Queens. Then, just as Glaze turned onto 139th Street in South Jamaica, the hustlers lost sight of him. Undeterred, they knocked on doors asking, "Is this Momma's house?" according to Tyler. After meeting with cold stares or slammed doors at several residences, one homeowner pointed the crew to 114-21 139th Street, the home of Fat Cat's mother, Louise Coleman.

Just after 12:30 AM, in an eerie echo of the Arjune incident of November 1987, the Brooklyn hustlers tossed a firebomb through the front window of Coleman's three-story frame house. Coleman, her husband Amos, Fat Cat's sister Mary, and three of Mary's children were home at the time. The fire swept quickly through the house, but the family had enough time to escape thanks, ironically, to gunfire that rang out through their block just after the firebomb was tossed. One of the Brooklyn hustlers had fired sixteen wild shots from a semiautomatic weapon, striking two cars on the block, both

of which belonged to the Coleman family. The brother of Supreme
Team lieutenant Bimmie—who happened to be on the block talking
to several Nichols organization members when the fire broke out—
shot back, but missed his target. All but Fat Cat's sister Mary, who
had suffered a stroke and was confined to a wheelchair, were able to
flee the fire. Louise Coleman attempted to pull Mary out of the fire
but to no avail; she was far too heavy to lift, and Mary was burned
alive in her wheelchair.

Behind bars in Wallkill State Prison, Fat Cat raged. His beloved
sister was dead, and though extracting revenge was entirely within
his means, any violent action coming from his organization in the
post–Edward Byrne era would bring even more unwanted law
enforcement scrutiny. To soothe his anger, Fat Cat applied to prison
officials for leave to attend Mary's funeral. The request was denied,
and Fat Cat furiously composed a letter to his relatives to be read at
the service: "Dear Momma," Fat Cat wrote, "I was informed by my
lawyer that I would not be able to attend the funeral because the
administration feels that it would be too much a security risk to
bring me down. I know you know that this is just another way of
them trying to torture me by not letting me say good-bye to my sister. A lot of things are going through my mind right now, but I'd just
like to take a moment to say times like these is when a family really
needs to stick together. I'm sorry that I can't be there to give my
support and that I can't be there to show my love. As I'm sitting here
writing this I keep thinking about Babysister. I remember how
sweet she was. I say to myself if there's a heaven, she's there. If in
any way I'm the cause of this I'm sorry because you know I would
most definitely trade places with her." The letter was signed: "I love
you, Lorenzo." 'Preme also sent his sympathies to the Nichols family; these came not in a moving letter or a condolence card but in a
flower arrangement in the shape of an S.

The extraordinary violence promulgated by Fat Cat had come
full circle to take the life of one of his closest family members. But
even with the cops of TNT flooding the streets of southeast Queens
and both major newspaper editorial boards and Mayor Koch
inveighing against the crews, the killings continued. Just after 9 PM

on May 28, 1988, a gunman strafed the 202nd Street home of hustler Raymond "Rashid" Blair. Believing that rival Shane "Qasim" Fells was responsible for the shooting, Blair and an associate named Gary "Pep" Steadman set off for Fells's home at 202nd Street and 109th Avenue to exact revenge. At around 10:25 that evening, Steadman and Blair fired several shots into Fells's house; Fells was spared but his mother, Maxine Peterson, was struck with two bullets as she stood in the kitchen holding her six-month-old son in her arms and talking on the telephone. Her son survived, but Peterson died at the scene.

As Peterson's lifeless body dropped to the kitchen floor, the gunmen fled down 109th Avenue, firing at least eighteen more shots. When cops from the 103rd Precinct arrived on the scene they found enormous piles of shell casings covering the sidewalks. The shooting was planned and executed with such carelessness and cruelty—the gunman had made a snap judgment that Fells was responsible for the initial firing at his house, and he strafed his home with no regard to whom they might kill—that southeast Queens was plummeted into a fresh sense of despair. Mildred Green, Edward Byrne, Mary Nichols, and now Maxine Peterson: The neighborhood's body count was steadily ticking upward with no reversal of the trend anywhere in sight.

These remorseless killings helped push the crack era to the brink of destruction, but incompetence, hubris, and plain bad luck played a part in its demise, too. Fat Cat's lieutenant Mark "Country" Garnes was a proud money man for the Nichols organization (as well as the suborganization run by his brother Glaze) who strode fearlessly through airports, train depots, and bus stations armed with duffel bags stuffed with cash meant to be laundered or brought to a distributor. On June 9, 1988, Robert Mallon, an alert agent with the Los Angeles Airport's Narcotics Task Force, spied Garnes (who was accompanied by two underlings from the Nichols organization) at the Continental Airlines ticket counter. Mallon and his partner Deputy Ricky Ross noticed Garnes scanning his surroundings suspiciously. Moving in close with his partner to observe Garnes, the pair overheard him ask for a cash refund for a Los Angeles–to–New York ticket. When Mallon and Ross trained their eyes on Garnes and he fidgeted nervously as he made eye contact with Mallon, the pair decided to approach him.

"You're not under arrest," Mallon said as he faced down Garnes at the ticket counter. "You're free to leave. But can I have permission to speak with you briefly?" Garnes agreed to talk, explaining that he'd asked for a refund on his ticket because the flight had unexpectedly been rerouted through Denver. Mallon listened to Garnes's story and asked to see his receipt from the airline. The Continental Airlines receipt Garnes handed to Mallon bore the name Antonio Brooks. Mallon's suspicions about Garnes seemed to be confirmed. "I work for the Narcotics Task Force," Mallon said to Garnes. "Are you carrying any large sums of money?" "Eight hundred dollars," Garnes replied. "May I have permission to search your bag?" Mallon continued, "I'll strictly be looking for narcotics or money." Garnes unzipped his duffel bag and handed it to Mallon. Inside the duffel bag was a red cardboard box holding thousands of dollars in cash. "How much money is here?" Mallon demanded. "Somewhere between thirty and thirty-two thousand dollars," Garnes replied calmly.

Mallon escorted Garnes back to his office in LAX. Garnes had stayed cool during the initial confrontation, but he was becoming visibly nervous, offering a wildly improbable story about the cash being used for the rental of a Malibu home and the purchase of a car. Mallon wasn't buying it, and he summoned DEA Agent Charles Bullock to his office to reinterview Garnes and inspect the duffel. Bullock found $31,295 in the bag along with a receipt for a Rolex and a contract for a beeper. When Bullock ran a background check on Garnes, he discovered that he had been arrested for narcotics-related offenses in New York. Bullock seized the cash—under federal law, money can be subject to forfeiture if it is believed to be proceeds from a narcotics sale—but allowed Garnes to leave. As Garnes walked out of Mallon's office, he cursed himself for taking such a big financial hit, though he was happy to avoid spending the night in prison. Unbeknownst to him, however, he'd provided the feds with another crucial piece of evidence in their case against Fat Cat. They now had a fresh lead in their investigation of Glaze's group.

When he returned home to southeast Queens in July 1988, there seemed to be no end to Garnes's run of bad luck. He and Gibbs were constantly fighting with Fat Cat's sister Viola, whom they had hired (with the permission of Fat Cat) as a bagger for their organization. It was a terrible decision: Viola's crack addiction was making her a slow, unreliable bagger. She would sit in an apartment at 1533 155th Street in South Jamaica with all the tools of the trade—clear plastic bags, rubber bands, and a stamper reading HIT MAN (the brand name of heroin sold by Gibbs's group)—yet bag only about $4,000 worth of the drug a day. Gibbs and Garnes expected at least double that amount, and they chided Nichols for her poor performance. Nichols was also cutting their heroin with too much quinine, which turned their pure product (dubbed "P") into low-quality stuff with a horrible street rep. Compounding her bad work ethic, Nichols asked for loans and raises. "They just took $33,000 from me!" Garnes shouted angrily to Nichols in response to a request for a bonus, referring to the incident at LAX.

The problems presented by Nichols's shoddy work paled in comparison to the other forces rocking Glaze's business. He and Garnes were convinced that they, along with Fat Cat and his crew, were being watched and wiretapped by the feds. So they instructed their baggers, enforcers, and lieutenants to communicate only in Pig Latin or a street slang bred in the South in which Zs were inserted into the middles of words. It was a crude, poorly thought-out ruse (indeed, wiretaps of Glaze's workers saying things like "Police ran in the spi-zott and di-zid every-thiz-ing up" were later presented at his trial), and nothing could prevent the Gibbs and Garnes organization from coming apart at the seams. The feds were bearing down on them, and the crack-addicted Nichols was working too sloppily and for too many crews, thus exposing her bosses to buy-and-busts. So blatant was Nichols in disregarding street protocol that she was even dressed down by hand-to-hand dealers. "Don't talk like that on the phone, sweetheart," said a worker at one of Glaze's drug spots after Nichols spoke freely about her drug-packaging operation. "Don't talk like that on the phone?" Nichols responded, unsure of what the worker meant. "Package and all that, *don't*," the dealer said curtly. "Why can't I say that?" Nichols said. "I'm not talking about no drugs on the phone."

The lack of discipline affected all of the crews and ultimately cemented their downfall. After making an enormous undercover purchase of heroin (some $70,000 worth) near Big Mac's Deli from Fat Cat's distributor Man Sing Eng in late July 1988, the feds moved on Glaze's and Fat Cat's crews simultaneously. Just after 6 AM on August 11, 1988, FBI Agent Dixie Vaughn led a raid on 111-32 146th Street, the South Jamaica home of Garnes's girlfriend Linda Astbury. The action by the feds was perfectly timed: Garnes and Astbury pulled up on a motorcycle soon after a team of agents knocked on her front door. The pair submitted to arrest without incident, but during the car ride over to FBI headquarters Astbury complained to Vaughn, "I thought the FBI only went after big criminals. We're small potatoes."

Astbury's remark did have some truth to it; Glaze's organization may have been doing decent business on the streets of Brooklyn and Queens, but it couldn't compare to the sheer size and profit-making abilities of Fat Cat's crew. As the dozen or so federal agents were taking down Glaze's group, an army of nearly four hundred law enforcement officials descended on Fat Cat's drug spots throughout southeast Queens, seizing property (including the firebombed home of Mary Nichols at 114-21 139th Street in South Jamaica) and arresting more than thirty Nichols organization enforcers, runners, lieutenants, and suppliers. Fat Cat himself was rousted the day of the raid, moved by federal agents from his cell in Wallkill State Prison in upstate New York to administrative segregation in New York City's federal Metropolitan Correctional Center. When assistant U.S. Attorney for the Eastern District of New York Leslie Caldwell announced the indictment the next day, the roster of hustlers named was so vast—"Jughead," "Ninja," "Bugout," and "Shocker," among them—that nearly every southeast Queens street guy seemed to be implicated.

By the end of 1988, Fat Cat, Mickens, and James "Wall" Corley were all imprisoned on federal drug conspiracy charges, facing the stiffest prison sentences of their long criminal careers. Fittingly for hustlers who cut such dissimilar profiles on the streets, each handled his fate in a strikingly different manner. Fat Cat resigned himself to spending the rest of his life in jail and even sent word from prison through lieutenants like Joseph "Bobo" Rogers that he didn't mind if female family members such as Viola Nichols testified against him in order to receive reduced prison sentences. Many took him up on his offer. Fat Cat also allegedly cooperated with the feds in their prosecution of Pappy Mason for the killing of Edward Byrne. "Because of his cooperation," says a former law enforcement source, "he'll be able to realize his dream of coming home to his grandchildren." But the extent of Fat Cat's cooperation—or even if he cooperated at all—isn't clear. All that is known is that Fat Cat was transported from his prison cell to the U.S. Courthouse in downtown Brooklyn for a secret session in which a plea was entered. When asked by a *New York Times* reporter about the proceeding, U.S. Attorney Andrew Maloney said only, "Sealed pleas are extraordinary measures taken by the government."

News of the secret proceeding spread quickly on the streets of southeast Queens, but it nonetheless did little damage to Fat Cat's reputation. Cooperating with law enforcement in the prosecution of Pappy Mason was understandable, because the senseless murder of Edward Byrne would forever sully Fat Cat's legacy, especially now that Arjune's home had been turned into a memorial to the fallen cop.

George Bush campaigned in the fall of 1988 with Byrne's badge in his pocket as a symbol of his "get tough" approach to the war on drugs, and by the end of the year, Congress passed the Anti-Drug Abuse Act of 1988, which stipulated a mandatory minimum sentence of five years for a first-time offender's possession of more than five grams of crack cocaine and applied the death penalty provision to drug dealers. During the signing of the bill at the White House on November 18, President Reagan stood side-by-side with Byrne's parents, and he hailed the fallen cop as a national hero. "With us today are Matthew and Ann Byrne, who join us as we give their son's comrades the valuable tools they need to carry forth the fight for which young Eddie so valiantly gave his life," Reagan proclaimed. "We salute Eddie Byrne. We salute his family for their determination that his death will not have been in vain." Soon after the Anti-Drug Abuse Act of 1988 became law, legislators began work on the the Crime Control Act of 1990, which authorized nearly $900 million for a new program called Edward Byrne Memorial State and Local Law Enforcement Assistance and codified a Crime Victims' Bill of Rights in the federal justice system.

Fat Cat, though, wasn't looking for payback against Pappy or to salvage the reputation of the Nichols organization—what he really wanted was a reduced sentence for his beloved "Momma," Louise Coleman. Pappy, typically, was in no mood for self-sacrifice even though *his* mother faced a lengthy prison sentence. "I couldn't believe he was gonna let his mother go to trial," says Joseph "Bobo" Rogers, sounding still angry at the memory. "I said, 'Pap, how you gonna do that? How you gonna let your mom go to jail?' " Pappy, according to Rogers, responded, "I'm not lettin' these crackers roll me." Worse, Pappy, locked up with Rogers at the Metropolitan Correctional Facility (MCC) in Manhattan, began threatening parole officers, thus reinforcing the image of Fat Cat's crew as cop killers just as they were about to go to trial. Rogers made his unhappiness with Pappy known, and Pappy in turn issued a threat against Rogers's life through a Nichols organization member named Shocker. "Pap said that I'd better be ready," Rogers says, "and I told Shocker, 'Cut off your dreads, put them in an envelope, and give them to Pap.' " Shocker didn't cut off his dreads but he told Pappy of Rogers's slander against Pappy's Rastafarian lifestyle. The Rogers-Pappy beef grew so serious that all of MCC seemed tense.

Pappy made his move one day during visiting hours at the prison when members of the Nichols organization were meeting with their attorneys. He showed up to the meeting room sporting "war gear" (prison slang for a jumpsuit stuffed with books meant to protect the wearer from punches and stabbing attempts). He also hid a crudely made shank underneath his T-shirt. "I ran back to the cell to get my shank, which had a rope attached to it," Rogers remembers. "I wrapped the rope around my wrist and when Pap passed by I grabbed him by his dreads and stabbed him." Pappy responded unpredictably, knifing Garnes, who was standing at a nearby pay phone. Furious, Rogers wrestled Pappy to the ground, taking multiple stab wounds. A huge crowd—which included several prison officials, Nichols organization lieutenants, and none other than John Gotti—stood watching the melee until Fat Cat stepped in and separated the men. Fat Cat was able to broker a cease-fire between his two lieutenants afterward, but Rogers never forgave Pappy for not standing up for the Nichols organization's women.

Mickens, meanwhile, was fighting the charges against him with the tenacity and pure bluster that marked his time on the streets. In Brooklyn federal court, ubiquitous criminal defense attorney Robert Simels portrayed Mickens as both an admired community leader and the beneficiary of a massive, multimillion-dollar inheritance from one of southeast Queens' most iconic numbers runners, Thomas "Lucky" Harris Sr. With Mickens's help, Simels was able to round up half a dozen of Harris's old gambling cronies, all of whom testified about Harris's purported millions. Their testimony was offset, however, by assistant U.S. Attorney Kirby Heller's presentation of evidence that Harris had a measly $3,000 life insurance policy before he passed away, hardly the stuff of a street millionaire. In another courtroom coup, Simels put New York Knicks point guard Mark Jackson—who went to St. John's University in Jamaica, Queens, and was friendly with Mickens—on the stand as a character witness. In the courtroom, however, Jackson seemed less than enthusiastic about the task. "Tell us, Mr. Jackson," Simels said, "among the people you know who know Tommy, does he have a reputation for honesty?" "Could you repeat that?" Jackson said. Simels carefully repeated the question. After a long, uncomfortable pause Jackson said blandly, "Yes."

For several members of the jury, the media attention (Mickens was profiled in the *Times*), the celebrity pals of Mickens, and the prospect of handing down a guilty verdict against one of the most dangerous (and beloved, by some) drug kingpins proved too much. One juror after another passed handwritten notes to U.S. District Court judge Thomas Platt asking to be dismissed. "The codine [sic] is wearing off," wrote one juror. "Can [I] ask my doctor for a topical, local anestisia [sic] for the future?" Wrote another: "[My] grand-mother pass [sic] on Saturday . . . in Washington, North Carolina. I would like to be in North Carolina Wednesday night . . . to attend the funeral." In the end, the jurors overcame their reluc-tance to adjudicate on the high-profile case: In December 1989, after deliberating for just three days, they found Mickens guilty on charges of drug conspiracy, money laundering, and tax evasion.

Mickens was defiant as he addressed Judge Platt at sentencing. "There were no drugs around me," he said, dressed sharply in a cream-colored suit, crisp white dress shirt, and black-and-white tie. "They found no drugs or weapons in my house or my mother's house. They want to get me because of my lifestyle, because I am young, and because I had money." It was a mere recitation of defenses presented at the trial, rather than the sort of conciliatory speech Mickens could have given to plead for leniency. Unsurpris-ingly, Judge Platt was harsh in doling out the sentence. He con-sulted a life expectancy table and, calculating that Mickens had about forty-four years left to live, he sentenced him to thirty-five years in prison and a $1 million fine.

At 'Preme's trial, Simels mounted an equally novel defense. The feds had the wrong guy, Simels said, because Queens Narcotics informants could not differentiate between the numerous hustlers in southeast Queens who referred to themselves as Supreme. Dur-ing his cross-examination of Detective William Tartaglia from Queens Narcotics, Simels pushed this theory so hard that he made Tartaglia seem unsure of his own testimony. "Which Supremes are you referring to?" Tartaglia said at one point during the trial, sound-ing like a flummoxed witness who had taken the stand for the first time. "Not Diana," Simels shot back, "I am talking about the people in Queens County." These bizarre courtroom tactics didn't work; the feds and Queens Narcotics had built an even stronger case against 'Preme than they had against Mickens. Indeed, the November 1987 raids yielded not only drugs and weapons but also jackets and signs bearing the Supreme Team name.

Experienced in the ways of the judicial system, 'Preme could see that a guilty verdict was virtually certain. Unlike Fat Cat or Pappy, he was deathly afraid of prison; 'Preme wasn't a street fighter, and he could vividly imagine suffering at the hands of those who were. He pled guilty to operating a continuing criminal enterprise in exchange for receiving a reduced sentence of twelve years. There was no Mickens-like last stand at sentencing, just rote affirmations of the crimes he had committed. "The government has that in connection with the plea to this superseding information, that I should ask you whether you were involved in at least three narcotics offenses in connection with engaging in the continuing criminal enterprise was set forth in the superseding information," the judge explained to 'Preme. "Were you?" 'Preme admitted that he was. Did 'Preme serve as "organizer, supervisor, and manager" of the Supreme Team? "Yes," 'Preme answered. "Willfully?" continued the judge. "Yes," 'Preme said. "Intentionally?" Again: "Yes." Finally, the judge asked, "No one forced you to do it?" to which 'Preme responded, "No."

The humbling 'Preme received in the courtroom was eased by the light sentence handed down by the judge. Fat Cat and Mickens were going away for decades; with good behavior, 'Preme could be out in less than ten years. By acknowledging that he ran the Supreme Team, 'Preme insured that his rep would survive his time away; all he had to do was endure his short stint in prison.

Just as the Supreme Team's titular founder was sent away, its heir was coming home. Buttressed by a web of connections to Colombian cocaine distributors he'd made while in prison, a newly freed Prince set his sights on reviving the crew. To celebrate his release from prison in the spring of 1989, Prince bought himself a $65,000 BMW and, in one of the boldest moves in the Supreme Team history, had corrupt New York State parole officer Ina McGriff accompany him to the car dealership. The bulk buys of cocaine were fattening Prince's profits, and the cash, especially during a moment when hustlers were grindin' for small change, had the added effect of making his status on the street skyrocket. Colombians were actually approaching Prince with offers to do business. One Colombian distributor, Gus Rivera, practically begged Prince to go into business with him, offering to slash his prices and even suggesting that they rob rival distributors together. Flattered, Prince accepted Rivera's offer to sell cocaine on the cheap to him and gave him a job with the Supreme Team.

Rivera was part of an expanding roster that included Ernesto "Puerto Rican Righteous" Piniella and Shannon Jimenez (returning as lieutenants) as well as a host of low-level southeast Queens hustlers like David "Bing" Robinson, who agreed to allow their homes to be used as stash houses. When the stash houses were raided, Prince had a crew of teenagers and small children in his employ to move the drugs just before the cops showed up or, more boldly, even afterward. During a raid of a stash house run by Bing in southeast Queens, a neighborhood kid nicknamed "Pee Wee" walked out of the home with a kilo of cocaine tucked in his waistband. A pair of Supreme Team workers were arrested down the street at the corner of Foch and Sutphin Boulevard, but Pee Wee escaped.

This was an amazing feat of lawlessness but Prince's ego, and the increasing crack use among Supreme Team members, meant such successes would be rare. When cops seized $13,000 of Supreme Team cash from lieutenant Trent "Serious" Morris, Prince marched over to the precinct house and got the name and phone number of the arresting officer and the voucher number for the seized cash in hopes that he could one day retrieve the cash. Prince also demanded that Supreme Team members forcibly take over housing project apartments or even entire floors of buildings to use as a base from which to sell drugs. "Take the third floor," Prince gruffly told enforcer Roy "Pookie" Hale during a wiretapped phone call. "Make that home." Prince was referring to 116-80 Guy Brewer Boulevard in the Baisley Park Houses, a building that the founding members of the Supreme Team had called home in the early 1980s but which had since become a high-rise crackhouse under Prince's guidance. His crew members took over numerous apartments and prowled its halls and lobby. "That third floor of the Baisley Projects was like 5th Avenue at Christmas time," assistant U.S. Attorney Leslie Caldwell said later. "Peddlers started selling without having to worry about retaliation."

Despite their struggles with crack addiction and the regular busts of stash houses and hand-to-hand dealers, business still flourished for the Supreme Team. Gus Rivera, the cocaine distributor who had pleaded with Prince to sell drugs to the Supreme Team, was introducing the crew to new and bigger connections. Rivera's friends Fernando and George, a pair of Colombian distributors who only went by their first names, were fast becoming the favorite suppliers of the Supreme Team. The duo would bring major weight to 116-80 Guy Brewer Boulevard at a moment's notice. "Gus would beep Fernando and George," assistant U.S. Attorney Caldwell explained, "and they would show up with a duffel bag and the deal would be done." These transactions were so effortless that the pair of Colombians seemed to have no idea who they were dealing with. In July 1989, Supreme Team enforcer Roy "Pookie" Hale decided to give them a taste of the crew's power.

Hale's plan was to ambush Fernando and George for their drugs and cash. No matter that the Supreme Team would have to find new cocaine connections afterward; the display of power took precedence over any practical concerns. Hale assembled a crew of the Supreme Team's toughest members including Wilfredo "C-Justice" Arroyo and Ernesto "Puerto Rican Righteous" Piniella to help execute his plan. But before they made their move on Fernando and George, the crew first needed permission from Prince, who was back in jail again serving one of his many short sentences on state narcotics charges. Prince gave the order to take out Fernando and George to Piniella over the prison phone. "Do it," Prince commanded during the call, "just as if it were me." Piniella wanted to do his boss proud, so the night before the July ambush he gathered the entire Supreme Team security force at the Baisley Park Houses. Addressing the large crowd, Piniella was purposefully vague: There would be a major transaction tomorrow, he explained, and the entire crew needed to show up, no excuses.

The next day, the Supreme Team security members showed up

outside 116-80 Guy Brewer Boulevard just as promised. Only the increasingly unreliable Julio Hernandez (Shannon's brother) was absent; he was out somewhere in Manhattan smoking crack. Everyone was surprisingly calm given what was about to take place except Gus Rivera, who was anguished that the distributors he'd introduced to the Supreme Team were about to be murdered. Rivera managed to put his game face on and when Fernando and George showed up with their duffel bag full of cocaine, he accepted the shipment without betraying his nervousness. Arroyo, Jimenez, and Hale then led the Colombians up to apartment 3K, a one-bedroom unit that Hale was renting. Soon after arriving in the apartment, the trio forced Fernando and George to the ground and tied their hands with rope. A dresser was then pushed up against the door to block anyone from entering. "Take the cocaine," Fernando pleaded, "just don't kill us."

Hale smacked Fernando in the head with a gun to quiet him. The mood in the apartment was suddenly becoming tense. Arroyo instructed Piniella to go downstairs to see if anyone was waiting outside for Fernando and George. After a quick bit of surveillance, Piniella noticed a pair of Hispanic-looking men sitting in a car. He ran back upstairs and asked for instructions from Arroyo. "Go outside and get them," Arroyo said, assigning Piniella and Jimenez to the task. When Piniella and Jimenez went downstairs they noticed that one of the men was on a pay phone while the other was still sitting in the car. Piniella, who spoke Spanish, said to the man on the phone, "Fernando would like to speak to you inside." He followed Piniella to 3K where he was pushed to the floor along with Fernando and George. But Arroyo wasn't satisfied. "Go back out and get the other guy," he barked. Piniella went back outside and said in Spanish to the other man, "Fernando wants to see you inside." But just outside apartment 3K, the man started to panic so Piniella drew his gun, pushed the man to the floor, and brought him inside where the trio of Colombians waited.

The Supreme Team's original plan was to murder only Fernando and George but now four men were lying in wait to be executed. Arroyo struggled to come up with a method of murdering the entire group. "What should we do, slit their throats?" he asked Piniella. Frustrated with the crew's bickering, Piniella left the apartment. "I'm going out in the hall," he said. "You decide." As Piniella waited outside, Supreme Team enforcer Harry Hunt arrived. "What's going on?" he asked excitedly. "Are they here yet?" When Piniella nodded his head, Hunt rushed inside. Hunt was a true sadist, and his presence spurred the Supreme Team to action: The Colombians were strangled with ropes and beaten in the head with hammers. Just as the killing was taking place, Prince phoned a downstairs apartment, 1K, from prison. "How much do you think you got, how much cocaine?" Prince asked Piniella, clearly excited about the potential take of cocaine. "Five," Piniella answered. "You didn't get ten?" Prince said. Piniella responded meekly, "He only brought five. C-Just said it was five." Prince was becoming irritated. Their haul of drugs was modest, and there were certainly going to be plenty of bodies to dispose of. "What are you doing with the guys upstairs?" Prince demanded. "They're chilling," Piniella said coolly. "They're on ice." Prince paused a moment and tried to put Piniella at ease: "Don't worry, I'll take care of it."

But Prince was in prison, and the responsibility of disposing of the corpses of the Colombians fell to his enforcers. The crew hogtied the Colombians, wrapped their bodies in huge garbage bags from the New York Housing Authority, and then tied the bags with ropes in order to keep the bodies in place. As Piniella served as lookout, the lifeless Colombians were brought out one by one to a blue Ford Taurus driven by Jimenez. The last body to be removed from 116-80 Guy Brewer Boulevard—George's—was so bloodied that the enforcers were forced to wrap it in a thick piece of carpet pulled from apartment 3K. As Piniella dragged George's body down the stairs, he slipped and fell on the blood that had been seeping from the corpse. His fellow Supreme Team members got a huge kick at the sight of Piniella knocked off balance and wiping George's blood from his shirt. "Righteous got all soaked up in blood!" Harry Hunt said, barely controlling his laughter. After the bodies were loaded up in the Taurus, they were dumped at a series of locations—145-40 155th Street and 167th Street and 120th Avenue, 174th Street and

116th Avenue—all just blocks from the Baisley Park Houses. The Supreme Team's enforcers didn't even bother to remove the New York Housing Authority garbage bags from the corpses, and they left on one body a green laundry bag of a make that was used in the Baisley Park Houses.

Speaking in Five Percenter code that night, Arroyo informed Prince that the deed was done: "Born, Cipher, Divine, Whys," an acronym for bodies (*C* alternates with *O* in Five Percenter–speak). Prince was satisfied with the Supreme Team's work, but instead of lying low after the quadruple homicide he decided to strike again. Jaime Padro, the distributor Prince had met on Riker's Island, was offering to connect the Supreme Team to a new pair of even more formidable Colombian cocaine dealers, Fernando Suarez and Pablo Perlazza. With Fernando and George now vanquished, the Supreme Team desperately needed new cocaine connections, so Prince immediately took Padro up on the offer. Prince put Arroyo in contact with Padro, who then introduced Arroyo to Suarez and Perlazza. The Colombians were happy to have new clients and the Supreme Team was thrilled to have their supply lines functioning again. Just as Fernando and George had done so many times before, Suarez and Perlazza would show up at apartment 3K at 116-80 Guy Brewer Boulevard in the Baisley Park Projects with a duffel bag of cocaine and then leave with ample Supreme Team cash.

The Supreme Team's relationship with Suarez and Perlazza was beneficial to both parties, but Prince and Arroyo were feeling greedy. They were still disappointed at coming away from the killings of Fernando and George with a mere five kilos, and were lusting after a truly big score. So, just after 6 PM on August 22, 1989, Arroyo called Suarez at his New Jersey home to request a major shipment of cocaine. When Suarez and Perlazza arrived at 3K, they placed their duffel bag on the dining room table and unzipped it to reveal just two kilos of cocaine. The Supreme Team enforcers were not dissuaded by the small quantity of drugs: As he had often done in previous meetings with the pair, Arroyo walked back to the bedroom to get the cash. But this time, Arroyo reached down to the living room floor and grabbed a gun hidden beneath a beach towel.

Suarez and Perlazza were frozen in fear; they faced not just an armed Arroyo but several Supreme Team strongmen including Julio Hernandez (who had rejoined the crew), Roy Hale, and Harry Hunt. (Piniella was absent as he'd been having a crisis of conscience since the slayings of Fernando and George.)

"Why are you doing this, CJ?" Suarez pleaded to Arroyo. Arroyo offered a lame explanation about the Supreme Team's suspicions that Suarez and Perlazza might be cops or informants. He then ordered Hernandez and Hale to tie the hands and feet of the Colombians with black electrical tape. Hernandez went one step further, placing plastic bags over the heads of Suarez and Perlazza. But the grim sight started to spook Hernandez. "I could see the plastic bags like sucking into their mouths," he said later, "and them trying to gasp for air." Hernandez stumbled back into the dining area; he wanted to separate himself from what he knew was about to take place even though it was much too late for that. Hale scowled at Hernandez and then picked up a baseball bat and took one mighty swing after another at Perlazza and Suarez. "He was banging them in the chest because they were making a lot of noise and moaning and groaning," Hernandez said, "and he hit Pablo in the head and then blood started seeping out of the bottom of the bag and after a while they stopped moving."

With expertise gleaned from the killings of Fernando and George, Arroyo and his enforcers dispatched Suarez and Perlazza quickly, hog-tying their bodies, covering them with laundry bags, and then carrying them out to a waiting car. Once again, the Supreme Team had difficulty transporting a body out of 116-80 Guy Brewer Boulevard. Hunt struggled to slide Perlazza's body, which was hemorrhaging blood, down the stairs. Once he got downstairs, he simply stuffed Perlazza's corpse into a shopping cart the Supreme Team had stolen from a nearby supermarket and wheeled him away from the Baisley Park Houses and into the getaway car. This time, the Supreme Team took a little more care in disposing of the bodies of Suarez and Perlazza, dumping them into thick, wooded brush in a remote area of southeast Queens near 135th Avenue and Cranston Street.

Meanwhile, Gus Rivera was panicking. The Supreme Team's killing of his friends Fernando and George was frightening enough but the slaughter of Suarez and Perlazza had him shaken to the core. Rivera began wearing a bulletproof vest, and Piniella confirmed his suspicion that the Supreme Team had targeted him for death during a phone call just before Piniella stopped working with the crew. On August 18, Hernandez and Arroyo staged an argument after a Supreme Team meeting at 116-80 Guy Brewer Boulevard. Thinking he was safe with the crew embroiled in the fracas, Rivera left the building without even a glance at his surroundings. As Rivera pushed open the door and walked outside, Harry Hunt sprang from behind a pillar, put a .44 Magnum to Rivera's head, and fired. "We got to about the end of the courtyard and a shot rang out," Hernandez explained. "I turned . . . and I seen Rivera falling face first hitting the ground and Hunt standing behind him with a small black gun . . . an aura of smoke around him."

Rivera miraculously survived taking a bullet to the head and was treated at Mary Immaculate Hospital on 89th Avenue in Jamaica. The Supreme Team, naturally, considered the job unfinished, and when Rivera was released from the hospital on August 28 Arroyo followed him back to his girlfriend Toni McGee's home at the Jade East Motel on South Conduit Avenue in South Jamaica, near JFK Airport. On the way, Arroyo, accompanied by enforcers Hernandez and Hale, stopped at apartment 3K to pick up their weapons. Arriving at the hotel just a few minutes later, Arroyo and Hale spotted McGee, who had just left the room she was sharing with Rivera, in the parking lot. Approaching McGee, they coolly asked for her room number. She refused to divulge it. "You tell us," Hale demanded. "*You tell us or we'll kill you.*" McGee relented: "Three hundred twenty," she said, and then nervously handed over the room key. Arroyo and Hale moved quickly. The pair didn't want Rivera to get lucky one more time. They ran up to room 320, slid the key into the lock, and then burst through the door and opened fire on Rivera. He was killed instantly, but in the volley of bullets one shot hit Hale in the hand. He stumbled down the stairwell of the Jade East, droplets of his blood hitting the floor as he made his way out into the sunlight. The Supreme Team's beef with Rivera would have provided cops with potent evidence linking the crew to the killing, but Hale's blood at the crime scene ended up making law enforcement's case irrefutable.

At the end of the eighties, this sort of violence gave the residents of southeast Queens the impression that the Supreme Team ruled the streets. But the endless murders were a sign of desperation, not of power. The Supreme Team had nothing to gain from the killings other than relatively small amounts of cocaine, and they had everything to lose. The murder charges that followed would bring prison sentences—including seven concurrent life terms for Prince, six life terms for Wilfredo "C-Justice" Arroyo, and two life terms for Harry Hunt—far exceeding the punishment meted out even to Fat Cat. "The four legs of the stool" of major drug dealers operating in southeast Queens had been broken, an unnamed law enforcement source boasted to a reporter from *Newsday,* referring, of course, to the indictments of Fat, 'Preme, Mickens, and the Corley Family. Nonetheless, the Supreme Team was still standing and, fueled by crack addiction and a sick sense of power gained from the killings of the Colombians, they were behaving like the undisciplined freelancers who were beginning to dominate the streets.

Like the Supreme Team under Prince's management, these new jacks on the streets of southeast Queens and in equally tough neighborhoods in Brooklyn and the Bronx were engaging in senselessly violent, open-ended free-for-alls that ratcheted up New York State's murder rate to previously unseen heights (in 1990 alone, 2,606 people were killed) and brought increased law enforcement heat to the streets. By the end of the eighties, stories began appearing with near-daily frequency in the media, often emphasizing the randomness of the killing: "Random Killings Are Latest Weapon in Crack War," blared a typical Associated Press headline.

The crack game freelancers frightened the streets in ways that the bigger, more organized crews—even at their murderous late-eighties peak that wrought the slayings of Edward Byrne, Maxine

Peterson, and Mildred Green—could not. Rolls-Royce-driving hustlers like Mickens and multimillionaire empire builders like Fat Cat were behind bars, but few were feeling safe. Indeed, the lower stakes made the streets of southeast Queens even more deadly by the early nineties. Hustlers were grindin' simply to survive; disagreements over turf and product that would have been settled or dismissed were now cause for war. Even the media could sense the closing of an era. On December 31, 1989, *Newsday* marked the end of the eighties with an article that perfectly captured the moment: "The Decade When Queens Was King." That royalty came with a price—and not merely for the leaders of the Supreme Team and the Nichols organization. The avalanche of "get tough" legislation that passed in the wake of Edward Byrne's murder helped the population of federal and state prisoners skyrocket from approximately 500,000 to nearly 2 million currently. The United States has become, in University of Buffalo professor Michael Niman's memorable phrase, an "Incarceration Nation"; it's a trend that began with President Nixon's initiation of the war on drugs in the early seventies but truly took off only with the reign of the game-changing, iconic hustlers of southeast Queens.

Left to right: Chris "Jughead" Williams, a member of the Nichols crime organization; rapper Kurtis Blow; and Lorenzo "Fat Cat" Nichols.

Left to right: Lorenzo Nichols, James "Wall" Corley, Kenneth "Supreme" McGriff.

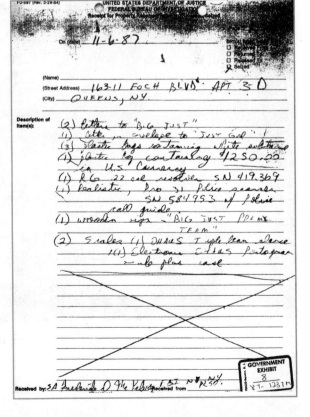

Arrest warrant from November 1987, which sent McGriff back to prison just months after he was released. The arrest of 'Preme and others led to a shake-up in the Supreme Team leadership, until Gerald "Prince" Miller regained power from prison.

FBI record from search of Supreme Team stash house, November 1987. This was one of many such raids undertaken after a string of murders in the summer of 1987 attracted the attention of law enforcement.

James Corley and Kenneth McGriff.

P E D I G R E E   S H E E T

1. Magistrate Case Number: 87-1257 M (CR 87-750-1)

2. DEFENDANT'S NAME: McGriff Kenneth (NONE)
   (Last)   (First)   (M.I.)

3. Defendant's Telephone #: 718 527-8699

4. Defendant's Address: 161-12 Foch Blvd., Quens, NY (mother's Home)

5. DATE OF BIRTH: 9-19-60   AGE: IN DET   SSN: N/A

6. Citizen of: US   Needs _____ Interpreter

7. Name of Interpreter used today: _____

8. Removal proceeding: _____ Yes ___No___ Other District: _____

9. ARREST WARRANT ISSUED: yes   DATE ISSUED: 9/5/87

10. Date and time of arrest: 4:20 pm 11/9/87   Deft. in custody: ✓ yes ___No

11. TITLE: 21   SECTIONS(S): 841(a)(1)

12. BAIL SET AT: Temp QP   ; BAIL HEARING DATE & TIME: 11/16/87

13. Arraignment on Complaint held: ✓ yes   _____ no

14. Time of Arraignment on Complaint: 2:45 /pm 11/10/87

15. (a) STATUS CONFERENCE SET FOR: _____
        (Date)   10 AM CRR   (Time)

    (b) Preliminary hearing set for: 11/20/87 ; or waived _____

16. ASSISTANT U. S. ATTORNEY: Kirby Heller   Ext. 7541

17. DEFENSE COUNSEL'S NAME: David Cohen / Michael Vald
    ADDRESS: 125-05 Queens Blvd., Kew Gardens, Queens NY
    _____ CJA _____ RET. _____ LEGAL AID _____ NONE
    TELEPHONE NUMBER: (718) 793-1553

18. Excludable Delay Code (if any): _____   Start Date: _____
                                              End Date: _____

SWORN TO BEFORE ME THIS 10th DAY OF Nov , 19 87

H S C
UNITED STATES MAGISTRATE

By Mag Chrein Complaint unsealed 11/10/87 @ 2:45 P.m

Court form filled out by Kenneth McGriff after his arrest in November 1987.
Despite getting off easy on previous arrests, 'Preme was sentenced to twelve years;
he only served eight and was released in 1995.

```
UNITED STATES DISTRICT COURT
EASTERN DISTRICT OF NEW YORK

------------------------------------x
                                    :
UNITED STATES OF AMERICA            :
                                    :
     -against-                      :
                                    :
LORENZO NICHOLS, HOWARD MASON,      : Indict. No. 88 Cr. 496 (ERK)
LOUISE COLEMAN, AMOS COLEMAN,       :
VIOLA NICHOLS, JOANNE McCLINTON,    :       AFFIDAVIT
NICHOLS, IDA NICHOLS, MARICA        :
NICHOLS WILLIAMS, MARTHA CRAFTS,    :
CAROL CRAFT, CLAUDIA MASON, WILSON  :
SKINNER, KAROLYN TYSON, MARK        :
GARNES, PARIS WILLIAMS and MAN      :
SING ENG,                           :
                                    :
          Defendants.               :
                                    :
------------------------------------x

STATE OF NEW YORK   )
                    ) ss.:
COUNTY OF NEW YORK  )
```

LORENZO NICHOLS, being duly sworn, deposes and says:

1. I am a defendant in the above-captioned matter and I make this affidavit in support of the annexed application.

2. On August 11, 1988, I was brought to the Metropolitan Correctional Center ("MCC") from the New York State Correctional System. I was placed in what I later learned was Unit Nine South. Since that time, I have been kept in what I have now been informed is called administrative segregation. Essentially, this status has prevented me from having attorney-client visits between the hours of 8:00 a.m. and 8:30 p.m.; has interfered with my

Prison complaint filed by Lorenzo Nichols several months after the murder of policeman Edward Byrne, orchestrated by Howard "Pappy" Mason without approval from Nichols. Fat Cat felt he was treated unfairly by the police after the murder, and he was allegedly furious at Mason.

opportunity to telephone my attorney, and even my family; and has also prevented me from visiting and utilizing the main law library in the facility.

3. I was advised upon my placement in a two-man cell in which I am locked in 24 hours a day that this was a temporary measure subject to my being classified in the institution. I have never received any further notifications, nor had any further review of my status. No one ever advised me that I was a security risk. On or about September 13, 1988, I had an occasion to speak with the Warden who advised me for the first time that my status was a result of security concerns. To my knowledge I have never been a security risk in the state facilities in which I was incarcerated, nor had I created any security risk to the MCC.

4. On September 19, 1988, I was advised by Mr. Holt that I was being moved from "behind the glass" and stepped down a level in my administrative detention status and, that if I did not create any problems for a week or a week and one-half, I would be placed in general population. On September 20, 1988 at approximately 4:00 p.m., Officer Gonzalez handed me the annexed Special Housing Review pink form. It is my belief that the apparent efforts to now comply with the appropriate law and regulations governing the Bureau of Prisons have been made in anticipation of the pending hearing before this Court.

-2-

5. The restrictions I have been placed in significantly impair my ability to prepare for trial. Although the MCC claims that I have access to the unit law library, that "privilege" is of no value. The main law library has a law student who is able to advise inmates as to what books or materials are available for a particular problem or question than an inmate might pose. I am not sophisticated enough to prepare written requests for materials without access to that librarian. Furthermore, on numerous occasions I have contacted my attorney's office and requested Mr. Simels to come to the MCC to meet with me. He has repeatedly advised me that his efforts to arrange visits are usually frustrated by his inability to reach staff members at the MCC to arrange such visits, or even when he is able to contact them, they are often unavailable, so that said meetings cannot occur. The assertion that I am being detained in administrative detention because I am a security risk is inconsistent with the fact that I am able to have regular visits with all other inmates from my floor. Further, the efforts to prevent my contact with co-defendants also seriously impairs my ability to review and discuss the facts and potential defense in this matter. As I have been incarcerated since 1985, almost all of the alleged activities set forth in the complaint occurred with my co-defendants and others. The only method of my learning the true facts is to

-3-

discuss them with my co-defendants. There is obviously a further inconsistency in the effort to segregate me from my co-defendants, which is apparent from the fact that when I am brought to court, I am placed in the same holding cell with co-defendants and other prisoners in the MCC for hours.

7. All of the areas that I have referred to in this affidavit make clear to me that I am being discriminated against in an arbitrary manner by the Bureau of Prisons, and that their efforts to now serve upon me documents to justify their prior actions or inactions should not be countenanced by this Court. I respectfully request that this Court direct that I be placed in general population so that I can have regular visits with my attorney, the opportunity to meet on a regular basis with my co-defendants, as all other inmates on my high security floor are permitted to do, and to review tapes from the extensive interceptions acquired by the government in this investigation.

Lorenzo Nichols
LORENZO NICHOLS

Sworn to before me this
21st day of September, 1988

Robert M. Simels
NOTARY PUBLIC

ROBERT M. SIMELS
NOTARY PUBLIC, State of New York
No. 31-4619798
Qualified in New York County
Commission Expires Sept. 30, 19__

-4-

Kenneth McGriff, Lorenzo Nichols, James Corley, and others.

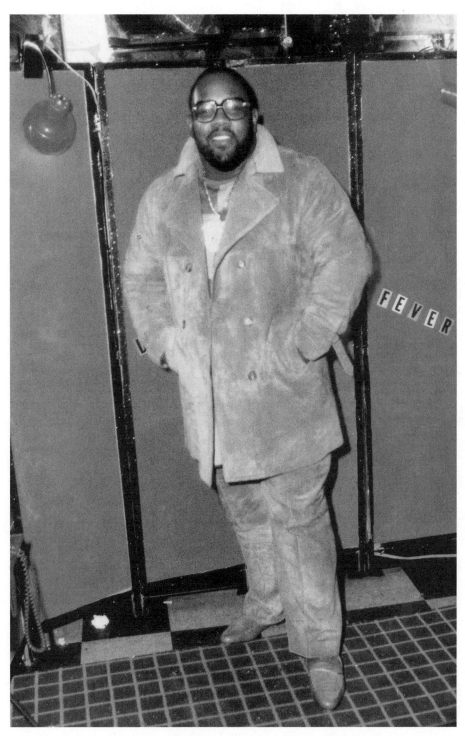

Lorenzo Nichols at a nightclub called Fever.

Lorenzo Nichols and his beloved Louise "Momma" Coleman, who was deeply involved in his organization and helped run the business from Mom's Deli until she was convicted on drug charges.

Lorenzo Nichols and one of his highest-ranking lieutenants, Joseph "Bobo" Rogers.

Maxine Peterson was murdered in 1988 when her house was
strafed with gunfire by two men trying to kill her son,
Shane "Qasim" Fells.

Left to right:
Gerald "Prince" Miller,
"Big Cee," and Shane Fells pose
at Leavenworth Federal
Penitentiary, 2005.

Complaint about police harassment filled out by Gerald Miller, who claims his business as real estate. Prince once even went to a precinct in person to demand the return of $13,000 seized as drug money.

AFFIDAVIT FOR SEARCH WARRANT
CRIMINAL COURT OF THE CITY OF NEW YORK
COUNTY OF QUEENS

State of New York)
County of Queens)

Det. William Ryan, Shield #848, assigned to the Queens
Narcotics District, being duly sworn, deposes and says,

1. I am a police officer and have been for 6 years. I have
been assigned to investigate narcotics cases for 2 years.

2. I have information based upon the following:

A. I am currently assigned to an investigation of alleged
cocaine traffic at 139-18 249th Street, Queens County, City
of New York, more particularly, the basement and first floor
apartments.

During the course of this investigation, your affiant and
fellow officers have made surveillances and observations which
are described below.

B. On January 4, 1990 I debriefed an individual who is not
a regular police informant but who has in the past furnished
reliable information leading to 20 arrests and two seizures
of narcotics regarding the drug organization known as the
"SUPREME TEAM" which is presently being orchestrated by Gerald
"Prince" Miller. During the debriefing, this individual("CI")
stated that he was employed by Gerald "Prince" Miller as an
enforcer, and that Wilfredo "C-Just" Arroyo is Miller's top
lieutenant in charge of security. Wilfredo "C-Just" Arroyo
no longer resides in the Baisely Projects. However, according
to the CI, Arroyo in addition to his position as head of
security, continues to actively sell crack which is contained
in black top vials in the Baisely Projects. The CI also
states that Arroyo presently resides in the Rosedale area of
Queens, New York. During the course of this investigation,
I have discovered that Wilfredo "C-Just" Arroyo resides at
139-18 249th Street, Rosedale, Queens, New York (the subject
premises).

C. On December 15, 1989, from 8:20 pm to 10:15 pm, a
surveillance was set up in the vicinity of the Baisely Houses
by *Det. John Sullivan. He informs me of the following:

    10:00 pm - Standing together in front of 117-06
               Guy R. Brewer Blvd., Queens, New York
               were:

        DAVID "BING" ROBINSON
        NYSID #4261171M

        HON. JAMES E. ROBINSON
                            Judge.

WILLIE COLON
NYSID #6178962K

GERALD "PRINCE" MILLER
NYSID #4356050R

WILFREDO "C-JUST" ARROYO
NYSID #4278853Y

During this period, Robinson was standing
in front of Arroyo trying to shield Arroyo
from Detective Sullivan's view. This lasted
for about 10 minutes and at 10:10 pm, these
individuals started walking toward 116-80
Guy R. Brewer Blvd. During this period,
Robinson continued to shield Arroyo from
Detective Sullivan's view.

* At the time of this surveillance Det. Sullivan was a police
officer, however, since the date of this writing he has been
promoted from police officer to Detective.

D. On January 11, 1990, from 4:25 pm to 4:50 pm, a
surveillance was set up at 139-18 249th Street, Rosedale,
Queens, by Detective John Saager. He informs me of the
following:

    4:39 pm - Wilfredo "C-Just" Arroyo is observed
              exiting a vehicle together with two
              females, a young male and an infant,
              and Arroyo together with these in-
              dividuals are observed entering the
              subject premises through the side en-
              trance on the left side of the house.

E. On January 18, 1990, from 4:40 pm to 5:40 pm, a
surveillance was set up at the Baisely Houses by Detective
James Phelan. He informs me of the following:

    4:40 pm - Detective Phelan observed a group of male
              blacks congregating around Gerald Miller.
              Also observed in this crowd was Wilfredo
              Arroyo. Det. Phelan observed Miller in
              conversation with this group for about
              fifteen minutes. During this time,
              Miller had the attention of the group and
              was waving his left hand in which he was
              holding a notepad and pointing to each
              individual in the group. After the
              meeting ended and the group dispersed,
              Miller and Arroyo continued to converse.

    4:55 pm - Arroyo is observed walking toward a
              double-parked vehicle and engaging in
              conversation with two black males inside

the vehicle. The conversation lasted for approximately five minutes. and after the vehicle left the area, Arroyo walked back toward Miller.

F.   On March 17, 1990, from approximately 10:10 am to 12:00 noon, a surveillance was set up at 139-18 249th Street, Rosedale, Queens, (subject premises) by Det. James Phelan. He informs of the following:

> '10:55am - Wilfredo "C-Just" Arroyo is observed exiting from the left side door, ground level of the subject premises. Arroyo is further observed getting into a vehicle and leaving the area.

G.   A citizen informant has related information to Det. Wayne Pollaci, who in turn has informed me that Wilfredo "C-Just" Arroyo has been living in the subject premises, specifically the first floor and basement apartments since September of 1989.

H.   Your affiant also states that on March 17, 1990, United States Postal personnel were interviewed by Det. James Phelan. Det. Phelan informs me that since September of 1989, United States mail and parcel post has been delivered to the subject premises in the name of Wilfredo Arroyo, and that Wilfredo Arroyo accepts same.

3.   As part of this investigation, my fellow police officers and I have been monitoring telephone calls from the telephone number (718) (465-2680) at 223-31 110th Avenue, Queens Village, N.Y., pursuant to Eavesdropping Warrant SP11-90 authorized by Justice John J. Clabby. In addition, my fellow police officers and I have been monitoring telephone calls from the telephone number (718) (481-6904) at 116-80 Guy R. Brewer Blvd., Queens, N.Y., pursuant to Eavesdropping Warrant SP9340-89 authorized by Justice John J. Clabby. The following is a partial list of telephone calls in which Wilfredo "C-Just" Arroyo is a party:

CALL #	DATE	TIME	DESCRIPTION
202	12/13/89	5:35 pm	Miller tells Arroyo to "get the best possible...prices...for the stuff they spoke about yesterday".

In my opinion as a police officer trained in narcotics investigations, I believe Miller and Arroyo are talking about cocaine because the term "stuff" is a street name for cocaine and had been used by the various targets in this investigation to refer to cocaine.

HON. JAMES E. ROBINSON
Judge.

Affidavit for search warrant in case against Gerald "Prince" Miller and the Supreme Team. Nineteen eighty-nine was the year Prince returned from prison and reinvigorated the organization's drug-dealing efforts through a series of Latino connections he'd made in prison.

Irv "Gotti" Lorenzo outside the Brooklyn Criminal Court
on the day of his indictment on federal money-laundering charges.
(AP/Wide World Photos)

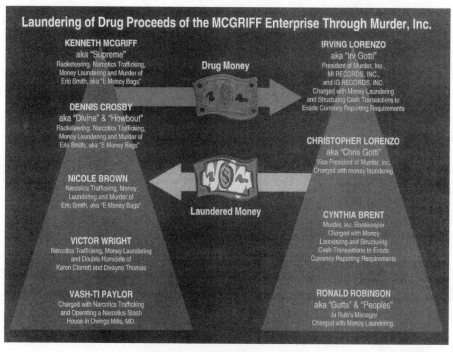

Flowchart from federal prosecutors used in the case against Kenneth McGriff, Irv Lorenzo, and Murder Inc.

Jay-Z and DMX onstage at the Amazura Ballroom in Queens in 1998, at the show where the beef began between Ja Rule and 50 Cent. At center, in the background, is Colbert "Black Just" Johnson, a Supreme Team associate who was murdered in 1999. (Photo provided courtesy of Black Hand Entertainment)

Left to right: Darren Ebron, Bernie Mac, his manager, and Curtis Scoon.

Seated, left to right: Tupac Shakur, Ed Lover, Eric "E Money Bags" Smith.
Middle row, left to right: Lil' Jay Nichols, Freddie "Nickels" Moore, Notorious B.I.G.
Top row, far left: Randy "Stretch" Walker

Part II:
HIP-HOP

5

The Rap Game

The chances of surviving the streets of southeast Queens in the eighties were slim. No matter what their status in the crews, most hustlers of the era ended up dead, serving long prison terms, or confined to a wheelchair. Indeed, legendary street players wheeling around the 40 Projects, Hollis Avenue, and the Baisley Park Houses became a common sight in the early nineties and beyond. Given the risk, many hustlers started looking for legal ways to make money.

Hip-hop was one way out. In the early nineties, hip-hop was making few artists and producers rich: The terms of recording contacts with struggling independent labels like Profile and Tommy Boy were uniformly terrible, yielding just a few cents in royalties per album. It was particularly difficult for beat-makers, who were considered DJs, not musicians, and often didn't receive income from hip-hop hits. But hip-hop could provide a decent living, and touring provided an escape from southeast Queens and other rough neighborhoods, especially at a moment when drug crews were claiming countless victims.

Working as an informant was another means of escape. Before the crack era, the feds hadn't shown much interest in the crews but with the rise of organizations like Fat Cat's, prosecutors were intent on bringing racketeering and continuing criminal enterprise charges. These were complex cases, where the prosecutors connected far-flung players belonging to multitiered crews, and recruiting informants was an absolute necessity. The streets frowned on cooperating with law enforcement, obviously, but when faced with lifelong prison sentences many hustlers simply rolled over.

Potential informants were comforted by the example of iconic Harlem heroin kingpin Leroy "Nicky" Barnes, who accumulated such enormous power during his seventies-era reign that he appeared on the cover of *The New York Times Magazine* with the headline MR. UNTOUCHABLE. Barnes snitched on his associates after his arrest in 1977 but maintained an enormous influence on the streets because he made such powerful enemies (President Jimmy Carter reportedly ordered the effort to capture him) and unlike other informants, he served significant prison time (he was freed in 1998, after twenty-one years behind bars).

Modest, entrepreneurial-style hustling was perhaps the most popular outlet in Hollis for those drawn to the streets. In stark contrast to the flashiness of the crack era, freelancers who emulated the big crews but ended up murdered or in jail before they could make any real money, the entrepreneurs meticulously planned specific jobs (a bank heist, an ambush of a hustler carrying cash from a drug deal) while maintaining a low profile. The entrepreneurs also constantly changed their affiliations on the streets, usually recruiting a fresh set of players for each new job in order to limit their exposure to informants. In a sense, the entrepreneurs were street traditionalists; they belonged more to the "stick-up kid" era of the late seventies when street guys robbed banks and retail businesses. This model provided decent rewards for minimal risk instead of the high stakes of the crews of the late eighties.

Hip-hoppers, informants, and entrepreneurs inhabited separate social spheres but a number of them were bound by the place where they were raised: Hollis. As the star of South Jamaica rose (and fell) during the eighties, Hollis underwent a little-noticed renaissance of hustling and hip-hop. No single crew controlled Hollis, so entrepreneurial hustlers flourished, robbing banks and local shops, even terrorizing people for bicycles. "Baisley and 40 had bigger crews, and they seemed like they were more organized," remembers Irv Lorenzo, "while Hollis was just this loose band of rebels with chips on their shoulders."

A handful of hustlers in the neighborhood claimed affiliation to something called the Hollis Crew, but it wasn't an organized crew and invoking the name meant little. "Lots of street guys would say they represented the Hollis Crew," explains a former Hollis hustler, "but only a few could represent Hollis when it was time to go to war with other crews. And if you didn't represent Hollis when it was time to go to war, you were just using the name." For those too meek to hustle, there was refuge in the basements of the neighborhood's many single-family homes. Hollis rec rooms and basements were often filled with drum machines and turntables, luxuries made possible by middle-class parents working steady jobs for the U.S. Postal Service and the New York City Transit Authority.

Even for Hollis's more middle-class residents, hustling—and the heroin trade—was never far away. The Simmons family, father Daniel, mother Evelyn, and their three sons Russell, Joseph, and Daniel Jr. were typical of the African-American families who migrated to Hollis in the sixties. Daniel held a B.A. in history from Howard University and was an attendance supervisor for District 29 in Queens, while Evelyn was a recreation director for the New York City Department of Parks. Like their neighbors, the Simmons had a spacious split-level home on 205th Street and 111th Avenue—there was a large basement, an attic that served as a bedroom, and a driveway where two cars (a red Volkswagen and a green Mercedes) were parked. But during the seventies, the Simmons family watched as white families moved out and hustlers like Ronald "Bumps" Bassett moved in. Heroin was so prevalent and so cheap (three dollars per bag) that once well-maintained middle-class havens like 205th Street became overrun with dealers and addicts. "205th Street was the number one heroin block, and when heroin went away it became a big crack block," Russell Simmons recalls. "It was a terrible disaster for what would have been a lower-middle-class neighborhood. People who had every opportunity destroyed their lives. Instead of moving up a lot of kids moved down."

While in his early teens, Simmons inhabited both Hollis's middle-class mainstream and its hustling underworld. He experimented with drugs, tripping on LSD and selling chopped-up coca-leaf incense as cocaine to gullible druggies, and even had a short stint in a southeast Queens street gang called the Seven Immortals. Yet Simmons was known as one of the sharpest students at local elementary school PS 135, and his brother Joseph attended St. Pascal Baylon, a highly regarded Catholic school in the neighborhood. The Simmons brothers also had the good fortune to be watched over by a neighbor whenever their parents were at work. "I walked to school every morning with a family, the Sawyers, who lived next door to me," Joseph recalls. "I walked home from school with them and stayed with them until my mother came home. I was protected from the dope fiends, the weed spots, the cocaine. I considered myself a Simmons and a Sawyer as well."

Russell Simmons was a mediocre hustler and a terrible shot (he once fired a .45 caliber pistol at a man who had just robbed him and missed by a wide mark), and in 1975 he traded the street life for City College of New York, in Harlem. At first, Simmons reverted back to the ways of his adolescence in Queens, hanging out at the student lounge on weekdays and tripping on LSD on weekends. But when a close friend introduced Simmons to the hip-hop scene at a Harlem club called Charles Gallery, he finally found an outlet for his restlessness.

At the time, hip-hop was almost completely DJ-driven. There were few actual hip-hop songs, and DJs spun soul, jazz, and disco records like the JBs' "Blow Your Head," Bob James's "Take Me to the Mardi Gras," and Cerrone's "Rocket in My Pocket." These songs had percussive sections (or "breaks") that would inspire dancers to hit the dance floor or strange sounds (like the Minnie Mouse–like vocal on Cerrone's "Rocket") that, when scratched back and forth on the turntable, created an otherworldly effect. Hip-hop DJs even handled the role of MC, rapping on the microphone as they worked; one of the music's biggest stars was DJ Hollywood, who was equally adept at the turntables and on the mic.

To outsiders, hip-hop seemed little more than a faddish new

party scene. But to insiders like Simmons, the music was a dance-floor democracy that stood in stark contrast to the velvet-roped disco scene. Anyone could participate, and anyone did, even a failed hustler and bored college student like Simmons. Soon after attending his first hip-hop party at Charles Gallery on 125th Street, Simmons began throwing events under the moniker "Rush" (a nickname friends gave him for his frenetic style) at Harlem clubs like Small's Paradise and southeast Queens venues such as Fantasia, which was right around the corner from the 40 Projects. Simmons occasionally scored high-profile hip-hop talent like Grandmaster Flash for his parties but more often he showcased a City College pal named Curtis Walker, aka Kurtis Blow.

Like his hip-hop peers, Blow could DJ and rap (he was originally known as "Kool DJ Kurt"), but Simmons sensed that he could be a more potent talent with a DJ behind him. For that, Simmons turned to his brother Joseph who, though he was just thirteen at the time, was a quick study on the turntables. "At first, I was just the guy who would give out the flyers for Russell's parties," Joseph Simmons recalls, "but then I became the DJ for Kurtis Blow. I was known as 'The Son of Kurtis Blow.' " Joseph's quick cuts on the turntables earned him the nickname "Run," and Russell began to refer to him as "DJ Run, his disco son."

At this point in the late seventies, hip-hop was a truly underground culture. The scene thrived in small inner-city clubs and ballrooms, and its music was something of a secret zealously protected by insiders. (Bronx turntable legend Kool Herc removed the labels from his vinyl so rival DJs wouldn't know what he was playing.) That all changed in the fall of 1979 with the release of "Rapper's Delight," from an unknown Harlem hip-hop group called the Sugarhill Gang. The song captured hip-hop's groove-snatching sensibility—it rode a bass line from the disco hit "Good Times"—and it became a surprise pop hit.

Hip-hoppers like Simmons reacted angrily to the Sugarhill Gang's success not because they were jealous that the group had been the first to cross over to the mainstream, but because much of the lyrics from "Rapper's Delight" were borrowed from hip-hoppers Grandmaster Caz and the Cold Crush Brothers; moreover the group's MC Big Bang Hank was a bouncer, not a rapper. "Someone had taken our rhymes, our attitude, and our culture and made a record," Simmons wrote of the record in his autobiography *Life and Def: Sex, Drugs, Money, and God.* "And not one of us in the community had anything to do with it!"

As furious as Simmons was with the success of "Rapper's Delight," the song inspired him to make a hit of his own. Simmons created a new company devoted to representing hip-hop acts—Rush Management—and he signed on Kurtis Blow as his first client. Soon after, Simmons and Blow hunkered down in the studio to record a rap song called "Christmas Rappin'." The pair finished the record and, thanks to the crossover reach of "Rapper's Delight," secured a deal with a major label, Mercury Records. Mercury rushed to get "Christmas Rappin' " to radio in time for the holidays and to Simmons's surprise it was played on influential New York R&B radio station WBLS on Christmas Eve. It was Simmons's first hit and, though it was essentially a novelty, the song, like "Rapper's Delight" before it, established hip-hop's pop credentials. After years in the hothouse atmosphere of Harlem clubs and Bronx block parties, hip-hop was now an aboveground phenomenon.

There was perhaps no more potent symbol of hip-hop's viruslike spread in the early eighties than Simmons's own block in southeast Queens. Here, an aspiring DJ in his teens named Jason Mizell (who actually lived on 203rd Street but was drawn to the bustle of activity on 205th) spun records with one of the block's popular residents, Jeff Fludd, who served as his MC. Mizell and Fludd called their group Two-Fifth Down, a homage to their block and a subtle boast about the duo's street cred. "We were down but we didn't have to hang out on the corner to be down," Fludd explains. Indeed, 205th Street and 111th Avenue was so hip that its habitués didn't have to hustle out on the main drags of Hollis to have street cred. When Mizell and Fludd weren't performing together at parties or in friends' rec rooms, they would shoot hoops with portable rims set up on both ends of the block. The pair would also play in Police

Athletic League basketball games with neighborhood friend Mark Jackson, who would later play with the New York Knicks and testify as a witness at the trial of Thomas Mickens.

Fludd's relationship with Mizell was not one of equals. Fludd was three years older and considered himself to be a mentor of sorts to Mizell, who was often embroiled in high-risk robberies (like ransacking homes in the Jamaica Estates section of Queens) with friends like Harold "Lovey" Lawson from his 203rd Street block. "I'd say, 'Ya ain't gotta break into people's houses,' " Fludd remembers. "Come hang out with us." Fludd belonged to a smarter set in Hollis, and he and his best friend Curtis Scoon attended Brooklyn Technical, one of New York's most competitive high schools. Fludd's inner circle also included a talented young basketball player named Douglas "Butta Love" Hayes, Hollis hip-hopper Darryl "DMC" McDaniels, and Joseph "Run" Simmons.

Hayes was the rare Hollis resident to have connections on the streets and in the neighborhood's middle-class homes. He provided a crucial entrée to the streets for McDaniels, who grew up on 197th and Hollis Avenue and was considered an outsider by the neighborhood's hustlers, most of whom lived between 200th and 205th Streets. (Hayes himself was raised on 202nd Street.) "The kids from PS 192 would come over to St. Pascal Baylon and rob us kids for earrings and stuff," McDaniels remembers, "but they never messed with me because I hung with Butta Love. Everybody in Hollis would say, 'Oh, you hang with Butta—we ain't gonna rob you.' "

McDaniels says it was Hayes who introduced him to Jason Mizell. He and Mizell struck up an instant friendship, and Mizell offered McDaniels and Joseph Simmons his basement as studio space. Like the Simmons family, the Mizells were prototypical residents of Hollis. Both parents had jobs that placed them solidly in the middle class (Jesse was a social worker, Connie a public school teacher) and they moved to the neighborhood because they saw its single-family homes as a refuge from the inner city. And just like the Simmonses, there were three children in the Mizell clan: Jay, sister Bonita, and half-brother Marvin.

Jesse Mizell was proud of his two-story home at 109-83 203rd

St., and he worked hard on the upkeep of every part of the place, especially the finished basement. There, his son Jay and friends Darryl McDaniels and Joseph Simmons filled notebooks with rhymes and practiced DJing. At the time, Simmons was the DJing "disco son" of Kurtis Blow but after being asked to spin at a party in Hollis with local hip-hop heavy Darnell "Nellie D" Smith, Simmons decided to start his own group with McDaniels and Smith. It was an inspired choice—Smith was a DJ *and* a beat-maker and, like Simmons, he was mentored by Blow.

Record labels were still wary of signing hip-hop acts, but Russell Simmons was undeterred by the lack of interest. He urged his brother Joseph and Darryl McDaniels to make a record at the home studio of Larry "Larry Lar" Smith, a former bass player with a keen sense of groove who produced records for Kurtis Blow. Simmons dubbed the group RUN-DMC, after the nicknames of Joseph Simmons and McDaniels. During the late fall of 1982, with just the simplest of instructions from Simmons—"Go home and write about how the world is"—McDaniels and Joseph Simmons came up with "It's Like That," a darkly pessimistic song that addressed social issues like unemployment without the false utopianism of seventies R&B hits like the O'Jays' "Love Train." "It's like that," rapped Simmons and McDaniels on the song's chorus, "and that's the way it is."

Released in 1983, "It's Like That" was as blunt and precise as Grandmaster Flash and the Furious Five's iconic refrain "don't push me cos' I'm close to the edge" from their early eighties hit "The Message." According to McDaniels, their initial take of "It's Like That" wasn't nearly so powerful, since both Russell Simmons and Larry Smith insisted that RUN-DMC adopt the theatrical rhyming style of Harlem's popular DJ Hollywood. Hollywood's suave style, which was backed by disco beats, stood in stark contrast to the tough, authoritative rhyming of Bronx MC and producer Afrika Bambaataa. When Bambaataa thunderously rapped "socialize, get down, let your soul lead the way!" on his totemic single "Planet Rock," he was nearly as commanding a presence as James Brown. McDaniels worshipped Bambaataa, but Simmons had an affection for Hollywood that dated back to his City College days, and he greatly admired Hollywood's suave style. "At first the song was over some R&B beat," McDaniels remembers, "and I was like, 'Yo, Larry, this fucking shit is fake. We gotta make this shit up-tempo like 'Planet Rock.' When Joe goes, 'It's like that!' I'm gonna go, 'And that's the way it is!' So we did it that way. I wasn't into the Kurtis Blow and DJ Hollywood–type rap shit. I was into the B-Boy, Zulu Nation, street, rhyming-over-beats shit. Fuck rhyming over R&B records like 'Good Times' and 'Bounce, Rock, Skate!' "

Though the song sounded far different than he originally envisioned, Russell Simmons was thrilled with "It's Like That." "When Russell heard it he was like, 'D, you're a genius, I love you,' " McDaniels remembers. Simmons decided to shop the group for a record deal. No one was biting, primarily because record labels doubted that hip-hop, which until then had been dominated by singles like "Planet Rock" and "Christmas Rappin,' " could survive in the album format. "Nobody wanted to sign no rappers, they didn't believe in it," Russell Simmons recalls. "Every label turned us down." After enduring months of meetings with record company execs, RUN-DMC were finally signed by indie Profile Records during the spring of 1983. Unlike other record labels, Profile saw enormous potential in the stream of singles generated by this young genre. "They were an independent who was smart enough to know that there was profit in the 12-inch business," Russell Simmons says. If Profile's expectations for RUN-DMC were high, the advance it offered the trio was nonetheless meager. In his book *Life and Def,* Simmons says that RUN-DMC received a $25,000 advance from Profile, and he adds now that "we got a low royalty rate, and we can't even legally question whether we got all of our royalties."

Several sources close to RUN-DMC claim that the group received a royalty rate of 35 cents per album. These proceeds were split between Russell and Joseph Simmons, McDaniels, and Larry Smith, who served as both DJ and producer, sharing duties with Hollis DJ Davy D, aka Davy DMX, to whom RUN-DMC paid tribute on their single "Sucker MCs": "Dave cut the record down to the bone," Run rhymed, "and now they got me rockin' on the microphone."

Smith and Davy D were critical to RUN-DMC's minimalist

sound, but the group didn't hire a full-time DJ until about midway through the recording of their debut. Joseph Simmons and McDaniels turned to Jason Mizell of Two-Fifth Down for the job, because he brought street savvy to RUN-DMC that the pair lacked. "Jay could come play basketball with me and Butta or fuckin' play in the park with Joe," McDaniels explains, "but at the end of the night he was rollin' with the crazy niggas." Jay's friends suggested that he call himself "Jazzy Jay," but McDaniels fought their efforts because it was the stage name used by the DJ for Afrika Bambaataa's Soulsonic Force crew. "I said, 'He can't be *Jazzy* Jay, he gotta be *Jam Master* Jay,'" McDaniels recalls. "What that meant is that he's the master of a jam which is a party and the master of a jam which is also a record. Jay was like, 'Yo, that's hot, D—I'm Jam Master Jay.'" Although Jay didn't contribute to much of RUN-DMC's debut, McDaniels and Simmons worked hard to include him in the remainder of the record. "Even though he wasn't part of the group, he was in the group in our minds," McDaniels says. "We wanted to make a record that would put Jay on the map." The trio wrote "Jam Master Jay" ("J-A-Y are the letters of his name/Cutting and scratching are the aspects of his game"), and when they played "Sucker MCs" live they replaced Davy D's name with Jay's. The revised lyric—"*Jay* cuts the record down to the bone"—became so accepted among RUN-DMC's fans that it's often mistakenly remembered as the original verse.

Jay soon found he was something of a stepchild within RUN-DMC. He arrived too late to be included in the Profile contract and was excluded from royalties entirely. "The contract was with me and D, and Jay was the DJ," Joseph Simmons explains. "Rappers got the deals then and DJs didn't get the deals. He wasn't even involved; it was like, 'The record was made, now I go get Jay. I need a DJ.'" Moreover, Larry Smith, McDaniels, and Simmons took the majority of the potentially lucrative songwriting and production credits, excluding "Jam Master Jay," which had little chance of becoming a single anyway. Charles Fisher, the former manager of Rushland—a fan club that once represented rappers managed by Russell Simmons including RUN-DMC and LL Cool J—says that Simmons promised to sign Jay to a separate solo deal to make up for such shortcomings. "With Jay not being on the contract Russell could take him and do other things contractually like have him start his own label," Fisher explains. Told of Fisher's comments, Simmons replies, "I didn't promise Jay no label deal."

In any case, the hip-hop trio was billed as RUN-DMC and Jam Master Jay, and Jay had less than a handful of songwriting credits on the group's self-titled debut, which Profile released in 1984. Indeed, Jay's contribution to *RUN-DMC* barely went beyond scratching; it was Larry Smith's unique sound (thunderous hand claps and martial snares) and the authoritative rhyming of McDaniels and Simmons that made an impact. RUN-DMC's drum-machine-driven sonics resembled the percussive breaks on rock records like AC/DC's *Back in Black,* and the group's rhyming style was confrontational, almost punk (Russell Simmons often called hip-hop "outlaw black music"), which helped them reach a demographic previously off-limits to hip-hop: whites.

Thanks to MTV's support of the first single "Rock Box," *RUN-DMC* was a fast success—it would eventually be the first hip-hop album to sell more than 500,000 copies—and the trio hit the road to capitalize on their historic achievement. Touring is where musicians make up for inequitable record deals, and this was especially true of RUN-DMC. "We got three grand for the first show we did," McDaniels says. "It was a great take. We felt like all of our dreams were coming true." Occasionally, RUN-DMC performed three or more high-paying shows in a single night, earning them unprecedented amounts of cash. Feeling flush with success, RUN-DMC took several of their Hollis buddies on the road with them: Jeff Fludd served as their road manager and Darnell "Nellie D" Smith worked as a roadie. Though Fludd had grown up with RUN-DMC, he surprised both them and Russell Simmons with his ability to enforce a rigid sense of discipline on tour. "Jeff Fludd was one of the smartest people I'd ever met," Russell Simmons recalls. "He was a fucking genius."

While Joseph Simmons promised Jay a third of their touring takes ("We made a decision that because Jay's so great we're gonna give him a third of the money live"), Fludd says that initially only Simmons and McDaniels truly shared in the wealth. According to Fludd, Jay was just allotted two to three hundred dollars of the group's nightly take, which ranged from thirty-five hundred to five thousand dollars. Simmons admits that "I don't remember exactly when we started giving Jay a third of the money," but insists that Jay was cut in as an equal partner on tour, adding: "You can't trust anything Fludd says." Fludd also complains that his salary as road manager was one hundred dollars per show and that to keep from going broke he would "find a way to make money" after each show. McDaniels is more frank about how RUN-DMC supplemented their incomes: "Everybody had their hustle on. Jeff and Jay were selling drugs, me and Butta were selling weed."

RUN-DMC made a much more concerted effort to include Jay in its business dealings when they signed on to headline the Fresh Fest in June 1984, an unprecedented hip-hop package tour featuring Whodini, Kurtis Blow, Newcleus, and the Fat Boys, several of whom were managed by Simmons's Rush Management. Thanks to corporate sponsorship from Swatch watch and sold-out arenas greeting the tour wherever it went, McDaniels, Simmons, and finally Jay were splitting up to $20,000 per appearance while Rush Management was taking in $1,200 in commissions per show. In some cities, RUN-DMC would even get an additional twenty percent take of the night's gross. Fludd says that his salary, however, was upped to only $125 per show, which seemed particularly unfair since he put his life on the line serving as the middleman between parasitic promoters and RUN-DMC. After a show in Philadelphia where the promoter claimed that he lost money, Fludd was confronted backstage by Uzi-toting thugs. "I wasn't gonna give the money back," Fludd remembers. "I said, 'Y'all getting no money: You might as well kill me.'"

Fludd was exhausted and practically boiling over with frustration at his treatment at the hands of RUN-DMC. McDaniels and Simmons were equally fed up with Fludd, who they say spent more time partying than working. "Jeff would fuck up a lot because he was *us*," McDaniels explains. "You can't have your friend working your business." Tensions were exacerbated by the RUN-DMC team's use of hard drugs, a lifestyle to which Simmons and McDaniels were unaccustomed. "When we started getting RUN-DMC money we were getting ounces of coke," McDaniels remembers, "and I was buying cases of Olde English. When we went over to Europe—they didn't have Olde English—I shipped them shits over there." A defining moment occurred during a flight home from a show in Los Angeles. "Jeff was sitting in the smoking section rolling weed up and smoking cocaine cigarettes," McDaniels says. "He was thinking nobody would know but we knew. Russell was like, 'That's the last straw.' "

Russell Simmons made a tough call: Fludd had to be fired. "Jeff was always troubled," Simmons recalls. "We all abused drugs back then but he abused them more." (Fludd maintains that he resigned from the group after getting a girlfriend pregnant.) Simmons then hired Lyor Cohen, a Los Angeles–based nightclub owner and aspiring music business impresario, as Fludd's replacement. Russell Simmons saw a lot of potential in Cohen—"He was a hardworking kid, a nice guy, he would do whatever to help with the cause"—but the RUN-DMC crew was skeptical. Cohen booked not hip-hop acts but punk at his Los Angeles nightspot, called Mix Club, and when RUN-DMC played the venue he had only half the money he'd promised to the group.

RUN-DMC worried that Cohen, like Fludd before him, was too caught up in the partying lifestyle to be an effective manager. But Cohen's management prowess soon became evident to the entire RUN-DMC team. "Lyor was incredible, all business," McDaniels says. (Indeed, Cohen had a degree from the University of Miami in marketing and international finance.) "Lyor was a very, very good road manager," Russell Simmons says. "He learned to negotiate with the promoters to watch their numbers." More importantly, Cohen was a bold decision maker; he came aboard just as RUN-DMC was winding down the second Fresh Fest and he urged them to spurn another sure-to-be-profitable round of the tour for their own headlining show. RUN-DMC was hesitant to embrace Cohen's idea, as Fresh Fest had brought them tremendous nightly takes and unprecedented national exposure, but he worked hard to convince the trio that they were more popular than any of the bands with whom they shared the bill. After all, Cohen argued, RUN-DMC were hip-hop's only real stars, who in just a few years had achieved significant milestones such as being the first to receive MTV airplay. "Lyor was like, '*Guys, I'm looking at this shit and we can do it ourselves,*'" McDaniels says, imitating Cohen's Israeli accent, which earned him the nickname "Little Israel." Cohen's instincts about Fresh Fest and RUN-DMC's career turned out to be dead-on. "They thought they could go on without us," McDaniels says of Fresh Fest, "and they got their asses kicked."

Business couldn't have been better for RUN-DMC and Rush Management in early 1985, but Russell Simmons still did not have a label of his own, forcing him into mediocre deals with independent labels. A Long Island–born NYU student and aspiring hip-hop producer named Rick Rubin shared Simmons's frustrations with the music business. Rubin had produced rapper T-La Rock's "It's Yours," which, with its minimalist beats programmed by Rubin on a Roland 808 drum machine and jagged, almost tactile cutting and scratching from Jazzy Jay of Afrika Bambaataa's Soulsonic Force, was one of hip-hop's most outré singles. Nearly 100,000 copies of "It's Yours" were sold, and the song was getting played in downtown Manhattan clubs like Danceteria as well as Bronx hip-hop clubs like Disco Fever, but Rubin reaped meager monetary benefits because it was released by independent label Party Time. When Michael Holman, host of a hip-hop TV show called "Graffiti Rock," introduced Rubin to Simmons at a party, the pair discovered that they'd been experiencing nearly identical struggles in the business. Simmons also confessed that "It's Yours" was not just his favorite hip-hop song of the moment but also one of the "blackest" rap records he'd ever heard.

As Rubin's NYU dorm room had become something of a hip-hop hangout—he'd put his address on the record sleeve of "It's Yours," bringing visits from the likes of Jeff Fludd and Adam Horowitz of the Beastie Boys—Simmons surmised that Rubin would be the ideal person with whom to start a record label. For the imprint's first release, the pair turned to James Todd Smith, aka LL Cool J, a teenage MC from Queens who had inundated Rubin's mailbox with demo tapes. In the fall of 1984, Rubin called Smith into the studio, and the pair quickly recorded "I Need a Beat," an ideal combination of Rubin's drum machine minimalism (which he dubbed "reduced," not "produced") and LL's wild wordplay. (He boasted that his rhyming and the heavy drums backing him would give listeners a "percussion-cussion.") "I Need a Beat" hit record stores in November, and it was the first release of Rubin and Simmons's label, which they dubbed Def Jam, after a bit of Rubin-invented slang that had appeared on the sleeve of "It's Yours." By the time "I Need a Beat" was released, the Def Jam brand was more than just familiar; it already had a cult following among hip-hop fans.

With the birth of Def Jam and Rush Management thriving, Lyor Cohen sensed that he was missing out on a revolutionary moment for hip-hop while stuck out on tour with RUN-DMC. He lobbied Simmons for a position at Rush Management, but as Cohen's hard-driving style seemed better suited for the road than a record company office, Simmons only reluctantly hired him. With Cohen gone, Jam Master Jay reached out to Karl "Big D" Jordan, a childhood friend who lived directly across the street from him on 203rd Street in Hollis, to be their new road manager. To RUN-DMC, Jordan seemed the ideal candidate to fill the position: He was a smooth talker who rivaled even Russell Simmons in public relations finesse, possessing a maturity beyond his years ("When he was eighteen he looked like he was twenty-eight," says a friend from Hollis), and he had a rep as a fearless street guy thanks to a string of arrests ranging from criminal possession of a stolen firearm to reckless endangerment. But Jordan was also a confidential informant (C.I.) working for the Queens District Attorney's office. In 1985, Jordan testified as a C.I. in the trial of a Hollis hustler named Joseph "Money" Thomas on murder charges. Jordan's testimony—he alleged that Thomas confessed to him about the crime—brought Thomas a life sentence and earned Jordan the enmity of many in the streets.

To do their jobs well, informants must maintain significant contacts on the streets, and Jordan was no different. "D was good for a minute," remembers McDaniels, "but then a lot of street shit started happening. He wasn't able to separate who he was and being a businessman." Unfortunately, the street shit that occurred under Jordan's management was far more than a backstage brawl or two. During a tour stop in Virginia Beach, RUN-DMC roadie Garfield McDonald was shot in the head by an assailant in an elevator of a hotel. "Me, Big D, Garfield, and Jay were fighting these dudes," McDaniels says, "and Garfield got shot in the head. But he was a hardheaded motherfucker—literally—so he survived." RUN-DMC's touring expenses were also wildly out of control under Jordan. "He was spending a lot of money," McDaniels recalls. "We were taking limos, staying in suites. I would go into my room and there would be champagne, weed, and lobster. He was thinking, 'Yo, we living good, this is gonna go on forever.' He didn't know no better." Jeff Fludd maintains that Jordan was also stealing from RUN-DMC and that Joseph Simmons caught him in the act. McDaniels refuses to confirm or deny Fludd's allegations and Joseph Simmons will only say of Jordan: "He was good, but it was a time in my life when I couldn't see clearly what was going on."

Such drama did not affect Simmons's growing Rush Management and Def Jam empires, or even RUN-DMC itself. Indeed, the group had such incredible momentum coming off the 1984 release of *RUN-DMC* that they never stopped recording; less than one year after the release of their debut they put out their sophomore album, *King of Rock*, the cover of which featured a cropped shot of the heads of McDaniels and Simmons with Jay noticeably absent. Released on January 15, 1985, *King of Rock* quickly outsold its predecessor, making RUN-DMC one of the first hip-hop acts to have a track record in the album format; at the same time, the success of the group on the road proved that hip-hop could draw arena-sized crowds.

With RUN-DMC's career taking on a historical importance in the hip-hop scene thanks to first-of-its-kind appearances at the massive benefit concert for African famine relief Live Aid and on

American Bandstand and with LL Cool J's "I Need a Beat" followed up with hits from the Beastie Boys and Jimmy Spicer, Simmons and Rubin were being courted by major labels to sign a distribution deal for Def Jam. The pair signed with CBS/Columbia during the fall of 1985 and though the label—whose roster included established R&B singers like Gladys Knight and Bill Withers—had little experience marketing hip-hop acts, few majors at the time did. Simmons and Rubin also calculated that the exposure that they could get for Def Jam artists from a clueless major would be more significant than from a hip indie. (Indeed, they spurned an offer from Tommy Boy, the indie that released Afrika Bambaataa's "Planet Rock.") Though CBS had final approval over which artists signed to Def Jam, they allowed the pair to work out of their own space downtown.

Simmons and Rubin made the most of their independence from CBS, hunkering down in grimy, run-down studios to record debut albums from LL Cool J and the Beastie Boys, who released the first single to come out of the new Def Jam/Columbia deal, "She's on It." They were growing weary of working in disparate locations for each of their acts, however, and in July 1986 they purchased a four-story brownstone at 298 Elizabeth Street in a rough section of Little Italy. Simmons's friends thought he was crazy to invest in the neighborhood—particularly since he had used much of his advance money from CBS to make the purchase—but Simmons was undeterred, making expensive renovations to the building, which included a living space for Rubin. Occasionally, Rush Management employees would leave the building to find crackheads defecating on the pavement; on other occasions, fierce gunfights broke out in front of the building. "It was a little bit of a crack block," Simmons admits, "but it was great."

The same month Simmons moved to Elizabeth Street, RUN-DMC released their third and greatest album, *Raising Hell*. The record was made in the same studio where much of LL Cool J's debut *Radio* was recorded—a no-frills Chinatown studio dubbed Chung King—but RUN-DMC purposely shunned any Def Jam influences. During the making of *Raising Hell*, Joseph Simmons forbade the group from watching TV or listening to the radio to avoid hearing LL Cool J's music. It was a decision made partly out of a competitiveness with the younger LL. "It was like I was Richard Pryor and he was Eddie Murphy," Simmons admitted to RUN-DMC biographer Bill Adler. The group also felt that they needed to come up with something completely unique in order to top their first two records and best Def Jam's new talent. The approach worked, with *Raising Hell* yielding the anthemic "My Adidas" (Hollis's most prized sneaker brand at the time) and the Aerosmith collaboration "Walk This Way," which resuscitated the seventies rockers' comatose career. With *Raising Hell*, RUN-DMC's rock sensibility became so pronounced that the group's rap-rock sound became a genre unto itself. RUN-DMC followed up the multiplatinum success of *Raising Hell* with another profitable solo tour, and with three classic records to their name, their momentum seemed unstoppable.

Instead of heading back into the recording studio as they had always done—RUN-DMC released a record every year from 1984 to 1986—they began a long, drawn-out battle with Profile over the terms of their recording contract. "We was fighting the label, trying to get out of the deal, and we were also trying to not give them an album in the process," Darryl "DMC" McDaniels explains, "and as a result, they were penalizing us. We knew we deserved more; the label wasn't giving us more so we should have lived with it. But we were trying to fight—we should have put the album out first and *then* kept fighting."

RUN-DMC also squandered the promising post–*Raising Hell* period on an awful hip-hop movie called *Tougher Than Leather*. The movie had a ludicrous plot—RUN-DMC portrayed themselves as street vigilantes fighting everyone from drug traffickers to biker gangs—and it came in nearly $400,000 over budget. Prerelease hype—*Tougher Than Leather* graced the front page of the *Times*'s arts section—falsely raised expectations for what was essentially a muddled blaxploitation flick. Unsurprisingly, after a strong opening weekend in New York in September of 1988, audiences declined precipitously. It didn't help that the movie's studio, New Line, refused to release it nationally. *Tougher Than Leather* was such a disaster that Rick Rubin has referred to it as "my *Magical Mystery Tour.*" The movie, however, was more than simply a bomb: It reinforced the image of rappers as thugs. Critics were shocked that RUN-DMC would depict themselves as street fighters in light of an August 17, 1986, concert in Long Beach, California, that was overrun with street gangs, resulting in mass arrests and nearly forty injuries. RAPPERS' MOVIE DOESN'T DISPEL VIOLENT IMAGE was a typical headline greeting its release.

The failure of *Tougher Than Leather* didn't prevent Russell Simmons from expanding his empire at Def Jam. In January 1988, Sony had acquired CBS/Columbia in a $2 billion deal and thanks to the multiplatinum success of acts like LL Cool J and the Beastie Boys, Simmons and Rick Rubin signed a joint venture with Sony. It was a fifty/fifty partnership, but the deal stipulated that Sony could charge Def Jam for everything from production to marketing, thus taking a significant bite out of the imprint's bottom line. Like the CBS deal that preceded it, the partnership with Sony was fraught with negatives for Def Jam, but it was much better than what was happening to RUN-DMC. Karl "Big D" Jordan left the group under a cloud of accusations that he stole from them, and in 1989 Joseph Simmons was charged with raping a Cleveland woman. The case was later dismissed, but the ordeal led to the dissolution of his marriage.

Joseph Simmons was soon feeling desperate. "I was a big star but I felt empty," he explains. "I was at the very tip-top of the world and asking, 'What is this all about? Is it about more pussy, more food, more candy, more cars?' I thought it was about winning all the prizes." Russell Simmons worried that his brother was paralyzed by the ups and downs of life with RUN-DMC. "After Run recorded *Tougher Than Leather* he was having a very difficult time," Simmons says. "He wasn't appreciating his blessings, he was wrapped up in having to succeed and getting all the toys." Simmons found comfort in Dallas-based televangelist Robert Tilton, whose program on cable station BET (Black Entertainment Television) brought $80 million annually into his ministry. Simmons had a profound spiritual awakening while watching Tilton on TV one day in 1989. Soon after this revelatory moment, he offered Tilton a substantial donation as well as an appearance at one of his Dallas-based conferences. Tilton, in turn, agreed to fly Simmons and Jeff Fludd down to Dallas for first-class treatment, including four-star hotels and restaurants. "It was like a celebrity coming to town for a couple of days," Simmons says of his Tilton trip. "They had a conference and I was to go onstage, give my testimony, give my offering, and then leave." Not long after unpacking their bags, Simmons and Fludd realized that the televangelist wasn't going to make good on his promise. "After the sermon, Tilton said he wasn't gonna pay since Run had an entourage," Fludd remembers. Stunned by Tilton's treatment, Fludd called childhood friend Curtis Scoon back home in Hollis for help. Scoon was happy to help his longtime friends and he wired the pair one thousand dollars to spend on hotel rooms, salvaging their disastrous Texas trip.

As one of Hollis's most well-connected residents, Scoon was perhaps the most obvious choice for the pair to turn to in an emergency. He grew up around the corner from Jam Master Jay's house on 203rd Street, attended St. Pascal Baylon Elementary with Darryl McDaniels, went to Brooklyn Technical with Jeff Fludd, and was once so tight with Joseph Simmons that the pair would steal marijuana from Russell's stash. Even after RUN-DMC's career took off in the mid-eighties, Scoon remained close with the group, appearing in the video for the trio's early single "Rock Box." So Scoon didn't even care if he was paid back: He was thriving on the streets of southeast Queens as a hustler, and RUN-DMC seemed like struggling artists by comparison.

"To guys like me, hip-hop was a pie-in-the-sky thing," Scoon explains. "No one was making any real money." Scoon was a paper chaser—growing up, he did everything from taking pictures of tourists in Times Square to selling fireworks in Hollis to make money—and by his teens he was becoming the sort of street entrepreneur that made his neighborhood infamous. "Not everyone was rough enough to do robberies," Scoon explains, "or smart enough to be an entrepreneur. Entrepreneurs had to know how to make money for themselves—*and* they had to be able to do the same for the guys working for them."

Outwardly, Scoon looked like a Supreme Team strongman (he stands over six-foot-four and has the broad shoulders of a football player) but he was actually typical of Hollis entrepreneurs who, unlike their much poorer counterparts in South Jamaica, came from middle-class backgrounds and even earned college degrees. (Scoon studied political science at Hampton University, though he did not graduate.) During the mid-eighties, Scoon amassed a small crew of followers, which included William Morris, Ralph "Yaqin" Mulgrave, and, most notoriously, Gary "Pep" Steadman, one of the gunmen responsible for the killing of Maxine Peterson in 1988. Scoon is evasive about his crew's activities—"Let's just say we weren't making money the legal way"—though he admits to an incident outside a pizza parlor on the corner of Hollis Avenue and 203rd Street in late 1984 where a dispute with a rival brought charges of attempted murder, kidnapping, armed robbery, and felonious assault (all of which were later dismissed). Scoon was also a close friend of Joseph "Money" Thomas and watched with great surprise as Karl "Big D" Jordan ascended in the RUN-DMC camp after snitching on his Hollis pal.

Jordan solidified his status as a fast-rising star in the hip-hop business when Russell Simmons named him vice president of Rush Management. With hip-hoppers often settling beefs right in the office, Rush Management could be as tough as its crack-block surroundings and a former street guy like Jordan fit right in. But many of Jordan's detractors in his neighborhood and in the music business—Jeff Fludd in particular—were perplexed at how Jordan's résumé as RUN-DMC's failed road manager could have led to such a prestigious post. "The vice president of Rush Management?" Fludd remembers thinking upon hearing about Jordan's new job. "How the fuck did that happen?" Russell Simmons refuses to explain his reasons for hiring Jordan, saying only, "Big D is a family member; we love him, we're all close to him."

The hiring of Jordan may have been controversial, but he was praised around Rush Management's offices for his ability to spot young executive talent. Jordan brought on a number of sharp people to work with him at Rush, particularly a hard-driving Hollis-bred hip-hop obsessive named Donald Francois. Although Francois was just over five feet tall, rail thin, and had a baby face that made him look like a teenager, he had held his own in fights back home in southeast Queens. In conversations, he riffed about hip-hop at the speed of an accomplished MC and had an absurdist sense of humor that could make even the toughest street guys—including pal Curtis Scoon—break up with laughter. "I was a corny kid," Francois admits, "but I had people around me who did grimy shit." Francois also had a strong work ethic and a passion for hip-hop so intense that he'd do almost anything to work with his idols such as Big Daddy Kane, Eric B and Rakim, Public Enemy, and RUN-DMC. Naturally, the job at Rush—which entailed menial tasks befitting a personal assistant—was a gigantic comedown. "I started seeing everybody for who they are," Francois explains. "They're just regular motherfuckers."

Francois's greatest disappointment about the job was Jordan's ill treatment of him. "He was giving me the worst groups like the Ultramagnetic MCs and Tim Dog," Francois explains, referring to a pair of Rush Management's more obscure acts. "And he wasn't paying me well, maybe $100 every two weeks." Francois had learned from the Hollis streets that you have to work every angle you've got, no matter how unpromising, and he soon found new angles for himself. "I hooked up with someone over in Europe and started doing shows over there with my acts," Francois says. "Soon enough I was getting so many bookings that I was in Europe almost every week." Jordan was immediately suspicious of Francois's sudden success; to him, there seemed to be no legitimate way that his lowly assistant could be making serious money. "He started saying that I was stealing money and that I was selling drugs out of the office," Francois remembers, "and I was like, 'Fuck y'all! Y'all ain't paying me so I started doing my own shit. You brought me in and you tried to play me and now I'm getting mine.' " It didn't help that the underpaid, overworked Francois dressed as sharply as Rush executives Lyor Cohen and Jordan. "I was coming into the office looking fresh, with money in my pocket," Francois remembers, "so that's when Big D started with the rumors about me."

When the rift between Jordan and Francois became obvious to everyone in the Rush Management offices, the company's artists began confiding in the latter about their own problems with Jordan. Francois discovered that most of Rush Management's clients despised Jordan and a handful—Big Daddy Kane foremost among them—suspected that he was siphoning money from their touring takes. Tensions between Kane and Jordan grew so great that the rapper and his crew began to use Francois as an intermediary to relay threats to Jordan. "Something went bad with Kane and all of the sudden Big D stopped talking to him," Francois remembers. "And a guy from Kane's crew named Infinite said to me, 'Yo, Donald, he better start talking to me or he's gonna have problems.' I communicated that to D, but since he thought he was a tough guy he brushed it off." One day, Kane and Infinite came up to Rush Management's offices for a sit-down with Jordan. "They were like, 'What's up, D?' and Infinite turned to me and said, 'Go get me some beer,' " Francois remembers. "Since I'd always done this kind of thing for Rush artists I didn't think anything of it. But when I got to the store I realized, 'Wait a minute, *this guy don't drink beer.*' When I got back to the office, the whole place was wrecked. D was bleeding, the tables were turned over, and Lyor was on his phone like, 'Did they leave yet?' "

Infinite had sent Francois to a bodega for beer because he didn't want him to witness his brutal beat-down of Jordan; Jordan believed that Francois had been in cahoots with Kane's crew all along. "Big D thought I was involved with the whole thing," Francois remembers, "especially since I came back from the store with a bag of beer, all smiling. D looked at me funny, he had blood coming down his face, he's all cut up, his shirt's all ripped up, and I was like, 'I didn't have anything to do with it, son. I was just doing hospitality for my people.' " When Francois showed up for work the next day, everyone in the office was whispering that Francois had set Jordan up. Francois panicked; he knew there would be hell to pay by the time the day was up. Indeed, by 6 PM that night only Francois and Jordan remained in the office. As Francois finished a phone call with a touring contact in Europe, he began to suspect that he and Jordan would soon come to blows. When he went outside for a break a few minutes later, his suspicions were confirmed: Two men stood on the corner staring menacingly at him. "They started coming toward me and they were like, 'Your name is Frances?' " Francois remembers, "and I was like, 'Nah.' And they were like, 'You know a girl named *Frances*?' And then they swung at me. I ducked, so they punched me right in my glasses, my expensive Gucci glasses! Then they tried to jump me so I ran a couple of blocks and then I jumped into a cab so they wouldn't catch me."

Francois returned to work intending to confront Jordan about the ambush. "I was like, 'All right, your niggas tried to jump me!" Francois remembers telling Jordan. "He said it wasn't him but it *was* him." Soon after the incident with Infinite, Jordan announced his intention to sue Kane for assault. Kane, naturally, was furious, and he gave Russell Simmons an ultimatum: "Either you fire Big D or you get rid of me." Francois says that Simmons then fired Jordan. Rush Management employees were thrilled by Jordan's dismissal—none more so than its president Lyor Cohen who, unlike Jordan, actually had an impressive résumé before joining the company. "Lyor was waiting for an opportunity like this to get D out," Francois remembers. It was just the sort of revenge Francois had been hoping for, but it didn't change his life at Rush Management.

Fortunately, the connections Francois made through his persistent European bookings were starting to pay off. Both Busta Rhymes, who was emerging from an inventive group called Leaders of the New School as one of hip-hop's most charismatic MCs, and Jam Master Jay were pursuing Francois to work on tours with them. Jay's overtures were particularly persuasive, because in 1989 he'd started his own label, JMJ Records, and he'd secured distribution for the imprint through Russell Simmons's Rush Associated Labels (RAL). The creation of JMJ had eased Jay's depression over the bomb of RUN-DMC's 1990 album *Back from Hell*, and he was eager to sign creative and executive talent to the label. Jay offered Francois a job road managing JMJ's Jackson 5–inspired retro-soul act, Fam-Lee, which Francois readily accepted because he was growing desperate to leave Rush Management. "Jay put me on the road, which was great because I was like, 'I can't be sitting behind this desk as a gopher,' " Francois recalls. " 'I got a college education and I need to expand my career.' " At first, Francois balanced jobs at both Rush Management and JMJ, but Jay convinced a reluctant Lyor Cohen to let him go.

Francois's move to JMJ provided a salary increase and offered him the sort of challenges he was missing at Rush Management, but it was not without the kind of personal and professional turbulence that marked his time at his previous position. The label was a small start-up run by Jay and the brother-sister team of Randy Allen and Lydia High, both childhood friends from Hollis. The label's first signings were mostly friends of Jay's, and, unsurprisingly, the close, familial atmosphere at JMJ produced heated arguments on a near-daily basis. "Lydia wanted to control everything including how you got paid," Francois explains. "She was like, 'You shouldn't be doing that tour,' or, 'If you do a tour and the money's coming in it should be coming through me.' She was really a nightmare for me; I almost got into something physical with her." The breaking point came when High removed all of Francois's belongings from JMJ's offices. "One day I came into the office and my desk was out in the lobby," Francois remembers. "She moved my shit out into the lobby, and she told me, 'Work out in the lobby.' I said, 'I will fuck you up, bitch.' " The ferocious, often physical battles Francois fought at Rush Management had made him thick-skinned, but the family feuding at JMJ Records proved to be too much to handle. Francois began looking for another job, and he would leave the label just a few years later.

Francois was slowly making his way in the music business, but Irv Lorenzo couldn't even get in the door. Born on June 26, 1970, Lorenzo was the youngest child in a family of eight, headed up by his cabdriver father, Irving, and his housewife mother, Mary. Irving supported the entire clan on his hack's salary and in the mid-seventies he managed to move the family from a cramped two-bedroom apartment in the Brownsville section of Brooklyn to a single-family home at 215th Street and Hollis Avenue.

As teenagers, Irv and Christopher (his older brother by three years) spurned hustling for the Hollis hip-hop scene of the mid-eighties. Irv Lorenzo spun records at house parties and high school talent shows, but the neighborhood's established DJs dominated popular outdoor parties, dubbed "park jams," where they hooked up their equipment illegally to a power source such as a lamppost and rocked crowds of thousands during summer nights. Lorenzo's inexperience on the turntables wasn't the only factor working against him in his quest to play a park jam: Because he lived in the safe area above 210th Street he was dubbed a "backstreet boy," a neighborhood kid who couldn't hang out on the bustling blocks between 200th and 205th streets. "He was a corny little cat," says Jeff Fludd of Lorenzo. "He wasn't street at all." Even Chris Lorenzo admits: "I'm from Hollis, me more so than my brother—meaning that I was out fighting way more than Irv."

An outsider like Lorenzo had little chance of playing any of the park jams, particularly one at 202nd Street and Jamaica Avenue hosted by RUN-DMC crew members Darnell "Nellie D" Smith and Garfield McDonald. This was Hollis's premiere park jam, and Smith and McDonald had a virtual lock on the turntables. But during one summer night in 1988, Irv (backed by brother Chris, who was a football player at Bayside High School in Queens) made his move, imploring Smith and McDonald to give him a shot on the decks. At first, the pair refused Irv's request; he was one of many kids looking for a chance and a backstreet boy at that. Undeterred, Chris turned to Hollis tough guy Shane "Qasim" Fells, who was standing nearby the turntables, for help in getting his younger brother on the decks. The son of crack-era shooting victim Maxine Peterson, Fells was a renowned knockout specialist, a feared boxer whom few in the neighborhood would ever dare to cross, and with his help Irv finally got his chance on the turntables. He didn't disappoint. "Irv took the crown for our side of town," Chris remembers, "[and] that was the beginning for Irv." Irv, naturally, agrees with his brother: "I killed it—the park was mine."

After his surprise success at the 202nd Street park jam, Irv's DJing talents were in high demand. He sold mixtapes under the name "DJ Irv" for ten dollars a pop, often moving five hundred copies at a time. The mixtapes were highly accessible, almost poppy, featuring a cappella tracks from R&B records laid over hip-hop beats, and soon Irv's fan base extended far beyond Hollis to nearly all of Queens. "I sold my tapes in Baisley Park, the 40 Projects, Lefrak, I was pretty busy," Irv remembers. "Everyone in Queens knew me and fucked with me."

Inspired by his success on the mixtape circuit in 1989, Irv put together a hip-hop group featuring Hollis's finest talents: Rahzel, a beat-boxer from 199th Street and 104th Avenue whose vocals were often impossible to differentiate from a drum machine, and Romeo, an MC from 203rd Street and 111th Avenue who was formerly managed by Jeff Fludd. Romeo's fierce rhymes were so ahead of his time that RUN-DMC hired him as a ghostwriter. Chris Lorenzo managed the group and soon found that securing bookings for shows was even more difficult than getting his brother on the turntables at Hollis's park jams. The pinnacle in the group's career, winning a talent show hosted by legendary Queensbridge producer Marley Marl at a roller-skating rink on Jamaica Avenue in southeast Queens, brought little but shattered expectations. The winner of the contest was promised a record deal and an on-air shout-out from iconic hip-hop DJ Mr. Magic during his popular show on radio station WHBI. But the deal never materialized, even after the group recorded tracks at Marley Marl's Queensbridge home; the Lorenzo brothers were finding that they'd have to work with the ferocity of a street entrepreneur to make it in the music business.

6

Straight Outta Hollis

In the early nineties hip-hop was still a homegrown phenomenon of talent shows, homemade mixtapes, and modest independent labels that at best brokered less than lucrative deals with majors like CBS. The scene yielded hit records—RUN-DMC's *Raising Hell,* the Beastie Boys' *License to Ill,* and NWA's *Straight Outta Compton* among them—and it finally had a presence on MTV thanks to the show *Yo! MTV Raps.* But no album had set hip-hop on an entirely new commercial direction in the manner that *Jaws* or *Star Wars* led to a surge of special effects-laden movies and big event-style releases. For the music itself, this was a good thing: Like Hollywood in the seventies, which saw the rise of personal filmmaking from auteurs like Martin Scorsese, Robert Altman, and Francis Ford Coppola, the late eighties and early nineties were a golden age for hip-hop. The music was a gloriously fragmented universe of political rap (Public Enemy), street provocateurs (NWA), afrocentrics (Brand Nubian), and even comics (Biz Markie). There was no single formula for a hip-hop hit, from the wild-style sampling of De La Soul's *Three Feet High and Rising* (which incorporated music from the sixties rockers the Turtles to eighties pop duo Hall and Oates) to the street polemics of Bronx crew Boogie Down Productions' *By All Means Necessary,* which featured strident anti-drug-war tirades like "Illegal Business."

In December 1992 hip-hop's *Jaws* finally arrived with the release of Dr. Dre's solo debut *The Chronic.* Dre, born Andre

Young, was a Los Angeles–based producer and DJ with a storied beat-making history, working with the World Class Wrecking Crew (whose space-age electro was so futuristic that songs like "Surgery" are played by techno DJs) and NWA (whose music Dre imbued with a striking mix of soul samples and noisy sound effects like police sirens). In the hip-hop scene, anticipation surrounding *The Chronic*'s release was sky-high. "As far as I'm concerned, Dr. Dre is the leading producer in the business," Russell Simmons told *The Los Angeles Times* on December 15. "Hands down, he's the man." At Dre's label, the Time-Warner-distributed Interscope, expectations for *The Chronic* were equally huge. Interscope honcho Jimmy Iovine—who had previously produced major rock acts like U2— dubbed Dre a musical genius and backed up the praise with a multimillion-dollar deal for Dre's Death Row label.

To skeptical music critics, however, *The Chronic* promised more of the same shlocky thuggishness of NWA's chart-topping 1990 album *Niggaz 4 Life* from a producer whose life seemed to mirror too closely the rhymes of his artists, many of whom had just left the street life for hip-hop. Indeed, the week *The Chronic* hit record stores, *The Los Angeles Times* ran an article that cataloged Dre's misdeeds—a battery charge in the beating of a New Orleans police officer, a $20 million lawsuit filed by a Fox TV personality who claimed that Dre assaulted her—and paid little attention to the album itself.

Though Dre had just released a single called "Deep Cover" (whose chorus featured the phrase "187," street code for killing a cop), much about *The Chronic* was alien to listeners not raised in the streets. Its huge posse of unknown California MCs like Dat Nigga Daz rhymed with Zs wedged within their words (*The Chronic* became "The Chr-izonic"), just as Fat Cat's crew had done to frustrate law enforcement wiretaps. Even the album's name itself— slang for high-grade marijuana—was unfamiliar to many. When Dre and Snoop appeared on *The Arsenio Hall Show* in 1993, Dre was asked to explain to his audience just what "the chronic" was.

While the slang of *The Chronic* was unfamiliar to most, its music was completely accessible. Rejecting the sample-heavy style of popular hip-hop producers like the Bomb Squad, Dre instead utilized a single sample to drive a song; his hit single "Nuthing But a 'G' Thang," for example, was based on a snatch of an orgasmic-sounding gasp from soul singer Leon Haywood's 1970s-era hit "I Wanna Do Something Freaky to You." Lawsuits from rockers against sample-centric acts like De La Soul made this stripped-down approach to sampling a legal necessity but Dre nonetheless used it to his artistic advantage. Unlike many MCs who wove dense narratives, Dre used the verse-chorus-verse structure of pop with the hook itself sung by R&B vocalists.

The Chronic received terrible reviews—Greg Kot of *The Chicago Tribune* wrote that the record "offers the same, tired gangster litany of big guns, big libidos, ribald jokes and angry threats," while *The Village Voice*'s Robert Christgau railed against it as "sociopathic easy listening . . . bad pop music"—but it became a mainstream phenomenon, spending nearly all of 1993 in the top ten on *Billboard*'s pop and R&B charts, competing with pop juggernauts like Whitney Houston's *Bodyguard* soundtrack. The album's cultural effect went far beyond its album sales: White kids were using those slangy Zs in conversation, Dr. Dre earned a nearly unprecedented amount of MTV airplay for a hip-hopper, and street hip-hop began an ascendancy that continues today. By the end of 1993 *The Chronic*'s importance was obvious even to pop's gatekeepers. "The advance of hip-hop and rap at the expense of traditional R&B in 1993," wrote J. R. Reynolds in *Billboard* in late December, "seemed to serve as a signpost of things to come."

To the streets, *The Chronic* only confirmed trends already occurring within the hip-hop scene—namely, Irv Lorenzo's blends of hip-hop and R&B and the migration of hustlers into the music business. The latter trend was best personified by Dre's partner and Death Row founder Marion "Suge" Knight. A former football player with the University of Nevada at Las Vegas who just missed a shot at going pro, Knight cut an imposing figure. He was also a quick study in the music business. When he failed at his first ventures, concert promotion and music publishing with rapper Vanilla Ice, Knight decided to become a freelance consultant to musicians who believed that they were being victimized by the recording industry. "You can get fucked real quick in this industry if you don't have the power and the know-how," Knight told *Newsweek*. "I decided that I wanted to look into people's contracts and see if I could help them."

In 1990, Knight hooked up with Dr. Dre and together they parsed the details of Dre's contract with Ruthless Records, the label that was home to his former group NWA and was run by the group's leader Eric "Eazy-E" Wright and his middle-aged white business partner Jerry Heller. Knight and Dre claimed that Ruthless was paying Dre a substandard royalty rate and had him released from his contract. Eazy-E, however, had a far different take on how Dre left Ruthless, claiming in a lawsuit that a pair of men armed with baseball bats hired by Knight forced him to release Dre from his record contract. Eazy-E's lawsuit was later dismissed but the tale of bat-wielding thugs working over music industry execs took on mythical status within the hip-hop industry. Budding hip-hop impresarios studied Suge's hardball tactics with great envy, especially as they resulted in the multiplatinum, game-changing *Chronic*.

Back home in southeast Queens, Irv Lorenzo and Jam Master Jay absorbed the lessons of *The Chronic*. It was time, Jay decided, to turn away from the kitsch of the seventies-style soul of the Fam-Lee and embrace hip-hop's more street-credible direction. Ironically, Jay glimpsed the future in a group of friends—Fredero Starr, Sticky Fingaz, Big DS, and DJ Suave Sonny Caeser—who were performing not hip-hop but house music in southeast Queens clubs under the moniker Onyx. "They were dancers, not really rappers," explains Jay's longtime friend Eric "Shake" Smith, "but Jay thought that he could remake them in a very different image." Jay insisted that Onyx's new image—gangsta and grimy over house music glam—could be achieved only through a radical makeover. "Jay said, 'Y'all gotta cut *all* your hair off,'" Smith remembers, "and the Onyx guys were like, 'No-o!' They were totally reluctant." Jay also suggested that Onyx sport black jumpsuits and hoodies to burnish their gangsta looks. The group acquiesced to Jay's demands in hopes that new image and their connection to RUN-DMC could someday bring them *Chronic*-like record sales.

To Jay's credit, instead of simply relying on his name to sell Onyx records he promoted the group relentlessly. "At the end of every RUN-DMC show, Jay would play Onyx records," Smith says, "and by the time the crowds left they'd be chanting Onyx's lyrics. It was incredible." When Onyx's debut *Bacdafucup* was released in 1993, the streets—and the mainstream—were ready. The album cover featured a photo taken from the perspective of someone of who had just taken a beat-down from the glowering, bald-headed members of Onyx. And the group's pogoing, punk brand of hip-hop, epitomized by the single "Slam," managed to blend the aesthetic of both West Coast gangsta rap and rock-influenced East Coast groups like House of Pain. As Jay had a significant share of the songwriting and production credits on *Bacdafucup* (which was mostly recorded at the home recording studio dubbed "24/7"), he was primed to make his first real payday if the record became a hit. In fact, *Bacdafucup* ended up far exceeding Jay's expectations, selling more than 3 million copies.

Onyx was Jay's first real success as a music business entrepreneur, but there were significant problems developing at JMJ. After working with Onyx on their first tour, Donald Francois left the label out of frustration with Lydia High. The label's artists were also fighting with Lydia's brother and JMJ partner Randy Allen, who, according to Francois, was perceived as having an imperious attitude. Francois says that in 1993 a disagreement with Allen and JMJ accountant Jay Battles eventually led to Onyx angrily trashing JMJ's offices. And though the streets had initially embraced Onyx, a backlash was brewing about Jay's manipulation of the group's image and sound. Onyx's transformation from happy house music dancers to scowling gangsta rappers who growled songs like "Blac Vagina Finda" was raising eyebrows among even their devoted fans. "We knew that Randy and Jay made over Onyx from [a] house music group," Francois explains. "They'd had extensions [in their hair] and platform boots. That was the truth."

Like Jam Master Jay before him, Irv Lorenzo looked at the success of *The Chronic* and hungered for an act that could bridge the gap from the streets to the mainstream. In 1993, the Lorenzo brothers scoured nightclubs and talent shows in southeast Queens for promising MCs, and before long they found just what they were seeking. At a talent show at Bayside High School in Queens, Chris Lorenzo's alma mater, the pair discovered a teenage MC named Mic Geronimo whose rhyming style was an original, tough-to-peg mix of scatting, fast-talking rappers like Das Efx and the more deliberate flow of traditional lyricists like Rakim. After winning the show at Bayside, Geronimo simply disappeared, and the Lorenzo brothers, even with their extensive connections in Queens, were unable to find him. When a friend of Irv's mentioned that he saw Geronimo at a local department store, Irv pounced on the tip, driving out to a mall in Valley Stream, Long Island, where he found the rapper working the cash register at a Stern's.

Geronimo was impressed with Irv's persistence, and the pair headed straight into the recording studio. The result was "Shit's Real," which had a *Chronic*-like chorus—"Shit's real, I smoke a twenty bag of buddha and then I'm ready to peel"—but with an even more pop-friendly, R&B gloss comprised of lush, almost pillowy synthesizer sounds. The Lorenzos then shopped a deal for Geronimo, signing with Blunt/TVT, a label whose executives were so impressed with Irv's discovery of Geronimo that they hired him as an A&R representative. (An A&R, or Artist and Repertoire, representative is essentially a talent scout.) "Irv came from a family of entrepreneurs, so he was driven to succeed in the best possible way," remembers former TVT urban music executive Tom Sarig. "He was very focused. He wanted to get paid." "Shit's Real" didn't meet TVT's commercial expectations—"It was a New York hit that never really grew," Sarig says—but the Lorenzo brothers were convinced that they had a genuine star in Geronimo.

The Lorenzos' instincts about Geronimo's commercial potential were later proven wrong, but the rapper was crucial in connecting them to aspiring Hollis hip-hop talent: In addition to being a solo artist, Geronimo worked with a posse of rappers who called themselves Cash Money Click (CMC). The Hollis-bred hip-hoppers were an ideal group for the post-*Chronic* era, as CMC member Chris Black had a reputation in the neighborhood as a fearsome street fighter. Irv signed CMC to Blunt/TVT in 1993, but he was concerned that one group member, Jeffrey Atkins, aka Ja Rule, would not pass muster with the streets. Like Darryl McDaniels of RUN-DMC, Atkins was a Catholic-school kid raised in the tame section of Hollis below 200th Street. "Ja was a sweet kid," remembers a former TVT executive. "He was half the weight that he is now. It seemed like he weighed no more than one hundred pounds." Lorenzo's worries were eased when CMC went into the studio: Ja had a gravelly voice that sounded tough on record. Better still, with Chris Black on board it would be difficult for hip-hop fans to second-guess the group's street pedigree.

Irv, however, wasn't in the mood to take chances after Mic Geronimo's failure, so he tapped all of his hip-hop contacts for guest spots on CMC's debut. The most promising of Irv's roster of MCs was Jay-Z, a Brooklyn lyricist who was so gifted that he didn't keep rhyme books but simply improvised entire songs on the spot. Irv met Jay-Z while touring Europe in the early nineties as a DJ for a rapper named Jaz-O; on the road one day, the pair discussed their plans for making it in the music business and Jay was so impressed by Irv's empire-building ambitions that he gave him the nickname "Irv Gotti." Irv also tapped an aspiring MC from Yonkers named Earl "DMX" Simmons who, while not nearly as agile on the mike as Jay-Z, had a doglike bark of a voice and an indisputable street pedigree. "DMX was robbing everybody," Chris Lorenzo remembers. "He was making it real bad in Yonkers."

With this lineup, CMC's debut seemed guaranteed to provide the hit TVT needed. But just as the group's debut was about to be released, Black was sentenced to five years in prison on an assault charge stemming from a confrontation with a cabdriver. "Chris was arrested right when Cash Money Click was on the cusp," remembers Chris Lorenzo, "so Irv is fucked again. He had to get more artists." With Black's arrest, the Lorenzo brothers' substantial efforts for Cash Money Click had been all for naught; worse, Irv claims that TVT CEO Steve Gottlieb passed on much of the major new talent he brought to the label. "I signed Mic Geronimo and Cash Money Click and I brought Jay-Z, DMX, and DJ Clue," Irv explains, "but they passed. I was frustrated because I thought these were the best rappers in the game."

There is no disputing the fact that post-*Chronic* rappers like CMC's Chris Black and DMX came from rough neighborhoods and occasionally hustled to make ends meet. But instead of rhyming about grindin' for meager amounts of money, most MCs boasted about moving weight, commanding Fat Cat–sized crews, and gunning down rivals with automatic weapons, thus shrouding their modest pasts in a mythology worthy of the southeast Queens streets of the eighties. Though few hip-hop fans realized it at the time, real street guys were not behind the mike but behind bars, thanks to tough sentencing passed in the wake of the Edward Byrne killing and the Giuliani administration's quality-of-life policing, which drove hustlers off the streets.

This was apparent to those in the life in the time, perhaps no more so than to Curtis Scoon. "After Giuliani came into office, most street guys were in jail or had moved out of town to get their money," Scoon explains. With hip-hop's stock rising and the streets looking more dangerous (and less profitable) than ever, Scoon decided to change his life for good. In 1993, Scoon began throwing after-parties for hip-hop tours and, with the help of Jeff Fludd, he started a record label called Hollis Crew Productions. The company flamed out quickly but the after-party business brought Scoon in close contact with new hip-hop talent as well as the next generation of hip-hop executives.

During the spring of 1994, Scoon rolled the dice on a lavish, expensive after-party in Baltimore for female rappers Salt N Pepa and a then-unknown R&B singer from Chicago named R. Kelly. His copromoter Darren Ebron had thrown some of the wildest, most extravagant parties the city's hip-hop scene had ever witnessed, and Scoon believed this could be a breakout event for him even though he worried that Ebron often went far over budget. "If Darren threw an indoor beach party it would have a real beach," Scoon remembers. "He lived for the night. For him, it didn't matter if any of the parties were profitable." Scoon was much more business-minded than Ebron, and he expected a return on his investment—which he says was "quite a few thousand dollars"—from the after-party.

The event began with some promise: Ebron had secured a much-coveted venue called the Baltimore Grand as well as the talents of hot New York DJ Kid Capri. But well before midnight, things began to unravel. Drug crews from Manhattan and Baltimore descended on the party to collect money they claimed Ebron owed them. Though Scoon was not responsible for the debt, he and a group of his most trusted associates called for a sit-down with the rival hustlers in the Baltimore Grand's office. "My right-hand man Talib broke the news to them that they weren't getting a fucking dime," Scoon explains, "and they got so angry that they didn't want my money; they just wanted my blood."

Scoon could have engaged the hustlers in a pitched gun battle but he decided to humiliate his rivals without firing a shot. "I said to my guys, 'Let's take the path of least resistance,' " Scoon remembers, "so I persuaded the police, who were already working security until 3 AM, to stay longer with the promise of additional pay." The cops acquiesced to Scoon's proposal, and outside the club the hustlers seethed, unable to shake down Scoon and his crew. "By the end of the night there must have been one hundred of these motherfuckers lined up across the street," Scoon says.

As the night wound down, Scoon realized that he shouldn't press his luck any longer. He gathered his crew, his cash, as well as several pricey bottles of champagne and headed for the Grand's rear exits, leaving the angry hustlers out front. Scoon's crew—which included Gary "Pep" Steadman, Ralph "Yaqin" Mulgrave, Freddie "Nickels" Moore, and an aspiring hustler and rapper named Eric "E Money Bags" Smith, who had driven down from his home in Queens to meet Scoon—then checked into the suite of a local hotel.

"We laughed about not paying the police," Scoon says, "and leaving Darren to face the mob on his own as he deserved."

Eric Smith was particularly impressed with the dramatic, yet bloodless escape from the Grand; he felt as if he were starring in a heist movie where the robbers make off with the diamonds without so much as tripping an alarm. Smith was raised in Lefrak City, a middle-class housing development in the Corona section of Queens; even though rappers from the area such as Noreaga dubbed Lefrak "Iraq" and nearby Queensbridge "Kuwait," the area was nowhere near as rough as South Jamaica or even Hollis. Lefrak City was dominated by low-level hustlers grindin' and chain-snatching bullies— not organized crews—yet even here Smith struggled to pass himself off as a tough guy. To bolster his street cred, Smith aligned himself with a cousin from Hollis who engaged in gunplay even during confrontations that did not call for such extreme measures. Smith's strategy fooled the young hustlers who dominated the relatively tame neighborhoods of Corona and Queensbridge, but experienced street guys saw right through it. "Bags's cousin, not Bags himself, is what made him formidable on the streets," explains Scoon.

Smith's mythmaking about himself was particularly well-received in Queenbridge's hothouse hip-hop scene, which boasted highly influential rappers and producers like Marley Marl and Nas. Growing up, Smith hadn't shown much interest in hip-hop, but in the early nineties he enviously watched the rise of street rap from Queensbridge and figured that he could muscle his way into the music business. Smith's instincts proved dead-on: He was able to convince rappers like Nas and Noreaga to collaborate on songs with him based on his inflated street rep.

That MCs like Nas—whose reminiscences in rhyme about Pappy and Fat Cat lent the impression that they had been peers—could be so easily intimidated led Smith to believe that he could ascend to the very top of the hip-hop business. All he needed, of course, was his own Suge Knight. For that, he turned to Scoon, who had more than proved his mettle in Baltimore. "Bags saw me as a Suge Knight figure," Scoon explains. "He meant that as a compliment but I was offended. To me, Suge is nothing more than a glorified bouncer.

Besides, I wasn't interested in what Bags had to offer: I was older than him, and I'd already been in trouble. Muscling nine-to-fivers is the easiest way to go to jail; I wasn't even going to go there."

Scoon did want to break into the music business; he just wanted to do it legitimately. After Freddie "Nickels" Moore introduced him to Irv Lorenzo, Scoon offered to help salvage the sinking career of Mic Geronimo. Scoon had connections at broadcasting powerhouse Radio One (which owns high-profile radio stations such as WKYS in Washington, DC), and he attempted to get spins for Mic Geronimo's single "Nothin' Move But the Money." Radio One didn't warm to the song, but Irv respected Scoon's tenacity. He introduced Scoon to Jay-Z and partners Damon "Dame" Dash and Kareem "Biggs" Burke, who had formed an independent record label called Roc-A-Fella, which was distributed by the midsized indie Priority Records. "Irv promoted the Roc-A-Fella guys as street guys and I dealt with them as such," Scoon says, meaning that handshakes, not contracts, would suffice if they were to enter into a business relationship. "But I immediately knew that Jay and Dame were not street. They were the kind of guys who could fuck each other over and then meet at a party and hug for the cameras."

In the post-*Chronic* era, it was becoming commonplace for rappers like Jay-Z and Eric "E Money Bags" Smith to flaunt their connections, however tenuous, to the streets. But few seemed as eager to prove their street cred as Tupac Amaru Shakur. While shooting a basketball movie called *Above the Rim* in New York during the fall of 1993, Shakur befriended a bevy of street guys from southeast Queens and Brooklyn including Curtis Scoon associate Freddie "Nickels" Moore, hustler Jacques "Haitian Jack" Agnant, and street-gang strongman turned hip-hop producer Jimmy "Henchmen" Rosemond. Though Shakur had a gangsta rep thanks to the militant rhymes of his debut *2Pacalypse Now* (which drew the ire of then–vice president Dan Quayle) and a starring role in the movie *Juice,* in which he played a Pappy Mason–esque killer named Bishop, the twenty-two-year-old rapper was out of his depth among his street acquaintances. As an adolescent, Shakur studied classical music and ballet at the Baltimore School of the Arts, and when he and his mother, Afeni (a former Black Panther who raised him alone), moved from Baltimore to Marin City, California, in 1988, Shakur was such a failure at hustling that he handed his supply back to his distributor.

With no experience on the streets beyond the botched attempt at drug dealing in the Bay Area, Shakur assumed that the showboating Agnant was the most fearsome of his new friends. "He is the epitome of what people think a gangsta is," Rosemond says of Agnant, "the jewelry, the diamonds, the cars, the crew." Shakur was so taken with Agnant that he told friends he was studying the hustler's every move to prepare for his role as a drug dealer named Birdie in *Above the Rim.* The rapper's friends warned him that his friendship with Agnant could lead to trouble ("Everyone told him he should stay away from Jacques," Shakur's longtime friend Watani Tyehimba told *The New Yorker*) but the pair became fast friends in large part because they shared a taste for theatrical displays of violence. "When I introduced 'Pac to Jack he clinged [sic] to Jack because Jack wanted to do the things he wanted to do," Rosemond explains. "They would beat up dudes together, they would do the bullshit that I wasn't doing anymore."

Though Shakur assumed that the plain, unassuming Rosemond (who is barely five-foot-seven, sports an unkempt afro, and spurns designer clothes for plain white sneakers and generic jeans) was Agnant's underling, Rosemond actually had a criminal history far more serious than Agnant's: During the eighties, he ran with homicidal West Indian drug gangs, and when he was just seventeen he was arrested and hit with a number of charges ranging from murder to weapons possession. (Eventually, all but the weapons possession charge were dropped.) Rosemond declined to take part in Agnant and Shakur's sparring, as any wrong moves on his part could send him to jail for the rest of his life. "Tupac didn't understand why I wouldn't get into the rumbles he wanted to get into," Rosemond says. "He would beat up people and I would jump in the middle and be like, 'Man, what the hell are you doing?' I was trying to restrain him."

Agnant, however, only egged Shakur on and the pair became inseparable, club-hopping together at New York nightspots with A-list celebrities like Madonna. One night in the late fall of 1993, Shakur met a starstruck nineteen-year-old fan at Nell's who he said fellated him on the club's dance floor; a few days later, Shakur and a posse that included Agnant allegedly gang-raped the young woman in a suite at a midtown Manhattan hotel. Shakur was accused of subjecting the fan to "sexual contact by forcible compulsion," and though prosecutors eventually dismissed the indictment against Agnant (he pled guilty to two misdemeanor charges instead), he allegedly told the victim that "he [Shakur] likes you so much he wanted to share you with his friends."

The nasty remark was a symbol of the casually cruel pose that Shakur had adopted in the post-*Juice* years. "I think that movie changed him," Bay Area rapper Klark Gable told *The Washington Post* on December 17, 1993. "That character that he portrayed, it wasn't him. But he tried to live up to it." Though he was facing serious prison time as a result of the rape charge, Shakur was still desperate to be seen as a peer of real hustlers like Agnant and Rosemond.

At Shakur's insistence, Rosemond and Randy "Stretch" Walker, a hip-hop producer raised on 210th Street and Hollis Avenue, took Shakur on guided tours of New York's roughest neighborhoods. "I showed him from example," Rosemond recalls. "I brought him to Brooklyn with me, and we were up with 'dreads [Rastafarians] in houses full of weed, full of guns, full of money. It was, '*This* is how we do it,' you know what I'm saying?" The mentorship of savvy street guys like Rosemond and Walker ultimately had little effect on the impulsive Shakur, who seemed more interested in causing confrontations than avoiding them. Shakur's incorrigible bad behavior began to cause friction between Rosemond and Shakur; Rosemond worried that the rapper's insatiable appetite for needless acts of violence would land them both in prison.

"One time, me, 'Pac, Stretch, and Jack were riding in Queens on Linden Boulevard and some cops rolled up," Rosemond remembers. "I'm nervous as hell. I'm sure we're going to stopped. We got

Tupac in the car! I'm like, 'We all clean, right? And 'Pac says he's not. He had his bulletproof vest *and* his gun on him. After the police left—they didn't stop us—I told Jack, 'Pull the car over.' I screamed at 'Pac: 'Don't you *ever* get in a car with me with a gun without letting me know. We have stashes for that. We don't need to go to jail for you being stupid. We got problems in New York and even we don't need to have a gun. You with us, you safe.' "

Shakur's slipup in southeast Queens was compounded by his loose lips about the impending rape trial. The rapper spoke freely about the case with New York *Daily News* gossip columnist A. J. Benza, infuriating his inner circle of hustlers. "There was a picture with Madonna, [Haitian] Jack, and Tupac and a guy involved in the rape case," Rosemond remembers. "They had a quote from Tupac that said, 'These are the guys who did the rape; I didn't have nothing to do with it' or something to that effect." At the New York premiere of a movie called *A Low Down Dirty Shame* on November 25, 1994, Rosemond confronted Shakur about the interview. That Shakur discussed the case infuriated Rosemond, but he was particularly angry that Shakur had slighted his new friends by describing them as "hangers-on." Shakur was dismissive of Rosemond's complaints, because he regularly gave incendiary interviews to journalists, a PR strategy that paid off in almost daily attention from tabloids like the *Daily News*.

Though Rosemond's relationship with Shakur had become rocky, the rapper still felt a debt of gratitude toward him for his mentoring. On November 30, as Shakur was on trial in New York for the rape charge, he agreed to record a collaboration with Lil' Shawn, an aspiring MC managed by Rosemond. "He was trying to get legitimate," Shakur said of Rosemond in a *Vibe* magazine interview. "I thought I was doing him a favor." The superstar rapper, unsurprisingly, was in no hurry to get to the studio, making a stop to buy marijuana on the way; meanwhile, Rosemond, who was paying a pricey hourly rate at the Quad Studios in Times Square, began paging Shakur. Rosemond admits to being furious with Shakur but only because the rapper demanded cash for the session. "He started saying, 'Man, if you want me to do it you better have cash,' " Rosemond recalls. "I kinda laughed. It's like, ' 'Pac, what the fuck are you talk-ing about? Nigga, this ain't no drug deal.' Then I said, 'All right, you'll have your money, just be there.' " Shakur, however, told *Vibe* that he argued with Rosemond because Rosemond reneged on his original agreement to pay him $7,000. In any case, when Shakur showed up at the Quad at 723 7th Avenue, he was comforted by the sight of Lil' Cease—the sideman for rapper The Notorious B.I.G., aka Biggie Smalls—waving from an upstairs window. Shakur and Biggie were both born in Brooklyn and had long been friends, shar-ing the stage and even recording together.

As Shakur and his posse—which included Randy "Stretch" Walker and Freddie "Nickels" Moore—strode into the Quad's lobby, they received a less than friendly greeting. Shakur told *Vibe* that he was ambushed by a pair of men toting 9 millimeter weapons who demanded that he hand over the nearly $40,000 in jewelry he was wearing. When Shakur refused, the gunmen shot him five times and manager Moore once, but he later told *Vibe* that "the only thing that hurt was that Stretch and all of them fell to the floor" without putting up a fight. The final humiliation, Shakur said, was taking the elevator upstairs only to find Rosemond, Sean "Puffy" Combs, and Biggie waiting for him. "All of them had jewels on," Shakur explained to *Vibe*, "more jewels than me."

Rosemond says he was unaware of what was transpiring down-stairs and that his first contact with Shakur came just after 10 PM, when the rapper and a member of his entourage nicknamed "Shorty" emerged from the elevator. As soon as he stepped off the elevator, Shakur (who was bleeding heavily) blamed Rosemond for the shooting. "'Pac looks at me and says, 'Why you let them know I'm comin', man?' " Rosemond remembers. "I said, ' 'Pac, hold on. Come talk to me. You my nigga. Tell me what the fuck happened.' He wouldn't come to me. He kept screaming, 'Man, why! Why did you let them niggas know?' He looked at the engineer and said, 'Call the police.' " Shakur then gestured toward Rosemond, Puffy, and Biggie and proclaimed: "*These* niggas shot me, man."

With the NYPD on the way, Rosemond's street instincts kicked in. "When I hear the police, I'm at the elevator," Rosemond remembers. "I'm trying to get the fuck out. I'm at the elevator door and Shorty pulls out a gun and says, 'If 'Pac die, nigga, one of you niggas dying!' " As Rosemond negotiated with Shorty, the elevator door opened, revealing an angry and armed Randy "Stretch" Walker. "Stretch has his hand on his gun and he's like, 'Goddamn, Jimmy, like *this*?' " Rosemond recalls, "I'm like, 'Come downstairs and talk to me.' My gun is in my car. I'm trying to get to my gun because I don't know what is about to transpire now. So he was like, 'Nah, I'm not going downstairs.' I'm so glad I didn't have no gun because when I got off the elevator Biggie and Puffy were up against the wall and the police had them handcuffed."

As Rosemond, Puffy, and Biggie were questioned by the cops, Shakur was wheeled out on an ambulance gurney and snapped by swarming paparazzi with his middle finger raised in the air. The next morning, Shakur appeared in court wrapped in bandages and in a wheelchair, a display of his street cred that, a *Newsday* reporter noted, "bolstered his image as rap music's baddest bad boy." Even Rosemond appreciated Shakur's courtroom theatrics. "You bandage yourself up, you go to court, you get all of that sympathy, God bless him," Rosemond says.

The Quad provided the most powerful street theater imaginable for the drama-prone Shakur. It's an incredible story—a rapper takes five bullets from a pair of thugs after his street-savvy associates refuse to take them on—that has become central to the mythology surrounding Shakur. But Rosemond and a source who was with Shakur at the Quad that November night say that nearly everything about his story is false. "The truth as I know it is that 'Pac shot himself," Rosemond says. "They made everybody lay down and when they was laying down 'Pac went for his gun, it went off, and he got shot. 'Pac shot himself and he shot Fred [Moore]. When he came off the elevator, he pulled his pants down, and he had one wound in his thigh. We haven't been allowed to tell the truth because people want to gravitate to the lie." Rosemond adds that Randy "Stretch" Walker later confirmed his version of events: "Stretch told me that the only thing that happened to 'Pac is that he ended up shooting himself."

Shakur would later accuse Rosemond of orchestrating the ambush, but the latter's story is supported by the source who was with Shakur that night. The source says that Shakur entered the building armed with two guns because most of the men in his posse had criminal records and did not want to be caught with weapons. A pair of men confronted Shakur in the Quad's lobby, the source explains, and they pistol-whipped him. (Rosemond says that the attackers "gun-butted the fuck out of him.") As Shakur lay on the ground enduring a beating, members of his entourage reached over to him and popped his expensive jewelry from around his neck and then tossed it at the attackers in an effort to placate them. When that didn't work, the source explains, Shakur grabbed at one of the attackers' weapons and was shot in the hand by him; panicked and bleeding, Shakur then fired his gun but ended up shooting himself in the testicles (the bullet passed through to his thigh) and Freddie "Nickels" Moore in the stomach. An EMT who treated Shakur told *Newsday* that the rapper bragged about being shot in the groin area: "He kept telling his friend, 'Look! I was shot in the —, I grabbed the gun, man, I grabbed it and he shot me, he shot me.' "

Shakur's courtroom display of his wounds from the Quad may have elicited some sympathy from the jury—he was acquitted of two counts of sodomy, one count of attempted sodomy, and three counts of criminal weapons possession—but he was nonetheless convicted of first-degree sexual abuse. A few months later, in mid-February 1995, Shakur was sentenced to four and a half years in prison and then sent to the notoriously tough maximum-security Clinton Correctional Facility in upstate New York to begin serving his time.

Shakur and his defenders felt that both the sentence and the prison to which he was assigned were indicative of law enforcement animus toward the rapper. After all, Shakur had engaged in a series of high-profile clashes with the cops, the most notorious of which occurred in October 1993 when the rapper shot a pair of off-duty Atlanta police officers whom he believed were harassing a black man they'd pulled over. (The charges against Shakur were dropped after it was discovered that the cops were intoxicated during the incident and were also carrying weapons stolen from an evidence locker.) "The entire case reeked of impropriety," Shakur's attorney, the famed Harvard law professor Charles Ogletree, told *The New Yorker*. Profoundly embittered by his conviction on the rape charge and convinced that an East Coast cabal of Rosemond, Agnant, Puffy, and Biggie conspired against him at the Quad, Shakur signed with Suge Knight's Los Angeles–based Death Row. Knight stoked the rivalry between the coasts while Shakur was imprisoned, taking the stage at *The Source* magazine's awards show in August 1995 to publicly mock Puffy and his Bad Boy label. When Shakur was paroled in October, he intensified Knight and Death Row's jihad on songs like "Hit 'Em Up" where he called Puffy "weaker than a fuckin' block" and told Biggie, "You claim to be a playa/but I fucked your wife."

Shakur's beef with East Coast hip-hop players was garnering huge record sales, but it was also threatening to turn violent. So, in December of 1995, Puffy sent Rosemond as his emissary to a peace summit attended by Shakur, Suge Knight, and widely respected Houston-based hip-hop impresario J. Prince (who served as a mediator). "Puffy was like, 'Go over there and figure this shit out,' " Rosemond remembers. "I had to get J., who was neutral, so he ['Pac] didn't feel like an East Coast dude was closing the deal." During the meeting, Rosemond conveyed an offer from Puffy to record a collaboration with Shakur; to sweeten the deal, Puffy would allow Death Row to release what was sure to be a million-seller. "But 'Pac came in the room and he was like, 'That nigga shot me,' " Rosemond remembers. Shakur torpedoed the deal and Knight backed him up: "I gotta ride with my homie," Knight told Rosemond.

Emboldened by his humiliation of Rosemond at the peace summit, Shakur stepped up his campaign against him, spreading word around the music industry that Rosemond had orchestrated the Quad ambush. Furious, Rosemond confronted Shakur backstage at a concert by R&B singer D'Angelo at the House of Blues in Los Angeles in late December. "The whole Death Row clique was there and I remember going to him—I had some Crip dudes with me—and said, 'Dude, you gotta stop telling people that shit,' " Rosemond remembers. " 'For real, nigga, I don't give a fuck. . . . It could go down right now. *You* know what happened. You know who did this to you. Why don't you fuck with them? Why you blaming Puffy and Biggie? Them niggas ain't got nothing to do with this.' "

With members of Los Angeles's feared Crips gang backing him up, Rosemond put such a scare into Shakur that the rapper didn't even ask Suge Knight, who was standing nearby, for help. "I remember Suge calling over, "Pac, everything all right?" " Rosemond remembers. "'Pac knew better not to tell him that something was wrong because I was so angry." Months later, on September 7, 1996, just a few hours after Shakur and a posse that included Knight delivered a fierce beating to reputed Crips member Orlando "Baby Lane" Anderson in the lobby of Las Vegas's MGM Hotel (an incident that was captured by the hotel's security cameras), the rapper was shot four times while stopped at an intersection; he died from his wounds six days later. Rosemond's admission that he confronted Shakur with Crips in tow is astonishing as the Crips are believed to be behind his murder. But Rosemond claims that the Crips who accompanied him to the House of Blues were "Rolling 60s" Crips, not Southside Crips, the "set" Orlando Anderson belonged to.

It is also telling that Rosemond often uses the word *discipline* to characterize the Quad shooting, because hip-hop insiders have suspected that the motive for the incident was not robbery but Rosemond's wish to teach Shakur a lesson for being disrespectful toward him. Indeed, a source close to a Brooklyn associate of Rosemond's named Dexter Isaac says that Isaac confessed that Rosemond ordered him to attack Shakur at the Quad. Isaac, who is serving life in prison at a federal penitentiary in Pollock, Louisiana, on a murder charge unrelated to the Quad, adamantly denies any involvement in the incident, saying only, "You got the wrong information." Rosemond says that neither he nor Isaac had a role in the Quad shooting, and he blames Shakur's murder on the rapper's beating of Anderson, a fatal mistake he says no real street guy would ever make. "If you're not a gangbanger you don't stomp gangbangers out," Rosemond says.

Rosemond adds that he would have never jeopardized a hugely important (and expensive) recording session over personal animus. This explanation makes the most sense; scoring Shakur for a guest spot on a track for the relatively unknown MC Lil' Shawn was a coup, especially for Rosemond, who was then struggling as a manager. Rosemond says that after the incident he let it be known on the streets that anyone involved would face severe consequences. "I called the 'hood and said, 'How dare anyone do some shit like that at my session?' " Rosemond says.

Yet it also seems plausible that Shakur's attackers were associates of Rosemond's who simply meant to beat the rapper but found themselves in a more serious situation after he grabbed for their gun. Though he is loath to admit it, Rosemond seems to want to preserve his reputation as hip-hop's über-villain, which emerged from the Quad shooting; he seems particularly proud of the fact that when Shakur was incarcerated on the rape charge in 1995 his fellow inmates told him that Rosemond was far more fearsome than Jacques "Haitian Jack" Agnant. "He realized at that point that it wasn't Jack that was the danger," Rosemond says. "It really was me."

To this day, no one has been charged in the Quad shooting, but before his death Shakur recorded a song that would permanently cast a shadow of doubt over Rosemond's protestations of innocence. On the album *Don Killuminati: The 7 Day Theory* Shakur blasted Rosemond and Jacques "Haitian Jack" Agnant as coconspirators in the Quad shooting. Though rappers often fling accusations against enemies, the anti-Rosemond tirade—dubbed "Against All Odds"—took on historic significance because Shakur was dead by the time the album was released. Even if Shakur hadn't been murdered, the urgency of Shakur's lyrics—the song, Shakur rhymed, was the "truest shit I ever spoke"—would have been more than enough to convict Rosemond in the eyes of Shakur's fans. Rosemond, however, claims to not be bothered by "Against All Odds," which he says was just one of many gestures from Shakur intended to create controversy and generate record sales. "The one thing that 'Pac understood was how to entertain and that was entertaining to him," Rosemond says. "I know that if 'Pac were alive today he would say, 'Man, I was just rapping. I was just entertaining.' "

The raised middle finger outside the Quad, the display of his bullet wounds in a New York courtroom, the 1995 prison interview with *Vibe* in which he implicated his East Coast rivals in the Quad shooting, and the cultivation of high-profile rivalries though song all proved that Shakur was peerless when it came to creating a hip-hop theater that dramatized real-life events from the streets to self-serving effect. Soon hip-hoppers from both coasts would emulate Shakur's PR-seeking style, even though his naiveté about the streets and the real-life ramifications of his battle with East Coast rappers may have cost him his life. This was an unsurprising development to anyone who had been following hip-hop—by the early nineties, NWA, for example, had become completely calculated provocateurs thanks to songs like "To Kill a Hooker"—but it would transform hip-hop into a gangsta minstrel show while, more ominously, placing very real hustlers like 'Preme and Rosemond among the pretenders.

7

The Rise of Murder Inc.

For all the street bluster that marked the Supreme Team's reign in southeast Queens—the souped-up Mercedes armed with gun turrets and an oil slick, the matching jackets emblazoned with the crew's logo, the packaging locations crowded with dozens of baggers who were forced to work in the nude so as not to walk off with any drugs—Kenneth "Supreme" McGriff left the streets with barely a whimper in 1987. Mike McGuinness of Queens Narcotics simply rolled up on 'Preme at the corner of Foch Boulevard and Gabreaux Street in South Jamaica and arrested him. 'Preme didn't put up much of a fight in court either: He admitted to being the "organizer, supervisor, and manager" of the Supreme Team, and in 1989 he was given a relatively light twelve-year sentence on a continuing criminal enterprise charge.

'Preme's only moment in the spotlight since his conviction came when he showed up at the 1993 trial of nephew Gerald "Prince" Miller on narcotics, murder, and racketeering charges sporting black wraparound sunglasses and flanked by a pair of imposing bodyguards. So when 'Preme returned home to southeast Queens in 1995 after serving eight years of a twelve-year sentence, he set out to connect to those who did not directly experience his heyday and therefore mythologized him as a kind of omnipotent hustler—the wannabe Gs of hip-hop.

Thanks to wild stories about the crack era passed down from older siblings as well as an adolescence spent consuming tabloid headlines about the Supreme Team and the Nichols organization, young rappers and hip-hop executives like the Lorenzo brothers were enthralled by 'Preme. The ascendance of ex-street guys like Suge Knight and Shakur's partnering with real hustlers like Rosemond and Agnant also played a big part in the lionization of the likes of 'Preme.

The reality of 'Preme's post–Supreme Team life was much more mundane than his hip-hop fans imagined; he passed his time in prison by immersing himself in the books of Donald Goines, the ex-hustler from Detroit who managed to crank out sixteen books with titles like *Daddy Cool, Street Players,* and *Inner City Hoodlum* before he was murdered in 1974. 'Preme's favorite works from the Goines canon were *Black Gangster,* which told the story of a young hustler named Prince who rose from the streets of Detroit in the early seventies to become a crime kingpin, and *Crime Partners,* about a pair of stick-up kids named Billy and Jackie who turn to a savvy hustler named Kenyatta to elevate their status on the streets. 'Preme dreamed of turning Goines's novels—which were so popular in the federal prison system that illiterate inmates were buying the books and learning to read as they went along—into big-screen gangster epics like *The Godfather.* Since hip-hop in the post-*Chronic* era mimicked the ghetto realist qualities of Goines's novels, 'Preme believed that there could be a substantial mainstream audience for a Goines movie, especially if platinum-selling rappers could be convinced to contribute to the soundtracks. 'Preme was stuck in a halfway house in Queens dreaming about making it in Hollywood, but he was not disheartened by his fall from grace: There were hustles to be had, and perhaps this time they might even be legitimate.

While 'Preme dreamed of bringing the Detroit of Donald Goines's imagination to the big screen, Irv Lorenzo was trying to capture crack-era southeast Queens. Though he was in his teens during his neighborhood's hustling heyday and was therefore far too young to have known 'Preme or Fat Cat, Irv and the acts he managed were deeply nostalgic for the era. On Cash Money Click's "Get Tha Fortune," Ja Rule boasted that he was "representin' Hollis Ave. and 205th," while Irv insisted on featuring southeast Queens' eighties hustling landmarks in Mic Geronimo's videos. "For Mic Geronimo's 'Shit's Real,' we rode through the 40 Projects, Baisley, and Hollis Avenue," Irv explains. "We were representin' all of Jamaica." Irv devised a similar video treatment for Cash Money Click's single "Get Tha Fortune," except this time he decided to focus the action on a single section of southeast Queens: 'Preme's old territory on Guy Brewer Boulevard.

During the shooting of "Get Tha Fortune," Irv was shocked when a friend on the set of the video told him that none other than 'Preme himself was standing outside a nearby bodega. "'Preme comes out on the block and then BJ, who is a good friend of ours, says, ''Preme is here, he wants to meet you,' " remembers Chris Lorenzo. Irv, a backstreet boy who longed for the street cred of a hustler like 'Preme (or even his own brother), readily agreed to an introduction with the South Jamaica hustling icon. His initial impression of 'Preme, however, was not quite what he'd imagined. "My first response to seeing 'Preme was shock," Irv explains. "This was the notorious 'Preme? This guy was like five-foot-two, this little guy, this little green-eyed motherfucker. So my first response was, 'Wow, this is the guy that everybody's talkin' about?' "

Though their mutual friend BJ made the introduction, the more street-savvy Chris Lorenzo was surprised that his brother had agreed to meet with 'Preme in the first place. To southeast Queens natives the Lorenzos' Hollis home is considered Northside while 'Preme's South Jamaica territory is the rival Southside. Though these areas are so close geographically that they're almost indistinguishable, each has its own specific hustling history (Northside is known for freelancers, Southside for organized crews) and street guys from opposite sides of the neighborhood would often test each others' mettle. When Chris Lorenzo was an adolescent, he would take a bus home from school that stopped at a Jamaica terminal; as soon as he stepped off the bus he would be set upon by angry Southside hustlers. Chris was ambushed so often that he wore a backpack to school so he could have his hands free to fight them.

Coming from this background, Irv's embrace of 'Preme on the set of "Get Tha Fortune" was a street faux pas akin to a Blood cozying up to a Crip. "I get a call from my brother and he's like, 'Yo, I just met Supreme,'" Chris remembers, "and I'm like, '*Supreme* Supreme?' And he says, 'Yeah, Supreme.' And I'm like, 'Nigga, you good? You OK?' Hollis and Southside don't get along. I'm about ready to go and see if we got a fight. But he was like, 'No, it's all good, we finishing the video.'" Irv had made a major miscalculation by befriending 'Preme on Guy Brewer Boulevard that day, though he clearly didn't see it that way at the time. To Irv, it was the rare opportunity to meet a southeast Queens street legend. To 'Preme, the encounter offered something much more concrete: a sympathetic (and well-connected) ear for his movie pitches.

"He seen me shooting the video, and he said, 'Hey, I got this movie idea,'" Irv remembers. "He had a dream about doing movies. He wanted to do something with Donald Goines because when he was locked up Goines was his favorite novelist. He felt that Goines movies was gonna be big with the urban world." Irv wanted to help 'Preme out but he admitted that he could be of little help as he was just beginning to make headway into the music business. Irv says that he told 'Preme that he didn't shoot music videos but that he had a close friend—well-known music video director Hype Williams—whom he would happy to introduce him to. The chance meeting with Irv was a small, yet important step in the former Supreme Team CEO's quest to bring Goines to the big screen; he'd made his first real connection in the music business and, with hip-hop straining for street cred, more like Irv were sure to follow.

Meanwhile, in Hollis, another storied street guy—Curtis Scoon—was seeking to trade his hustling past for a hip-hop future. Though he'd helped friend Freddie "Nickels" Moore recuperate from the Quad shooting at Moore's 201st Street home in Hollis, Scoon still figured the music business to be safer than the streets. Indeed, by 1996 Scoon left the streets behind entirely, a decision that infuriated Hollis hustlers, especially because he had moved back to the neighborhood. Through an introduction made by Irv Lorenzo, Scoon pitched Roc-A-Fella Records about promoting Jay-Z's single "Dead Presidents II." Scoon was excited about working with Jay-Z, as he'd taken the rapper's boasts on songs like "Dead Presidents II" about moving "crazy weight" literally. But Scoon soon found that Jay-Z shared a background similar to Tupac Shakur's: He'd made his name not on the streets but as a hype man for Jaz-O. Scoon went ahead with his "Dead Presidents II" promotion anyway but discovered that radio programmers preferred to play the single's B-side, a duet with rapper Foxy Brown called "Ain't No Nigga." It was a disheartening moment for Scoon, but he wasn't giving up on hip-hop just yet.

Thanks to a chance meeting with Jam Master Jay on 203rd Street and Hollis Avenue, when Scoon loaned the RUN-DMC DJ $2,500 in exchange for an introduction to some of his music business connections, Scoon had a meeting with Def Jam's Lyor Cohen. Scoon and Freddie "Nickels" Moore had put together a tribute album for southeast Queens hip-hop legend and Tupac Shakur associate Randy "Stretch" Walker, who had been killed near his Queens Village home on November 30, 1995—one year to the day after the Quad shooting—and the pair were hoping that Def Jam would distribute the project. When Scoon arrived at Def Jam's Varick Street offices in September 1996 carrying commitment letters from the likes of Puffy Combs and Digital Underground frontman (and Shakur's former mentor) Shock G, he found that Cohen was much more interested in waxing philosophical about hip-hop's East-West rivalry than distributing the tribute album. "Lyor was talking a lot of bullshit about the tragedy of Tupac's death and how hip-hop violence was escalating," Scoon says. "He wasn't telling me anything I wanted to hear."

It was obvious to Scoon that Jay's stature in the music business had been greatly diminished with the fall of RUN-DMC. "Nobody gave a fuck about Jay," Scoon says. "And when I realized that, I asked for the money back." A few months after the meeting with Cohen, Scoon confronted Jay in a park beside PS 192 in Hollis, pulling him aside from a group of people he was talking to and asking for his money. Scoon says that Jay confessed that he didn't have the money but would pay him as soon as he did. Two months later, Scoon says, the $2,500 was paid back in full.

Jay's connection to Cohen may not have resulted in a deal for Scoon's "Stretch" Walker tribute album, but the former Hollis hustler was being eagerly courted by Irv Lorenzo. Irv made his move one night in early 1997 when Scoon was partying at the cavernous Manhattan nightclub Tunnel. "He compared me to Suge Knight," Scoon remembers. "He told me that he'd sought out a relationship with Suge and really admired what Suge was doing." Scoon was mystified by Irv's admiration for Knight; by then the Death Row empire was crumbling. After "gangsta rap" hearings in Congress and relentless criticism from anti–gangsta rap crusader C. Delores Tucker, Time-Warner sold its interest in Interscope back to the company in 1995; Death Row's biggest star, Shakur, signed to the label only after Knight bailed him out of prison after the rape charge, had been murdered and the East Coast was eclipsing the West thanks to the rise of Jay-Z and Biggie. Worst of all, Knight's thuggish behavior frightened off music industry executives from dealing with former hustlers. "He messed it up for guys like me," says Jimmy "Henchmen" Rosemond. "He made people feel like you can't let guys who have this kind of background into the business anymore." Irv, however, still saw Suge as an iconic hip-hop persona and believed that Scoon had the potential to be the same.

Irv's obsession with his own street cred was particularly strange at a time when his career was vaulting him beyond hustler acquaintances like 'Preme. The work he'd put in with Cash Money Click and on Jay-Z's instant classic *Reasonable Doubt* caught the attention of Lyor Cohen, who hired him as an A&R executive at Def Jam. "It was a unique time because Lyor had nothing," Irv says. "They were gonna fire Lyor and take Def Jam from him. So basically the guy just ran with me."

Def Jam had slumped in the post-*Chronic* era, signing third-tier talent like a female MC named Boss (whose 1992 debut *Born Gangstaz* was a rote take on the West Coast sound) and Los Angeles–based one-hit wonders like Domino. "We were pretty cold," Russell Simmons admits. "We didn't have no hit records."

Simmons, however, rejects the notion that the label's dry spell was caused by the West Coast's dominance of the hip-hop scene in the early nineties. "Trends are bullshit," Simmons says. "We just didn't make good records. We weren't very focused." Whatever the reason, the label's lack of focus began affecting the bottom line: Where once Def Jam was making massive hit records with modest budgets now it was a multimillion-dollar money pit with major label backing. In 1994, Sony decided that it had had enough: The company sold half its stake in Def Jam to PolyGram for $33 million.

Cohen believed that Irv Lorenzo could reverse Def Jam's flagging fortunes, but Irv says that most of his colleagues were not convinced by his signings. DMX was Lorenzo's most controversial new Def Jam artist: His dark, paranoid lyrics and growling voice were starkly at odds with hip-hop's optimistic mid-nineties moment epitomized by Puffy's smiling, pop-friendly stable of rappers. "The people who worked there used to clown with me and say, 'Who's gonna buy his record? *Dogs?*'" Irv remembers. " 'What the fuck is this bullshit? He's barking. No one wants to hear that shit.' But I thought they were clowns up there. I was like, 'Y'all don't know what's going on the streets.' " Fortunately for Irv and for Def Jam itself Cohen ignored the chorus of Lorenzo critics at the label, many of whom called him "Snotty Gotti." "Lyor gave me carte blanche," Lorenzo explains. "He let me do what I wanted to do."

While Irv Lorenzo was solidifying his status at Def Jam, Curtis Jackson was just beginning to make his presence felt in the southeast Queens hip-hop scene. Jackson was born on July 6, 1976, in South Jamaica, to an absent father he never knew and a teenage, drug-addicted mother, Sabrina. Most of Jackson's family was immersed in the drug trade—as an adolescent, he was sent on drug runs to pick up cocaine for partying relatives—but his mother was a hardcore hustler who worked for an organization in Fat Cat's territory on Sutphin Boulevard and 150th Street. "Sabrina was slinging rocks out on our block for a dealer named Hilda," remembers former Nichols organization lieutenant Joseph "Bobo" Rogers. "It was a small operation, full of crackheads, but it didn't bother us any." Sabrina may not have rankled Fat Cat's crew but out on the block she exposed herself to the very worst the streets had to offer. Unsurprisingly, after years of hustling on one of southeast Queens' most dangerous blocks without protection from a major player like Fat Cat, Sabrina was murdered. Someone—the assailant has still not been caught—poisoned Sabrina and then left the gas on in her home, killing her.

After his mother's death, an eight-year-old Jackson moved to his grandmother's house on 161st Street in South Jamaica, where he fell under the hustlers' spell. "I looked up to them because they had everything that we was looking for," Jackson told *New York* magazine. "When you grow up without finances it starts to feel like finances are the answers to all of your problems. And when you're like twelve years old and you're having a hard time in school and they're telling you, 'You can do well in school for eight more years and have the things you want,' a kid's curiosity leads him to the 'hood. And he finds someone who got it and didn't go to school. They persuade you, they tell you, 'No, you can get paid like *this.*' You go off into a whole other zone, it's, 'This is how I gotta do.' And even if you're only generating enough finances to purchase a vehicle, you're still taking care of yourself better than your people can. . . . So I had to tell my grandmother I was in an after-school program; it gave me a few hours to be doing whatever I had to do."

In stark contrast to the days of the Supreme Team's reign, when drugs were sold on the busy, densely populated blocks of Guy R. Brewer, Jackson hustled alone on the boulevard's more desolate stretches. If the multitiered Supreme Team was structured like a Fortune 500 company, Jackson's two-person crack cocaine and heroin dealing operation resembled a corner store. Jackson and his sixteen-year-old partner Taiesha Douse had a simple hustle down pat—customers would approach Jackson for drugs and he would flash his fingers at Douse indicating the number of "nicks" (five-dollar vials of crack) the customer requested, and then Douse would bring the drugs over.

Just after 11 PM on June 29, 1994, Jackson and Douse were working their usual hustle near 134-25 Guy R. Brewer, and just as they had done so many times before they repeated their workman-like scheme. This time, however, Jackson and Douse's customer was a Queens Narcotics officer named Kathleen Kragel. The pair were cuffed, brought to One Police Plaza in downtown Manhattan, and booked on charges of criminal sale of a controlled substance in the third degree. But Jackson's problems with law enforcement were just beginning: A few weeks later, a search warrant was issued for Jackson's home at 145-40 Rockaway Boulevard and cops seized seven bags of crack, an envelope containing heroin, an air gun, and $695 in cash.

It was a small bust that brought modest time—seven months in a shock incarceration boot camp—and Jackson admits that he was most upset about disappointing his grandma, especially as he had been caught with nicks at high school just prior to the bust. "After I got caught I had to tell my grandma," Jackson told *Playboy.* "She asked me if the charges were true and I don't lie to my grandma. As crazy as it sounds, I felt like I got caught because I was hiding it from her. I told her I did it and I told her I was going to keep doing it. . . . She said, 'Don't call here when you get in trouble.' "

Jackson's arrest on charges of criminal sale of a controlled substance had chastened him; it was time, he realized, to find a more legitimate hustle. So Jackson began writing rhymes and rapping as "50 Cent," a name he borrowed from a stick-up kid named Kelvin Martin who was raised in the Fort Greene section of Brooklyn during the eighties. Taking the name of a Brooklyn hustler may have seemed an odd choice for an aspiring rapper from southeast Queens, but Jackson felt a kinship with his namesake that went beyond the boundaries of the five boroughs. Martin robbed Brooklyn businesses with a sense of fearlessness that bordered on the psychotic; it wasn't unusual for him to hit several liquor stores in one day, often on the same block.

Martin was a street legend, but his hustles were often comically unsophisticated; friends would watch, dumbstruck, as he would put on a Halloween mask just before robbing a mark. Unlike the street CEOs of southeast Queens Martin was eminently approachable, too, and he was well-liked in his neighborhood even by the rappers he robbed. "If I was going to take a gangster's name," Jackson wrote in his autobiography *From Pieces to Weight: Once Upon a Time in Southside, Queens*, "then I wanted it at least to be that of someone who would say 'what's up' to me on the street if we ever crossed paths." Jackson's move stood in sharp contrast to his hip-hop peers who had assumed the names of drug cartel and Mafia bigwigs. "I couldn't see Gotti or Escobar giving me the time of day."

Jackson sought to apply Martin's antiestablishment attitude to hip-hop's iced-out icons like Puffy, who were growing smug and increasingly removed from the streets. "50 the street guy didn't care about anything and 50 the rapper wanted to be the same way," explains Jimmy "Henchmen" Rosemond, who served time in a juvenile facility with Martin.

50 also looked to Brooklyn for his rhyming style, imitating the boastfulness and fast-paced flow of Jay-Z. He soon found this more derivative than inspired, and he sought out a mentor at home in southeast Queens to help him refine his art. In a stroke of good fortune, he ran into Jam Master Jay on the streets of Hollis. "He said he was developing his label and looking for new artists and I was like, 'Yo, I'm a new artist,' " 50 remembers. "I was hustling my way into it with conversation. I didn't have anything to show. But then he gave me a beat tape and I wrote some rhymes to it. He loved the rhymes but some of them weren't right. One was too long, one was too short. And I was stopping when I felt like the statement should stop. He taught me how to count bars, the song structure; all that comes from Jam Master Jay." Jay also cautioned 50 to resist the lure of the drug game, which 50 had yet to leave behind. "Jay was like, 'Stay focused,' " 50 remembers. " 'Focus on your music if this is what you want to do.' "

Jay was an important mentor for 50—the RUN-DMC DJ got the rapper his first-ever guest spot, on Onyx's 1998 single "React"—but the road constantly called him away. So, eventually 50 turned to Chaz "Slim" Williams for help. Born in Harlem but raised in southeast Queens during the seventies, Williams had become a master of takeover robberies, a brazen form of bank heist where the bank itself—not just a teller or two—is commandeered by the assailants.

(Takeover robbers dismiss those who slip bank tellers notes as mere "note pushers.") While serving out a long prison sentence for armed robbery in the seventies, Williams joined a gang called the Black Hand which fought off attacks on African-American inmates by white supremacists.

Upon release from prison in the early nineties, Williams, like Curtis Scoon, attempted to break into the music business through party promotion. Williams threw highly popular after-parties for Mike Tyson in Las Vegas and even befriended the fiery pugilist. Sensing hip-hop's move to the mainstream, he moved out of the party business and into the music industry in 1996 when he founded Black Hand Entertainment, which he wisely headquartered in the heart of southeast Queens at 89-139th Street off Grand Central Parkway. One of Black Hand's first clients—signed with a handshake, not a contract, according to Williams—was a young and hungry aspiring rapper named Curtis Jackson, who was already calling himself 50 Cent.

'Preme was also looking to Williams as a way into the music business as the Lorenzo brothers were still uncomfortable with his presence. "In the beginning stages, I didn't even meet 'Preme," Chris Lorenzo explains, "I would just get the call from Irv, 'Yo, I'm at the club and 'Preme is here.' He's letting me know; we're Hollis niggas and this dude is the epitome of Southside. Who knows what might happen?'" 'Preme was eager to find contacts outside of the Lorenzo camp to help him realize his dream of bringing Donald Goines's novels to the big screen. With young hip-hoppers like DMX and 50 Cent knocking down the doors of Black Hand's 139th Street office in South Jamaica, Williams was an obvious choice, so in 1998 'Preme suggested to Williams that they produce a film version of *Black Gangster* together. Though Williams didn't have the finances or Hollywood connections to make the movie happen, he devised a counteroffer. He'd put together a soundtrack to *Black Gangster* featuring rising southeast Queens hip-hop stars like 50 Cent and Ja Rule. If the project took off, Black Hand would consider making the movie itself. To prove just how serious he was about the project, Williams flew out to Los Angeles to purchase the rights to *Black*

Gangster from Holloway House, the publishing company that controls the rights to Goines's catalog. 'Preme agreed to the novel idea, thinking *Black Gangster* would impress hip-hop entrepreneurs and, with storied ex-hustler Williams at the helm, would give the newly released 'Preme an extra boost of street credibility.

As 'Preme neared completion of his first project and the Lorenzo brothers finally gained a foothold at Def Jam, the new, street-centric approach of the southeast Queens hip-hop scene had yet to be validated by the mainstream. That all changed on May 19, 1998, with the release of DMX's Def Jam debut *It's Dark and Hell Is Hot.* During its first week in stores, more than 250,000 copies of *It's Dark . . .* were sold, knocking country music superstar Garth Brooks off the top of the charts. But what made the first-week sales even more impressive was that DMX had received almost no MTV or radio play. The Lorenzo brothers had created buzz for the record almost entirely through the mixtape scene.

"When X came," Irv explains, "it was a tidal wave. It was just one of those special things in hip-hop. . . . People was just tired of the Puffy way of doing things and he just came and landslided the whole fucking country." Like *The Chronic, It's Dark and Hell Is Hot* helped alter hip-hop's compass: Suddenly, hits like Will Smith's 1998 Puffy-piggybacking "Getting Jiggy Wit It" seemed ludicrously outdated. The streets were primed for a takeover of the mainstream led by an army of ex-hustlers and music business impresarios from southeast Queens.

Everyone in the Lorenzo brothers' camp—including former Cash Money Click member Ja Rule and DJ Clue (who helped push DMX's music on the streets)—was ecstatic. Not only had their bosses scored their first multiplatinum success, they'd also secured them deals with Def Jam. Ja celebrated the newfound status of the Lorenzos and southeast Queens in a freestyle piece for a Def Jam live album called *Survival of the Illest,* which featured DMX, Jam Master Jay, stalwarts Onyx, and the label's supergroup Def Squad. A memorable freestyle can kick-start a young rapper's career; it had happened with Nas with his freestyle on "Live at the Barbeque," from a Queens group called Main Source, and Ja looked to make a huge impression. He also sought to solidify the Lorenzo brothers' connection with 'Preme even though there was still lingering discomfort from Chris Lorenzo about the former Supreme Team CEO. Ja boasted on the freestyle that the Lorenzos were backed by "'Preme Team representatives" and he also name-checked former Supreme Team member Hobie "Robo Justice" Townsend and even Black Hand's Chaz "Slim" Williams.

Williams appreciated the shout-out from Ja; he was in the final stages of production on the *Black Gangster* soundtrack with 'Preme and was holding studio sessions at the Black Hand headquarters on 139th Street in South Jamaica well into the morning. Even before the album's in-store date, the hard work was paying off: Williams secured contributions from Jay-Z, DMX, Ja Rule, and 50 Cent. DMX was in especially fine form on *Black Gangster*; his lyrics were unusually reflective, and his flow was deliberate rather than the aggressive, staccato rhyme style heard on *It's Dark and Hell Is Hot*. The performances Williams coaxed from the likes of DMX stood out even more against the production, which had the orchestral, moody feel of Ennio Morricone's soundtracks for movies like *Once Upon a Time in America*. Because *Black Gangster* was to be released independently, Williams was free to stick to the novel marketing scheme that he and 'Preme had devised for the project: *Black Gangster* would be sold not as a soundtrack exactly but a concept album "based on the novel by America's number one best-selling black author Donald Goines."

By the late nineties, Williams was becoming known as something of a kingmaker to southeast Queens hip-hoppers, a reputation solidified when former protégé 50 Cent landed a deal in 1999 with Columbia Records through storied hip-hop and R&B producers the Trackmasters. It was a paltry deal—50 says he received a $65,000 advance, almost all of which went to Jam Master Jay and the attorney who represented him during the deal—and Columbia was better-known for R&B singers and producers like Destiny's Child and Jermaine Dupri than hardcore hip-hoppers. But it was the first recognition of 50's talents from the music business, and he worked hard to overcome the modest deal's limitations, holing himself up at an upstate New York recording studio and churning out nearly forty tracks.

Later that year, back home in southeast Queens, 50 devised a scheme to make a more substantial impact on the hip-hop scene than his modest deal with Columbia would allow. "You only get to make a first impression once," 50 says. So he turned his sights on the Lorenzo brothers and, more specifically, Ja Rule, who he felt had treated him dismissively backstage at a concert at the Amazura Ballroom in Queens. "50 felt that Ja had completely brushed him off at the Amazura that night, that he didn't acknowledge his presence with a 'what's up?'," remembers Chaz Williams. Ja's middle-class background growing up in the tame Woodhull section of Queens made him an especially tempting target. 50 considered Ja to be a fraud, a "studio gangster," and he began cranking out numerous diss tracks aimed at the Lorenzos and Ja, accusing them of faking their southeast Queens street pedigree. For instance, 50 rapped that his rivals wrote "about bricks" of cocaine when they had "only dealt wit' dimes."

50's campaign to portray Ja as inauthentic was given a huge boost when Ja was robbed right outside his Woodhull home—by someone who was a close acquaintance of 50 *and* the Lorenzo brothers no less. A man whom Ja apparently knew pretended to greet him outside his home. When Ja embraced the man he said menacingly, "Give me your chain," according to Chris Lorenzo. Ja believed that the confrontation was a prank until the man growled, "I ain't playin', give me your chain." Ja handed the jewelry over and then appealed to the Lorenzo brothers for help in getting it back. "We got the chain back," Chris remembers, "it was no big deal. We all knew the guy so it was like [affects schoolmarmish voice], 'Johnny, will you give the chain back, please.'" Lorenzo won't say who the assailant was nor will he reveal whom he enlisted to reclaim the jewelry. But sources close to the Lorenzos say that Chris turned to 'Preme to retrieve Ja's chain. Indeed, according to an IRS affidavit filed in the federal investigation into The Inc., when Ja complained about the robbery to the Lorenzos, Irv contacted 'Preme, who "secured the return of the jewelry . . . using his reputation for violence to intimidate and threaten the robber."

50's opening shots at the Lorenzos struck the brothers as little more than insignificant tweaks from an upstart rapper. After all, 50 was still struggling to find an audience (he even admitted on "Life's on the Line" that "nobody likes me") while Irv Lorenzo was being eagerly courted by music industry heavies like Tommy Mottola thanks to the surprise success of DMX. At a lunch meeting with an emissary working for Mottola, which Irv believed was simply about the purchase of beats, Irv was instead offered a record deal. "Irv meets up with him at a restaurant, and they're sitting there and then something distracts Irv for a minute and he looks away and—smack!—the guy reaches into his pocket and pulls out a contract," remembers Chris Lorenzo. "Irv says, 'What the fuck is this?' He says, 'I don't care about buying no beats from you. I wanna give you a label.' Irv says, 'You serious?' Irv looks the contract over, and he throws the shit back on the table and says, 'Give me a fuckin' real deal.' Irv gets up and he says, 'No, I'm serious, Tommy Mottola wants to give you a deal.' Tommy starts calling Irv and once he did that the floodgates opened." No one would have blamed Irv for jumping to Sony. Chris Lorenzo says that his brother was making a mere $60,000 per year as an A&R exec at Def Jam; a source at the Universal Music Group puts Irv's salary at $30,000, adding that "Irv slept in the studio so often he might as well have been living there." But Irv was hesitant to abandon the rappers he'd brought to Def Jam, as he'd been building their careers since the early nineties.

The Lorenzos took a meeting with Lyor Cohen to relay the news of Mottola's proposal. Irv purposely kept the tone of the sit-down with Cohen cordial; he didn't plan to leave Def Jam, but he did want Lyor to match Mottola's offer. "Lyor said he couldn't do it," Chris Lorenzo recalls. "He could have; Lyor has a philosophy of getting talent at the cheapest cost possible. He has another philosophy of 'You should want to be with me because I'm the best for you. You should want to be here and take less money because it's gonna mean more for you.' "

Negotiations were at a stalemate until Edgar Bronfman Jr., then CEO of Seagram (the corporate giant that in 1998 purchased Poly-Gram, Def Jam's parent company, and renamed its combined music operations Universal Music Group), stepped in. "It took Edgar Bronfman to say, 'Cut Irv his check and get him his deal,' " Chris Lorenzo remembers, "or Irv would have been at Sony." Irv was given a $3 million check for the new label, which would be a fifty/fifty partnership with Def Jam, meaning that they would split promotion and marketing costs and profits down the middle. It was the first unambiguous victory in a career marked by frustrating stops and starts, and Irv was feeling invincible. He dubbed his new venture Murder Inc. after a team of Mafia hit men, and he named Murder Inc.'s downtown Manhattan recording studio the Crackhouse.

For Russell Simmons, the success of Murder Inc.—as well as the cash coming from Lorenzo's superstar signings like Jay-Z—meant that he could at last cash out of his Def Jam empire. "Irv Gotti was the best thing to happen to Def Jam since the eighties," Simmons explains. "Lyor and Kevin Liles managed the label, but Irv made the records. Irv did what I did. He was fantastic. He made a lot of money for us." Sensing that Def Jam was at its peak—thanks to Lorenzo the label had its best year ever in 1998, bringing in an astonishing $176 million in sales—Simmons offered his forty percent share of the company to the Universal Music Group for nearly $125 million. Universal balked at the asking price; 1998 may have been a solid year for Simmons but the pre-Lorenzo mid-nineties saw Def Jam rack up multimillion-dollar losses. (One source close to the label told *The Los Angeles Times* that Def Jam lost nearly $20 million between 1995 and 1997.) When the two sides came back to the negotiating table, they agreed on a number that wasn't far from Simmons's original offer: $100 million. Irv Lorenzo had not just resuscitated the fading Def Jam brand; he helped give its iconic founder one of the most sizable payouts of his career, all thanks to a business strategy that embraced the southeast Queens hustling ethos of the eighties. Irv may have been a backstreet boy back in Hollis but the from-the-streets success of DMX proved that he was as skilled in moving product as a Supreme Team lieutenant.

50's Insurgency

While the Lorenzos were celebrating their status as hip-hop's pre-eminent players, 50 Cent was plotting their overthrow. 50's debut was coming along better than anyone, including his mentors Jam Master Jay and Chaz Williams, had ever expected. The highlight of the record was a savagely smart single called "How to Rob," in which 50 imagines himself sacking hip-hop and R&B's blingy A-list, including Lil' Kim, Puff Daddy, Keith Sweat, and Juvenile, for all of their cash. Unlike most rap revenge fantasies, however, 50 didn't see himself emerging from the feuds rich and famous. "This ain't serious," an MC named the Mad Rapper chanted on the chorus of "How to Rob," "bein' broke can make you delirious." To make the point of his relative poverty even clearer, 50 also closed the song by sarcastically chanting the refrain—"Did you ever think that you would be this rich?"—from R&B singer R. Kelly's pompous late 1990s hit "Did You Ever Think." "How to Rob" was a rare thing: hip-hop satire. "I wanted to make it funny," 50 explains, "I felt I accomplished that." Executives at 50's label worried that "How to Rob" would alienate the hip-hop scene's biggest players—"The song was getting some buzz but they were afraid to make a video for it," Chaz Williams says—and, indeed, most of the rappers skewered on the song didn't get the joke and some even threatened 50 with violence.

The streets were savoring the subversive humor of "How to Rob," and 50's contribution to *Black Gangster* helped make the record a surprise hit when it was released during the summer of 1999. (The record managed to crack both *Billboard*'s Top 200 and its R&B charts.) 50 was fast making a name for himself as one of hip-hop's smartest young MCs, and enmity was growing between 50, the Murder Inc. crew, and even southeast Queens hustlers. At a Murder Inc.–hosted party in Atlanta in 1999, tensions between 50 and the Lorenzos came to a boil. When Williams spotted the Lorenzo brothers and Ja Rule at the event, he tried to make peace between 50 and the Murder Inc. crew. "Chaz sees us, he knows there's a beef between Ja and 50 and says, 'Look I got 50 over here, I want him to talk to you, I'm trying to manage him and I don't want to have no problems,' " Chris Lorenzo remembers. "We was good friends with Chaz. 'OK, cool.' So, Rule and 50 go outside to talk." During their conversation, Ja implored 50 to stop making records about him. "Rule's like, 'I don't even know you, why you making these beef records?' " Chris says, "and then all of the sudden Rule's like, 'What the fuck?' The next thing you know 50 snuffs Rule and they start fighting." The pair engaged each other in a fierce fistfight—at one point, Ja pulled 50's shirt over his head while he whaled away at his stomach—which spilled back into the hotel. "50 gets into the elevator and Rule throws a garbage can into the elevator," Chris says, "and Rule has to pay damages to the hotel. That's all it's been with this dude [50]—lawsuits."

Ja's anger at 50 paled in comparison to 'Preme's fury when the aspiring rapper's song "Ghetto Qu'ran (Forgive Me)" was leaked to the streets. On this track, 50 described the southeast Queens hustling scene of the eighties in novelistic detail. 'Preme, according to Jackson, was "the businessman" and his nephew Prince was "the killer." He also rapped about seeing 'Preme in his "bulletproof BM" and reeled off a roll call of former Supreme Team members including "Baby Wise." There were also shout-outs to Chaz Williams as well as new jacks like Eric "E Money Bags" Smith. But what made the song so memorable were 50's sharply observed details about Queens hustling icons. 50 rhymed about Thomas "Tony Montana" Mickens and his "Rolls-Royces with Louis Vuitton interiors" and lamented that he "used to idolize Cat," until he turned on Pappy

Mason. Former Nichols organization members brushed the track off. "I don't like 50 Cent," says Marcy, a close relative of Fat Cat's. "He doesn't know what he's talking about." Adds Joseph "Bobo" Rogers: "50 didn't know any of us, but we knew him way before he got big."

Chaz Williams warned 50 that many of the hustlers named in "Ghetto Qu'ran" would be unhappy with the song, and, sure enough, 'Preme was furious. He was trying to make it in the music and movie businesses and the last thing he needed was a rapper broadcasting his past misdeeds on a major label release. 'Preme was also angry that his nephew Prince came off as far more menacing than he in the song. So, according to a former Nichols organization member, he conveyed a stark warning to 50 through a surrogate in southeast Queens: "Stop rapping about me." That 'Preme took 50's rhymes so seriously surprised his hustling peers. Why, they wondered, was a storied street guy starting a war with a rapper close to twenty years younger than he was? The Lorenzo brothers had blurred the lines between hustling and hip-hop by aligning themselves with the former Supreme Team CEO but that was to be expected from such a street-cred-hungry pair. 'Preme, however, had nothing to gain by allowing himself to be drawn into a hip-hop beef.

50 is purposefully vague when talking about his relationship with 'Preme, but he does hint that once-friendly relations between himself and the former Supreme Team CEO chilled. "Me and 'Preme had a relationship," 50 explains. "At one point we would speak to each other, and we would say, 'Hey, what's up, potna', and we would kick it. We have so much in common we can't get along. His outlook on things is he should do what he wants to do and I feel exactly the same. So we clash. You know what I mean? He's not gonna like me and I'm not gonna like him." 'Preme's attorney Robert Simels dismisses the notion that the pair had a rivalry, pointing out that 'Preme and 50 are a generation apart. "How could he grow up with Kenny?" Simels asks. "He didn't know Mickens, he didn't know Fat Cat. It's all bullshit."

As much as "Ghetto Qu'ran" annoyed 'Preme, he struggled to focus his energies entirely on the new, formidable challenges ahead, specifically getting one of Donald Goines's novels into production. Though *Black Gangster* the album was an unqualified success (it sold nearly 150,000 copies according to Chaz Williams, the near-equivalent of a gold record for a major label), there was no interest from Hollywood in taking the project from a soundtrack to an actual movie. So 'Preme decided to attempt another novel from the Goines canon, *Crime Partners*. But this time, 'Preme would look to a production company far more powerful than Williams's Black Hand: Murder Inc. The Murder Inc. posse had grown so close to 'Preme since Irv's chance meeting with him on the set of "Get Tha Fortune" in 1996 that they were almost familial. "That's my man," Lorenzo says of 'Preme. "He knows my mother. He carries in groceries for my mother. He was on my wedding line. My brother was my best man and 'Preme was on my wedding line. He knows my whole family. *'How's Supreme? Is he doing all right?'* Niggas don't know my mother. *'Preme* knows my mother." Irv's closeness with 'Preme shocked friends and even business associates like Russell Simmons. "I saw Supreme [at Irv's wedding], and I was shocked," Simmons says, "because I hadn't seen 'Preme in 15 years. I didn't even recognize him. *Supreme?* You mean Supreme from Jamaica? Why? How? How? How?"

Partying nightly at New York clubs with Irv and even attending his family functions, 'Preme naturally felt comfortable approaching the Lorenzo brothers about investing in *Crime Partners*. Irv says that he gave $50,000 for a small piece of the film, and he also secured contributions from big-name artists like Jay-Z for the *Crime Partners* soundtrack and then convinced Def Jam to release it. "I was basically like, 'Yo, I'm giving him ['Preme] all my acts for the soundtrack so it's going to be in your best interest to control it,' " Irv explains. "Don't let me give him all of these acts and then he can go take this soundtrack to Warner Brothers or EMI or Capitol with it." A source at the Universal Music Group says, however, that Irv made a much different *Crime Partners* pitch. "Irv said, 'Here's a guy getting out of a life of crime,' " the source remembers. " 'Can you help?' " Regardless, 'Preme landed his *Crime Partners* soundtrack distribution deal with Def Jam for $1 million, $500,000 of which was paid up front.

'Preme then turned to the production of *Crime Partners* itself—he didn't want to be left with a movieless soundtrack the way he had been with *Black Gangster.* 'Preme, his sister Barbara McGriff, and a longtime friend from Queens named Jon Ragin formed Picture Perfect Entertainment to produce the film. ('Preme's attorney Robert Simels minimizes his client's role in Picture Perfect, claiming that 'Preme was only a "minority stakeholder" in the company.) With Def Jam on board as the distributor of the *Crime Partners* soundtrack, 'Preme and Picture Perfect were able to convince hip-hop icons like Ice-T and Snoop Dogg to take starring roles in the movie at sharply reduced fees. As a result, the entire budget came in around $1 million, less than the price of some expensive music videos, according to a source close to Murder Inc. As the film was self-financed, Picture Perfect decided to take *Crime Partners* straight to DVD, rather than release it in theaters. In straight-to-DVD production, marketing costs are minimal, and profits can be maximized if the producers own the project. At last, 'Preme had his first real entrée into the legit hustle of hip-hop.

The hustles of the past, however, were never far behind 'Preme. His Picture Perfect partner Jon Ragin (who was on lifetime parole for a cocaine conviction) and a friend named Derek Hayes established a sham side business called Tuxedo Rentals which they used as a front for numerous credit card fraud schemes. Working out of his apartment at 175-20 Wexford Terrace in Queens, Ragin defrauded American Express cardholders and customers with credit cards at chains like Home Depot for hundreds of thousands of dollars. In one cluster of charges to American Express alone, Ragin was able to electronically transfer $25,000 to his Tuxedo Rentals account at Chase Manhattan. Ragin also sold drugs such as Ecstasy via his pager, which transmitted messages to customers under the company name Picture Perfect Dude. In these schemes, Ragin used painfully obvious codes: "TylEnol pills" for Ecstasy, "Penny" (JCPenney), "Homer" (Home Depot), and "Wally" (Wal-Mart). It was a third-rate hustle bound for trouble.

Things quickly moved far beyond massive credit card fraud and Ecstasy dealing on December 11, 1999, when federal agents sur-

veilling Ragin witnessed an SUV registered to Tuxedo Rentals dropping off the body of Supreme Team member Colbert "Black Just"
Johnson at a hospital in southeast Queens. On that December day,
according to a source close to Eric "E Money Bags" Smith, 'Preme
and Johnson were approached in southeast Queens by Smith, who
had a long-running feud with Johnson over a debt he believed Johnson owed him. Smith and Johnson then exchanged angry words, and
Smith fired a gun at Johnson, hitting him in the leg. During the
Supreme Team's heyday, 'Preme wouldn't have been concerned
with taking Johnson to the hospital, but now that he was trying to go
legit, he worried about being connected to such a serious crime,
even if he had no direct involvement in it.

So, according to the source close to Smith, 'Preme packed Johnson in his SUV and drove around southeast Queens aimlessly for
hours in hopes of coming up with a plan. But as 'Preme maneuvered
the SUV through Queens, Johnson's life slipped away. Horrified that
a nonfatal shooting had suddenly become a murder, 'Preme
dropped Johnson's body by the curb at a Queens hospital. 'Preme
was wracked about guilt over his inaction, and he was furious at
Smith, so, according to police, he sought to "locate Smith to avenge
Johnson's death." (Robert Simels calls the allegation "the work of a
great fiction writer.") Charges have yet to be brought in the Johnson
case, but after his murder it was clear that Smith's brash hustles
were about to end.

The murder of a prominent Supreme Team member and Jon
Ragin's credit card schemes cast a cloud of suspicion over the *Crime
Partners* production, and even the Lorenzo brothers themselves,
but the Murder Inc. crew wasn't helping matters with the increasingly violent style in which they settled rivalries. On March 24,
2000, at the midtown Manhattan recording studio Hit Factory,
Chris Lorenzo, Ja Rule, and Murder Inc. rapper Ramel "Black
Child" Gill decided to take revenge against 50 Cent for his stream of
songs slighting them. "Ja was in the Hit Factory, and he found out
that 50 was there and he went ballistic," Chris remembers. As Chris

and his posse went studio-to-studio searching for 50, they bumped into hip-hop superstars like LL Cool J. "I finally found the right door," Chris Lorenzo recalls, "and 50 was in a studio that I never knew existed. . . . I'm not gonna say he was hiding but it wasn't one of the regular rooms. As soon as I walked in, the first thing out of his mouth was, 'Pass me my gun.' When he said that I snuffed him—boom—he fell back down." The Murder Inc. crew engaged 50 and his friends in a fistfight until someone switched off the lights. "The lights went out and 50 threw a speaker which cracked me in the head," Chris Lorenzo remembers. Lorenzo was left with a big gash in his head that required stitches; 50 was stabbed by Ramel "Black Child" Gill and later treated for a laceration to the chest and a partially collapsed lung at St. Luke's–Roosevelt Hospital.

While 50's debut had yet to be released for Columbia—it was set for the spring of 2000—"How to Rob" and the Hit Factory incident were lending him a reputation as a David taking on music industry Goliaths like Murder Inc. The label's effort to portray 50 as a coward for taking out an order of protection against the Lorenzos and Gill backfired; to hip-hop fans it seemed like another example of the increasingly imperious Murder Inc. empire attempting to intimidate an upstart. Besides, to the marketing-savvy 50 the Hit Factory incident was the latest chapter in a dramatic biographical narrative. In just a few years he'd gone from grindin' in southeast Queens to exposing the vulnerabilities of one of hip-hop's hottest record labels.

The brawl at the Hit Factory was soon overshadowed by a much more dramatic attack. On May 24, 2000, as 50 and a friend sat in a car outside his grandmother's house on 161st Street in South Jamaica, a gunman rolled up in a vehicle on his left side and pumped nine shots into his body, hitting him in the hand, hip, calf, chest, and face. 50 managed to drive himself to a nearby hospital and, after a few weeks of rehabilitation, made a full recovery. He was left with a hole in the left side of his jaw and a shard of bullet in his tongue that gave his voice a slurry sound.

50 instantly grasped the symbolism of surviving such a bold assassination attempt. After all, Tupac Shakur's mythology had begun only after the Quad Studios shooting. Unfortunately for 50,

Columbia Records didn't share his view of the incident. The label worried that 50 wouldn't live to see his major label debut, and they were petrified that his violent street beefs might somehow spill into the boardroom. (This wasn't an unrealistic fear; in the late nineties there was a rash of violent incidents at record companies, most notoriously Puffy's alleged beating of Interscope executive Steve Stoute inside his own office during the spring of 1999.) "After I got shot, they got afraid," 50 explains, "afraid of me in their offices. . . . After I got shot and I was taking a meeting instead of it being about music it felt like it was a psych evaluation. They were asking me more about my issues in the 'hood than in my music. I think the industry would prefer a studio gangsta rather than someone who actually comes from that background because it's less of a risk. 'Cos you're investing money in this person and shots could go off."

Soon after the attempt on his life in southeast Queens, 50 was dropped from Columbia. His major label debut *Power of the Dollar* was never released but thanks to the subversively funny single "How to Rob" it was bootlegged on the streets. That *Power of the Dollar* suddenly had a new life was an object lesson in the power of street marketing: 50 may have been without major label backing, but he had a chance to build an empire from the ground up.

As 50 was starting his career anew on the streets of southeast Queens, Curtis Scoon was turning his experiences hustling in the neighborhood into a screenplay. In early 2000, Scoon began work on a script called *Fall from Grace* about a group of four friends from the streets who meet with starkly different (but equally tragic) fates: Two are murdered while the other pair end up serving lifelong prison sentences. Scoon hoped to make a film about hustling that was gritty and tough, yet not exploitative in its depictions of violence, like 'hood genre films such as *Menace II Society*. "I felt I could make it real because I lived it," Scoon says. Soon after completing *Fall from Grace*, he sent a copy of the script via e-mail to Kojo Bentil, an executive at Motown Records, which, like Def Jam, was under the Universal Music Group umbrella.

"I was hoping that since he was in the Universal system that he could walk it into the movie department," Scoon explains. To Scoon's surprise, Bentil asked to set up a meeting with him. But when Scoon arrived at Universal Music's 8th Avenue offices in midtown Manhattan for the appointment with Bentil he encountered "the same old pomp that I'd had in my discussions with Lyor Cohen." Bentil says that he did take Scoon's project seriously—"I thought his script was really compelling stuff"—but Scoon left the building without a commitment to the film. Though the pair corresponded via e-mail in the months after their initial meeting, nothing ever materialized. It was an especially difficult time as Scoon had sworn off the streets entirely but had yet to see any fruits of efforts in the music business. "I knew that I could plug right back into the street matrix," Scoon says. "But I had made a clean break. There was no going back."

The Murder Inc. camp was also turning away from the streets: Chastened by the negative fallout from the Hit Factory incident, the Lorenzo brothers decided to chart a more mainstream course in the fall of 2000. *Rule: 3:36*, Ja Rule's sophomore album for the label, which Murder Inc. released in October, offered one empathic duet after another, albeit with a slightly street feel; in the video for "Put It on Me," Ja pledges his love to an R&B singer named Lil' Mo from a prison cell. With "Exstasy" Ja became one of the first hip-hoppers to embrace the love drug which had long been verboten in a scene dominated by marijuana. Ja made such a convincing "Love Thug" that when Irv Lorenzo released a dark, humorless Murder Inc. all-stars album called *Irv Gotti Presents . . . The Murderers*, it seemed schizophrenic. Though the album sold more than 80,000 copies in its first week in stores, sales quickly tapered off. Ja's gruff cry, "It's murda!" had been one of the label's trademarks but just a year earlier, 50 had taunted Murder Inc. with the rhyme, "Murder! I don't believe you!" on "Life's on the Line." After *Rule 3:36*, it wasn't hard to imagine hip-hoppers nodding their heads to 50's rhyme in agreement.

Murder Inc.'s executives and rappers may not have lived up to its moniker, but the label had one of the most credible of street connections in 'Preme. Unsurprisingly, his fellow hustlers were growing jealous of 'Preme's relationship with the Lorenzos, imagining that 'Preme was living the high life depicted in Murder Inc. videos. But the Lorenzo brothers maintain that 'Preme was struggling finan- cially; Irv claims that he didn't "have a pot to piss in" and Chris says of 'Preme, "Some people think he had money stashed from back in the day but this guy was broke. That's the 'Preme I know. We was good friends but he was a broke friend. I got a bunch of broke friends from the 'hood, and he's one of them." The truth would not have placated the envious hustlers; the fact that the Lorenzos chose 'Preme instead of them was enough to stoke their fury.

In the spring of 2001, at a birthday party for Irv in New York, a posse of southeast Queens hustlers which included Troy Singleton, Eric "E Money Bags" Smith, and former Supreme Team member Nathan "Green Eyed Born" May showed up at the event in hopes of confronting 'Preme, according to a source close to Murder Inc. "They wanted 'Preme to come outside so they could slap him around," the source says, "but instead Gutta [Ja's manager Ron "Gutta" Robinson] who was outside at the time got slapped in the head with a semiautomatic. Gutta was high on Ecstasy, and he got delirious. The group never made it into the party, but they managed to snatch a necklace with the Murder Inc. logo as a trophy. Irv was disappointed in 'Preme: Here he was promoting him as a gangster who's supposed to slap everybody around but everyone was slapping *him* around. 'Preme even offered to pay for the necklace." Irv says that Smith was not at the party but he admits that back in southeast Queens "a lot of people were jealous of our relationship. That's nor- mal 'hood shit. But we don't give a fuck."

Even if Smith was not present at Irv's birthday party, there was little doubt that he was becoming a major-league irritant to the biggest players in hip-hop and on the streets. 'Preme was furious with Smith for the 1999 shooting of former Supreme Team lieu- tenant Colbert "Black Just" Johnson, and Jay-Z was feuding with Smith about a rapper signed to his Roc-A-Fella label named "H Money Bags." Smith even confronted Jay-Z about his namesake live on New York radio station Hot 97. "I don't appreciate you having a nigga up there with my name," Smith protested, to which Jay-Z replied, "Yo, E, man, I don't respect this." Smith shot back: "Why you ain't respecting that I'm asking about a nigga with my name, dog?" Moments later, Smith hung up the phone, satisfied that he'd put the scare into hip-hop's premier rhymer.

Smith's strong-arm style finally came back to haunt him when, just after 9:45 PM on July 16, 2001, four gunmen sporting white gloves driving in a Mercedes pulled up alongside Smith's Lincoln Navigator, which was parked near Witthoff Street and 111th Road in Queens Village. Smith had just come from a nearby barbeque and was playing demo tapes of his music for rapper Prodigy of the Queensbridge hip-hop group Mobb Deep and Christopher "Maj" Walker, the brother of Randy "Stretch" Walker, when the first of ten bullets tore through his body. The gunshots were fired at such close range that 9 millimeter shell casings covered the SUV's interior. When police arrived at the scene in Queens Village, they found Smith's body in the SUV with his belongings intact (a diamond-encrusted Rolex, $40 in cash, and a .380 caliber handgun). It was an archetypal hit job; robbery was quickly ruled out as a motive.

The same month that Smith was snuffed out, 'Preme was pulled over in his BMW near a known drug spot in Harlem. When asked for his driver's license, 'Preme identified himself as Lee Tuten and claimed that he was an executive at Def Jam, according to cops. "I didn't know none of that," Irv says when asked if he was aware that 'Preme claimed in Harlem to be a Def Jam exec. "I'm pretty sure 'Preme said a lot of things I didn't know about." Officers searching 'Preme's vehicle found a .40 caliber Glock pistol and $11,000 in cash; when he was arrested and charged with weapons possession his true identity was revealed. The cops turned 'Preme's weapon over to the Bureau of Alcohol, Tobacco and Firearms (ATF), who traced it to a relative of Lorenzo's. Chris Lorenzo disputes the ATF's allegation while insisting that it was necessary for 'Preme to carry a weapon with him. "From what I know since he got home his life was tried four times," Lorenzo says. "Once in broad daylight by a gas station. He might want to keep a gun on him."

'Preme's weapons possession arrest in Harlem and the murder of his longtime associate Smith soon brought the sort of intense law enforcement scrutiny that marked the end of his days on the streets of southeast Queens in the late eighties. On August 20, 2001, 'Preme's fate was sealed: Cops searching a parking lot outside of an apartment complex at 4314 Flint Hill Drive in Owings Mills, Maryland, where a pair of men named Karon Clarrett and Dwayne Thomas had just been murdered, found a piece of paper with the number of 'Preme's two-way pager written on it.

This discovery, as well as the premeditated nature of the crime itself (Clarrett and Thomas were shot to death execution-style) strongly suggested a drug business dispute. It turned out that Clarrett and an associate named Victor Wright had been arrested with two kilos of cocaine during a routine traffic stop in North Carolina just a few months earlier, on April 5, 2001. At first, Clarrett allegedly contacted an attorney who often represented Supreme Team members, but then he told the lawyer that he wanted to seek his own representation, a clear signal that Clarrett was going to cooperate with law enforcement in his case. Soon after Clarrett spurned the Supreme Team attorney's assistance, 'Preme allegedly met with a fearsome Baltimore-based drug dealer named Billy Guy who owed 'Preme a substantial drug debt, according to a cooperating witness (C.W.) working with homicide detectives. During the meeting 'Preme allegedly gave the order to kill Clarrett in exchange for forgiving the debt. Guy, the C.W. said, agreed to the arrangement with 'Preme and then set up the Clarrett hit.

Scouring Clarrett's cell phone records investigators found the name and phone number of Vash-ti Paylor, which they traced to 4314 Flint Hill Drive—the apartment complex whose parking lot was the scene of the double murder of Clarrett and Thomas. Upon searching the Paylor residence, cops allegedly found significant amounts of cocaine and heroin as well as $30,000 in cash, a cell phone allegedly used by Clarrett, a certificate for a firearms training course in the name of Lee Tuten ('Preme's Def Jam executive alias), and a videotape depicting surveillance-like footage shot from an apartment window with the time stamp of July 13 through July 16,

2001. After sharing the tape with NYPD detectives, who had become involved in the case because of the alleged connection to 'Preme, investigators pinpointed the block as 111th Road near Witthoff Street, the location of the Eric "E Money Bags" Smith killing. NYPD detectives also helped in identifying the SUV in the video as the vehicle that Smith was driving when he was killed. After Smith was murdered, 'Preme allegedly boasted that former Supreme Team lieutenant Colbert "Black Just" Johnson could "finally rest in peace."

The year 2001 was fast becoming a bloody one, with bodies dropping at an alarming rate and connections to 'Preme cropping up in Maryland, North Carolina, and, of course, southeast Queens. On October 28, 2001, Troy Singleton, a southeast Queens hustler with a long, storied history in the neighborhood (50 Cent shouted him out in "Ghetto Qu'ran") was killed on October 28, 2001. Singleton was murdered execution-style—four shots to the body, one shot to the head—outside a sports bar called the Club Van Wyck on Liberty Avenue in South Jamaica, not far from where Howard "Pappy" Mason's hit men ended Edward Byrne's life in 1988. Given Singleton's long criminal history, the killing easily could have been attributed to a low-level beef. But on the streets, Singleton was perhaps best-known for his role in an incident that humiliated the Supreme Team. In July 1995, Singleton and an accomplice killed two men named Pierre Mitchell and Jamal Adams during a basketball game near the Baisley Park Houses, right in the heart of the Supreme Team territory. The double murder was a huge embarrassment to 'Preme and his crew, and Singleton's killing, like that of Eric "E Money Bags" Smith, vanquished yet another one of 'Preme's enemies.

As 'Preme's past was catching up with him, 50's was finally fading into the past. Surviving nine gunshots in southeast Queens in 2000 had given him a feeling of fearlessness, one that he smartly applied not back to the streets but to the music business. Sensing that cracks were growing in Murder Inc.'s empire thanks to 'Preme's growing recklessness on the streets, 50 decided that it was an ideal time to challenge Murder Inc.'s supremacy in the hip-hop scene. With the help of longtime friend Sha Money XL, 50 mounted a guerrilla marketing campaign to heighten awareness of their hip-hop crew which they dubbed "G-Unit" (Guerrilla Unit). Just as DJ Clue had done so successfully with DMX in the late nineties, 50 and G-Unit worked the mixtape medium to its fullest, releasing an almost overwhelming barrage of material to the streets. In May 2002, 50 fired the first shot in his new battle, releasing a mixtape called *Guess Who's Back?*, a title that played on the attempt on his life.

While 50's hip-hop had always had a real-life quality to it, he personalized his music even further on *Guess Who's Back?* In contrast to the "studio gangstas," who 50 says fail to write from their own experiences, he rhymed with a clear-eyed honesty about his life. Fortunately for him, 50 had more than enough biographical material to draw from. On "Fuck You," 50 addressed his May 2000 shooting in southeast Queens and named 'Preme as a suspect. "Get back to questions/like '50 who shot ya?' " 50 rhymed. "You think it was 'Preme, Freeze, or Tah-Tah?/Nigga, street shit should stay in the street/so keep it on the low/but everybody who's somebody already know."

Recording "Fuck You" was one of the savviest moves of 50's career, a ballsy shot across the bow of both Murder Inc. and 'Preme, who was particularly vulnerable at the time. It also established 50 as one of the few rhymers to work from his actual biography instead of an imagined street past (though 50 would abandon his fidelity to the truth when he hit the mainstream). 50 and the G-Unit crew weren't content to rest on the laurels of *Guess Who's Back?*, and they released a pair of back-to-back mixtapes in 2002, *50 Cent Is the Future* and *No Mercy, No Fear.* On the latter, 50 made an anthem out of his distaste for studio gangstas, whom he dubbed "wankstas." With 50's mixtapes outselling copies of major label releases on the streets, producers and record label executives came calling. Dr. Dre and Eminem began courting him for a record deal at their Interscope-distributed label Shady/Aftermath, sparking a frenzied bidding war. Only Eminem, who worked from his biography as smartly as 50, seemed to grasp the potency of 50's long history on the streets of southeast Queens. "His life story sold me," Eminem explained to hip-hop magazine *XXL*. "To have a story behind the music is so important."

While 50 was scoring a new record deal with reigning hip-hop's megastar thanks to music that boldly took on hip-hop and street icons, Irv Lorenzo was settling into a conservative groove. Inspired by Ja's successful duets, Irv produced odes to fidelity like "Always on Time" and "Down 4 U" for Murder Inc.'s marquee R&B singer Ashanti. These songs were trite, but they were all huge hits and enabled Irv to sign a new, better contract for his label with Island Def Jam. Success soon went to his head. In a July 30, 2002, profile for *Rolling Stone*, Irv and Jay-Z's partner Damon Dash tussled over who the reporter could dub the "hottest nigga in the building." After arguing at Def Jam's 8th Avenue offices, Irv and Dash bickered again over the phone—and then Irv continued the ludicrous debate by relaying both his and Dash's competing claims to *Rolling Stone* scribe Touré. "Dame called to tell me he's the hottest nigga in the building," Irv proclaimed. "He's not the hottest. I am the hottest nigga in the building." More ominously, Irv boasted in the interview about having sold drugs while he was growing up in southeast Queens. "I got lured into the bullshit," Irv said blithely. "I don't recommend it." This was news to those who grew up with Irv in Hollis and knew him only as a backstreet boy, and it was a claim that, along with the Murder Inc. moniker, would soon be taken literally by law enforcement.

9

Hard Times

Just as Irv was hitting the pinnacle of his career, back in southeast Queens Jam Master Jay was enjoying a creative peak not seen since his early days with JMJ Records and Onyx. The nineties were a brutal time for Jay: Russell Simmons ended JMJ's partnership with Rush Associated Labels. "Onyx was very successful but other than that there wasn't a lot of records," Simmons says. "He didn't make the right records. It just fizzled out." Though RUN-DMC's sixth album *Down with the King* (released in 1993) was moderately successful, the group had to perform more than 250 shows per year in the mid-nineties just to keep their heads above water. "The one thing we had was a good show," explains Darryl "DMC" McDaniels. "That's what kept us eating." Joseph "Run" Simmons agrees: "We were still RUN-DMC. We got our high performing the records. Even if we played a five-hundred-person club we gave them the same show we would have given to twenty thousand people in 1985. Our heart was still beating from the eighties."

Jay benefited from RUN-DMC's constant touring in the nineties, but unlike his bandmates, he was mostly cut off from the royalties (meager as they were) from the trio's most popular records in the eighties. Donald Francois says that Jay's financial situation was bleaker than that of new artists signed to JMJ Records. "Jay was like, 'I'm broke today, I'll make money tomorrow, I'm just living,'" Francois explains. "It was sad because you walk in the streets with him, and you see how people react to him—he's like a legend." Jay was significantly in debt to the IRS, he wrestled with a vast mortgage, and he was borrowing money from friends and even minor acquaintances like Curtis Scoon. Longtime friend Eric "Shake" Smith says that Jay would not have been so down on his luck if he hadn't been helping out so many friends financially. "Jay would have been straight if he was just taking care of Jay, his wife, and his kids," Smith says, "but it was like he was taking care of like a whole world. Cats would come around saying, 'I need help' and—bam—he would give it." He used to take care of Randy [Allen]. Randy didn't have no job. Randy was eating off Jay. Lydia [High], too. She didn't have no job. She was eating off Jay. There were many times when Lydia would come to Jay needing her rent paid and Jay would be like, 'OK.' And *he* didn't have it—but he would give it to her anyway."

By the mid-nineties, Jay had become so desperate that he began running small amounts of cocaine—two or three kilos at a time—down Interstate 95 from New York to Baltimore to one of the city's most well-connected distributors, according to a source who worked closely with the distributor in Baltimore. "Jay would buy three keys for sixteen thousand dollars each and then sell them to my man for twenty-four thousand dollars," the source explains. "That's not a bad profit for a weekend's worth of work but the only way you gettin' on that highway with a couple of keys is if you're desperate. Maybe he thought the police weren't gonna pull him over because he's Jam Master Jay."

By the fall of 2002, however, the worst seemed to be behind Jay: He'd secured a record deal with Virgin for Rusty Waters, a group that included his nephew Rodney "Boe Skagz" Jones and business partner Randy Allen, and was busily mixing their debut at his 24/7 Studio on Merrick Boulevard in Hollis. Jay was also working on a straight-to-DVD movie called *Just Came Home,* and he was in talks with Michael K. Williams (the actor who plays Omar on HBO's acclaimed series *The Wire*) to star in it while monitoring the progress of former protégé 50 Cent, who was finishing up his Interscope debut *Get Rich or Die Tryin'*. Most satisfyingly, after the thankless touring of the nineties and a 2000 reunion record called

Crown Royal, which was an embarrassing attempt to cash in on the rap-rock craze, RUN-DMC was enjoying a genuine comeback. The trio was performing all over the country with Aerosmith and Kid Rock, a tour that for the first time in nearly two decades brought them back to 15,000-plus capacity venues like Long Island's Jones Beach Amphitheatre. "Shit was starting to grow again," remembers Darryl "DMC" McDaniels. "It was like, 'Whoa, these guys will *always* be here.'"

The multiple projects meant that Jay was often overextended and stressed-out. He ignored phone calls from friends and business partners and in late October 2002 he decamped to the Milwaukee, Wisconsin, home of longtime friend Eric "Shake" Smith for nearly a full week. The pair holed themselves up in Smith's apartment, playing Xbox video games around the clock. Jay was so intent on evading responsibilities that he often handed over his two-way pager to Smith. "Niggas was paging me: 'Have you seen Jay? Where's Jay?'" Smith remembers, "and I was like, 'Jay, why ain't you hittin' these niggas back?' And he was like, 'Man, I'm tired. I just need a break.'" Jay's reluctance to answer the pages only brought more calls from friends like Randy Allen and Darnell "Nellie D" Smith. Allen was desperate for Jay to return to Hollis so the pair could complete the mix of the Rusty Waters album for Virgin. Seeking to release the pressure he was feeling from back home, Jay and Smith hit clubs all over the Midwest from the Velvet Room in Milwaukee to the House of Blues in Chicago, where they saw 50 premiere *Get Rich or Die Tryin'* material. It was one of best times Smith had ever had with Jay since first meeting him in the late 1980s. But Jay's visit made Smith uncomfortable. "He didn't want to go back to Queens," Smith remembers. "I don't know why. He just didn't want to go home."

Smith eventually confronted Jay about his intransigence. "I was like, 'Go home and get your shit tight,'" Smith explains. The next morning, October 30, 2002, Jay left. Before catching a plane home to New York, he made Smith promise to travel to Washington, DC, to meet him at a November Celtics-Wizards game where RUN-DMC was to perform. Smith didn't expect to hear from Jay until game day but he got a call from him soon after he arrived back in

Hollis. Jay thought he had left his two-way pager at the Velvet Room in Milwaukee, and he asked Smith to check if it was there. Jay notoriously misplaced cell phones, two-way pagers, and digital cameras, most of which were never found, so Smith wasn't expecting to retrieve the two-way when he arrived at the Velvet Room. But to his great surprise an employee of the club had kept Jay's pager in the lost and found. Jay instructed Smith to bring it to the Celtics-Wizards game. After retrieving the pager and arranging its return, Smith was going to get back to work. Jay wouldn't let him go, and the pair stayed on the phone for several hours. "We was talking, and I was hearing him and Boe and Randy getting a haircut and getting sandwiches," Smith remembers, "and I'm hearing Boe hollering at girls. Then Jay says, 'Hey, Shake, don't call my phone. I'm gonna go to the studio. If you need me call the studio.' "

Just after 7:30 PM that night, Jay and a RUN-DMC hanger-on named Urieco Rincon settled into the lounge of Mizell's 24/7 Studio on Merrick Boulevard, situated less than one block away from the 103rd Precinct house on Edward Byrne Avenue. It had been a long, exhausting day; Jay ran errands with Boe Skagz and Randy Allen most of the morning and spent the afternoon putting the finishing touches on Rusty Waters's debut and even fielded an unsolicited demo tape from an aspiring female rapper. When he finished, Jay fired up his Xbox to relax. His gaming partner was Rincon; Lydia High and Randy Allen declined to join in, opting to listen to the unsigned MC's demo in the control room while Boe left for a nearby barbershop to get a haircut. Suddenly, a pair of men sporting black knit caps burst into the studio; one stood guard by the door; the other strode fearlessly into the lounge. "Don't look at me, look at the floor," the attacker barked to High. Moving toward Jay, he pulled out a gun and shot him behind the ear at such close range that gunpowder burns covered his shirt. Jay crumpled to the ground; the bullet had traveled through his head and killed him instantly. The gunman squeezed off another round at Jay but instead hit Rincon in the leg. He then turned and fled the scene with his accomplice but not before Allen, who had heard the gunshots go off while sitting in the control room, gave chase, armed with a .380 semiautomatic. The killers had a jump on Allen and fled down Merrick Boulevard before Allen could catch up with them. Exhausted by the chase, Allen tossed the .380 in 24/7's parking lot.

A few hours later, Jay's former protégé 50 Cent was preparing to take the stage at outer-space-themed Times Square nightclub Mars 2112. It was to be one of 50's first hometown performances in support of his imminent major label debut *Get Rich or Die Tryin'*—but cops quickly stepped in and stopped the show. "They said they had information from valid sources that there is a hit out on my life," 50 remembers, "and I said, 'If you have information from valid sources why is no one arrested? They said, 'Do you think someone would do something to Jay to send 50 a message?' " 50 disputes the cops' theory. "Jay and me haven't made no money together in a long time," he explains. "There's a lotta people who could be shot if you wanted to go after a friend of mine. You don't go after Jam Master Jay, someone whose [murder] is gonna be heavily publicized. . . . If they trying to send him a message they gotta kill someone that nobody knows." 50's manager Chris Lighty seemed more resigned to the NYPD's action. "They didn't want 50 to go on, knowing that the shooting could have been foul play," he told *The New York Times*. "And we didn't want to go on after that. 50 was just too broken up. They didn't say that we were involved or anything, but it's rap. . . . I'm sure they thought, 'You're rap guys, you must know each other.' In this case, unfortunately, they were right."

Lighty's sentiments struck a nerve: Jay's murder did indeed reveal the tight-knit nature of the hip-hop scene. The RUN-DMC DJ had mentored 50 Cent, and he had also once been a candidate for Lighty's job at Violator Management. But to the streets of southeast Queens and law enforcement, Jay's murder was notable for its connections not to the hip-hop world but to eighties-era hustling icons like Fat Cat and 'Preme. Cops suspected that 'Preme had murdered Jay because of 50's high-profile campaign against him during a time when he wished for nothing more than to be invisible to law enforcement.

On the night of the murder, Scoon was holed up in his Brooklyn apartment working on a new screenplay based on the climactic spring of 1988, the months of Byrne's murder, and the toppling of Fat Cat's empire. Scoon named his new project *10:13*—NYPD slang for officer down—and, excited about the access he'd been granted to Fat Cat's crew (and even Fat Cat himself), e-mailed an early version of the script to Kojo Bentil, the Universal Music Group executive who had reacted positively to his earlier project.

Scoon was shaken out of his work routine by a late-night call from friend and former JMJ Records executive Donald Francois. "Did you hear what happened?" Francois shouted over the line. Scoon hadn't turned on a TV for weeks and had no idea what Francois was referring to. "They're saying on the radio that Jay got killed." Scoon assumed that the news of Jay's murder was a rumor; hoaxes had been commonplace in the hip-hop scene since the killings of The Notorious B.I.G. and Tupac Shakur. But the phone in Scoon's Brooklyn apartment didn't stop ringing that night and each caller informed him that Jay was dead. That same night, Joseph "Run" Simmons's beeper was flooded with incoming messages about Jay. "I was in church and I got a beep from DJ Scratch, 'Tell me this ain't true, somebody said Jay's dead,' " Simmons remembers. Russell Simmons received the call about Jay's murder while watching rehearsals of his Broadway show *Def Poetry Jam* at the Longacre Theater on 48th Street. "I got a phone call and I was like, 'Oh shit,' " Simmons recalls. "I didn't believe it, that was my first reaction."

The next morning, Eric "Shake" Smith awoke in his Milwaukee home to the ringing of phones—and page after page coming through Jay's two-way. "I wake up and my two-way is going bananas, *his* two-way is going bananas, my phone is ringing tremendously," Smith remembers. "I'm like, 'What the fuck is going on?' A friend called and said, 'Man, this ain't me saying this. Don't get mad at me. Somebody paged me and said, "Jam Master Jay got killed." ' " In a state of shock, Smith put down the phone but then it immediately rang again, this time with RUN-DMC crew member Darnell "Nellie D" Smith on the line. "He said, 'Jay's gone,' " Smith remembers, "and I said, 'Where'd he go? To the hospital?' He was like, 'Yo, Shake, he's gone.' And I said, '*Gone where?*' Then I heard people in the background crying. He put Lyor on the phone and he said, 'Somebody killed Jason.' I couldn't believe it. I started crying, and my girl came in and said, 'What's wrong?' My voice was gone. I couldn't get it to come out: 'Somebody killed Jay.' "

Smith picked up Jay's two-way pager for evidence that his friend was indeed dead. There were pages from hip-hop stars like Busta Rhymes and Dr. Dre, all asking if the news of Jay's death was real. "Everybody thought it was a rumor," Smith remembers. But as the minutes passed, the messages on Jay's two-way turned from inquiries about his life to condolences. The nephew of Joseph "Run" Simmons—a rapper named Chris Classic—left a particularly poignant message. As he had done with 50, Jay had taught Chris how to rhyme, and Chris was heartbroken by his mentor's murder. "Uncle Jay, thank you for your help, I'm not gonna let you down," the message from Chris Classic said. "I'm gonna finish what we started."

Overcome with grief, Smith called both Lydia High and Randy Allen but neither was answering the phone. So he began slowly packing his bags for Jay's funeral. The next morning he caught an early flight out to New York. As the plane prepared for landing, Smith recalled the many times he'd made the trip before to see Jay; except this time Darnell "Nellie D" Smith, not Jay, would be there to greet him at the airport. As he drove toward Hollis with Nellie D, Smith dialed Randy Allen's cell phone number. "I said, 'Randy, who killed Jay?' " Smith remembers, "and he said, 'Not on the phone, put Smith on the phone.' " Allen then told Nellie D to bring Smith to a Burger King located around the corner from the recording studio where Jay was killed. When Nellie D and Smith pulled into the Burger King parking lot in southeast Queens, Allen was waiting. Allen got in the car with the pair and instructed Nellie D to go into the restaurant. "Nellie D went into the Burger King and I was like, 'Randy, who killed Jay?' " Smith recalls. "He looked at me through the rearview mirror and he said, 'Shake, the nigga that killed your best friend and mine is Curtis Scoon.' I was like, 'How you know, Randy?' He said, 'Lydia looked him dead in his face.' And I said, 'Why he didn't kill Lydia then?' And he was like, 'He kinda liked Lu

Lu.' I was like, 'Damn,' because I remember the situation with Scoon back in the day."

Smith initially believed Allen—he'd heard about Scoon's loan to Jay in the mid-nineties—but he became suspicious when Allen explained that he'd withdrawn money from the bank account of his and Jay's Hot Ta Def production company, which he called "Erotic Money." Smith says that after Allen confessed to him that he took the money because he didn't want Jay's wife to get it, Smith accessed the account through a PIN number left on Jay's two-way pager and found that Allen had actually liquidated the account. In interviews following Jay's murder, Allen denied ever sharing a bank account or holding a business insurance policy with Jay, but law enforcement sources told the New York *Daily News* that he and "Jam Master Jay had an insurance policy naming each other as benefactor if anything should happen to either one." "I couldn't tell you how much was in the account," Smith continues, "probably seventy grand. Whatever it was it was supposed to go to [Jay's wife] Terri and the kids." Numerous attempts to reach Allen were not successful.

Meanwhile Allen was, according to Smith, naming Scoon as the killer to "everyone in shouting distance." Other associates of Jay's were simultaneously talking to the police about a man who threatened to "come up" from Georgia to settle an old debt. (Scoon had lived on and off in Atlanta.) Scoon didn't become aware that he was under investigation until references to Edward Byrne began cropping up in newspaper and radio accounts of Jay's murder. On November 1, 2002, unnamed NYPD investigators told *The New York Times* that "detectives also were looking into whether there was any connection to a once-powerful organization of crack kingpins who executed a police officer, Edward Byrne, in 1988 as he sat in his patrol car." (The source was likely not referring to the Nichols organization but to the Supreme Team; since the Supreme Team was subordinate to the Nichols organization in the southeast Queens street hierarchy and Fat Cat often moved weight to 'Preme, law enforcement did not draw distinctions between the two.) A report on New York radio station 1010 WINS even implicated Scoon in Byrne's murder.

Scoon, of course, had never been a suspect in Byrne's murder (nor had he ever been affiliated with the Nichols organization) so the 1010 WINS report baffled him. "Then I started piecing it all together," Scoon remembers. "The only connection I had to Edward Byrne was the script I wrote about him. And the only person who had that script was Kojo Bentil." Bentil acknowledges receiving Scoon's script, but he says, "I did not share it with anybody." He adds that "my first reaction when I heard about Scoon being named a suspect is that it's bullshit. . . . It's probably a fucking smoke screen. Because after Scoon gave me the script we had several conversations where I got to know him. . . . He had too much going for him for him to put his own life in jeopardy by doing something crazy."

Though Scoon had yet to be officially named a suspect in Jay's murder, the growing buzz in law enforcement circles and on the streets that he was the killer meant that his arrest was not far off. Scoon sought out the counsel of famed New York criminal defense attorney Marvyn Kornberg, who had represented everyone from Justin Volpe, the NYPD cop accused of brutally torturing Abner Louima, to John Gotti's son-in-law Carmine Agnello. Kornberg agreed to represent Scoon, during police questioning only, for a sum well under his usual fee and then publicly invited cops to question his new client. "If you want him, arrest him," Kornberg told *The New York Post* on November 5. The questioning never happened, even after unnamed law enforcement sources quoted in newspaper articles claimed that Scoon would be arrested. "Kornberg chastised the cops for the leaked stories, saying, 'Yes, he's here now, but the only way we're coming in is if he's charged,' " Scoon remembers. "Kornberg then turned to me and said, 'I love this fuckin' shit.' "

For Scoon, the entire experience was surreal. "I'd gone from writing a movie," Scoon says, "to living in one." The ordeal was even stranger because Scoon still hadn't been arrested and the likelihood of his arrest suddenly seemed remote. As cops started backing away from naming Scoon as a suspect, the credibility of the witnesses to Jay's killing began taking crucial hits. Suddenly, the assailants once described by Lydia High as knit-cap-wearing men were ski-mask-wearing men, making improbable Allen's contention that Lydia High had looked Scoon in the eyes. Then the attackers, who had been described in initial accounts as sneaking into the 24/7 Studio through the front door, were said to have been buzzed in by High. Scoon could not, as unnamed sources quoted in several newspaper accounts claimed, have been "coming up" from Georgia to settle the debt with Jay because he was living in Brooklyn when Jay was murdered; besides, the insignificant debt Jay owed him was settled in the mid-nineties. Scoon adds that even if Jay was indebted to him at the time he would not have killed him: "You can't get paid back by a dead guy." While Allen had named Scoon as the killer he neglected to mention that his brother Teddy had gotten into an altercation with Jay's cousin Alfonso at the 24/7 Studio just prior to Jay's murder that resulted in Teddy pulling a gun on him. This wasn't the only instance of gunplay at the studio during the fall of 2002: According to Eric "Shake" Smith, Jay waved a gun at a southeast Queens hustler nicknamed "Goldie" over an unpaid debt.

In other words, Jam Master Jay's killer could have been any number of people, yet somehow only Scoon had come under scrutiny, likely because of Randy Allen's early identification of him as the killer and a strong dislike of Scoon among Jay's friends and business associates. "Scoon ain't close to nobody," Russell Simmons admits. The dead-end leads were made more frustrating by the behavior of Randy Allen and Jay's nephew Rodney "Boe Skagz" Jones, who infuriated Jay's family by leaving Hollis for New Jersey to prepare for a promotional tour for their group Rusty Waters after Jay's murder. Jay's mother, Connie, called Allen and threatened to have him charged with kidnapping if her grandson didn't return home, according to sources close to Jay's family. Boe returned to Hollis to an uneasy peace and residual anger at how he'd handled the news of his uncle's death.

The night of the murder, Boe had pistol-whipped his mother's boyfriend at the Mizell home on 203rd Street because he believed that the man was connected to Scoon. (Scoon says that the man often invoked his name on the streets but had no relationship with him.) Boe also helped roust Hollis hustler Ronald "Tinard" Washington from Jay's family's home—to the consternation of the Mizells, who knew Washington as a suspect in the murder of Randy "Stretch" Walker, Jay had given him permission to sleep on the couch—because he believed that Washington had been involved in the murder of his uncle. To make matters worse, Boe caused a huge scene in front of the neighbors by throwing Washington's belongings onto 203rd Street.

While Boe was behaving erratically, Allen was vacillating about the identity of Jay's killer. During an interview with Hot 97, he suddenly dismissed Scoon as a suspect. "They may have had their little situation back in the days," Allen said, "but I don't think it was anything that would lead to Jay's death. I know it wasn't that deep of a situation." Smith was apoplectic upon hearing Allen's new story. "Randy is saying a different story than what he told me," Smith explains. "I think he was trying to throw people off, get people pursuing a false suspect. I could see him saying, 'Let's live by street code, let's not tell the cops,' but you would think he would tell the people who were close to Jay. This is Jam Master Jay, not a motherfucker that got shot on the corner. This guy is an icon. If RUN-DMC is the Beatles then Jay is John Lennon."

Smith is still furious with both Allen and sister Lydia High for what he believes to be their lack of cooperation with police. "Jay loved them people, Randy, Lydia," Smith says. "They owe him more than that. Let me put it this way: If I was in the studio that night either the dude that did that would be dead or me and Jay would be dead. It wouldn't be like the way it is right now: 'We wonder who did it?' This is not like when Biggie or Tupac got killed. 'Pac got killed and the car sped off." 50 Cent expressed similar sentiments about Allen during a guest spot on DMX's album *Grand Champ*. "Randy ass was there," 50 rhymed on a song called "Shot Down," "now he runnin' scared." (During the song 50 also compared himself to Fat Cat, Pappy Mason, and Mickens.) The most pointed criticism of Allen, however, came from Jay's mother, Connie, in an interview with the New York *Daily News*. "You're his friend for twenty years, and you don't want to talk to the police about what happened?" Mizell said. "You don't come to my house after he died? You want to say you don't know anything?" In that same *Daily News* piece the commanding officer of the 103rd Precinct detective squad said, "It's the people closest to Jason Mizell, his inner circle of business associates, who are not being entirely forthcoming."

A spokesperson for the NYPD refused repeated requests for comment about the investigation, but a source close to Jay's family says that detectives from the 103rd Precinct told them that they believe that they have been sent on a wild goose chase by High and Allen and that they fear the time lost pursuing false leads makes an arrest much less likely with each passing day. The source also says that the focus of the NYPD's investigation into Jay's murder is now turning toward those who were in the studio with him when he was killed. "Detectives want to know what their motive was in spreading false leads," the source says.

Complicating the investigation even further, names of potential suspects and new motives for the killing surfaced almost daily; during the fall of 2002, it seemed as though nearly all of southeast Queens was under the magnifying glass while, at the same time, the ghosts of the Edward Byrne era were being raised. Ronald "Tinard" Washington was floated as a possible killer; one absurd theory had Scoon and Washington committing the crime together. ("I wouldn't cross the street with Tinard," Scoon says in response.) Then, when Washington was arrested on armed robbery charges in the late fall of 2002, he claimed to have seen former RUN-DMC road manager Karl "Big D" Jordan and his son Karl "Little D" Jordan flee 24/7 Studio just after Jay was killed. "Everybody was a suspect," says Darryl McDaniels. "Jay was from Hollis, and he got killed just like any other motherfucker from Hollis. Jay kept his studio five minutes away from where he grew up. The thing he was trying to bring niggas away from is the thing that killed him. Whoever pulled that trigger is just like the motherfuckers that I grew up with."

Jay's murder had been greeted with fiery promises of justice from the streets of southeast Queens and hip-hop heavies like Lyor Cohen and Russell Simmons, but soon Jay's family and friends felt a profound sense of hopelessness. "There were a lot of rumors, he said, she said, it got very confusing," says Charles Fisher, the former manager of Rushland, "but the press didn't help at all. Because every week there was a different rumor in the newspapers about who killed Jam Master Jay. It was like, 'Who killed JR?' " Fisher worried that Jay's killing could turn into a great hip-hop unsolved crime à la Biggie and Tupac Shakur. "I was sick and tired with what happened with Biggie and Tupac where I felt the hip-hop community didn't get involved, and we never found their murderers," Fisher explains. "I said, 'This isn't gonna happen with Jay.' I wanted to find out who killed this guy and I was going to do something about it."

Fisher launched an anonymous tipline to help solicit leads in Jay's murder. At first, he was optimistic about the tipline's prospects: He says he raised nearly $250,000 in reward money from a single donor and he had a childhood friend at the 103rd Precinct who assisted him in vetting the dozens of leads coming in. The cash, though, worked against Fisher's efforts—"Everyone's thing was, 'Well, how am I gonna get the reward if my information leads to the capture?' " he says—as did his connection to the NYPD. A source close to Jay's family says that Fisher's announcement of such an enormous reward did little but attract false leads and that he never collected the $250,000 in the first place. Fisher attributes these allegations to a falling-out he had with Jay's family, particularly Jay's brother Marvin. "Marvin wanted the world to jump when Marvin said jump," Fisher says. "He felt that law enforcement should have caught the killer yesterday and that people should have given money to the foundation yesterday." Fisher also insists that he did collect the $250,000, which came, he says, from an anonymous donor.

Controversy also surrounded the establishment of the Mizell Children's Fund, which was set up by Russell Simmons to raise cash for the college education of Jay's three children, Jason, Jesse, and TJ. During a star-studded November 6, 2002, press conference featuring the likes of Puff Daddy, Lyor Cohen, and Chuck D, hip-hop's biggest names pledged five-figure sums to the fund. "Lyor Cohen and I gave money, but the single biggest artist donor was LL Cool J," Russell Simmons said at the press conference. "LL Cool J gave

$50,000, then Busta Rhymes gave $30,000. Then [we got] $10,000 from just about everybody. Kedar Massenburg, Kid Rock, Aerosmith, and the list goes on. Eminem, Dr. Dre, just so many people came forward. . . . It was a beautiful thing." But a source close to Jay's family says that several major pledges were withdrawn over concern about management of the fund. "A few people who promised to give up money didn't come through because they said that the foundation wasn't set up and they weren't sure where the money was going," Charles Fisher says. Russell Simmons admits that several artists did not follow through on their pledges to the fund but he adds that "that's what artists do; they say they're going to do something and then they don't do it. We called them and I wrestled with the idea of making it public doing that but Terri didn't want to do that." Simmons notes that he nonetheless collected over $200,000 for the Mizell Children's Fund, and that there's still nearly $100,000 that's gone uncollected.

The source close to Jay's family counters that hip-hop stars were reluctant to contribute to the fund because of Russell Simmons's involvement. "The feeling was, 'If I'm going to give money, I'm going to give it directly to the family," the source says. " 'I'm not going to deal with Russell.' " The source says that Jay's family was initially supportive of Simmons but soon became disillusioned with him after he reneged on a promise to assist them in the restoration of their family home on 203rd Street. "When the family confronted Russell he claimed that they never sent him the proposal, which wasn't true," the source says. Simmons says that the plan to refurbish Jay's 203rd Street home was "probably mentioned to me. But I got seventy different programs I'm working with. . . . I'm not restoring the home for [Jay's brother] Marvin. . . . I don't prioritize him on a list to give to. The priority is his children."

The wake of Jay's death brought false leads and the withdrawn pledges to the Mizell Children's Fund—even his funeral provided an unusually unsettling atmosphere. While eulogizing Jay at the Greater Allen Cathedral in Hollis, Joseph Simmons offered inappropriate metaphors about the murder of his former bandmate: "I don't know if I should say this," Simmons said, "but I believe this is

Jason's biggest hit ever . . . as big as 'Walk This Way.' " Simmons says now that his eulogy was misinterpreted. "People may say, 'Well, he seems not to be sympathetic,' " Simmons says. "I'm very sympathetic. I mourn with you but I realize another thing about death. I'm very understanding of it. . . . He went out in a very dramatic, hip-hop way. People may say, 'Wow, that's very mean of you, Run.' But he came, he saw, he conquered, he lived great, he died great." One close friend of Jay's calls Simmons's strange eulogy "not just inappropriate but heartbreaking as well. I think the hip-hop community has avoided talking about Run's comments out of respect for him. The embarrassment he gave himself is enough."

Soon after Jay's funeral, the streets and law enforcement began buzzing about 'Preme as a potential suspect, bringing a fresh sense of dread to southeast Queens. There was a rumor on the streets that 'Preme had sent a message to Randy Allen warning him that he'd be killed if he cooperated with law enforcement in the investigation into Jay's murder. This would have been easy to dismiss had Jay not had at least two connections to the former Supreme Team CEO: He mentored 'Preme's nemesis 50 Cent, and a number of sources close to Jay's family claim that his widow, Terri, carried on an extramarital affair with 'Preme while she was employed as a flight attendant. Terri Mizell will not comment on the alleged affair, and friends like Darryl McDaniels deny that 'Preme and Terri were ever an item. But a source close to Jay's family says that they have repeatedly confronted Terri about her relationship with 'Preme only to receive nondenials.

Tensions between Terri and her in-laws were raised even further when she left New York for Virginia almost immediately following her husband's murder. Terri, who won't comment on her relations with her in-laws, acknowledges moving to Chantilly, Virginia, soon after Jay's death. She also pointedly distances herself from Randy Allen and Lydia High. "I had no association with them," Terri says. "I never hung out in his studio. Those people never came to my home. My husband kept his work and his family life separate. I didn't know those people. They were not part of my social life."

As Jay's friends and family traded recriminations, law enforcement zeroed in on 'Preme. "The Mizell hit was obviously a professional killing, like a typical organized crime killing," explains a former law enforcement source who has extensive experience working in narcotics in southeast Queens. "He was there, they went in, told him to sit down, did what they had to do, they didn't intentionally hurt anyone else, there wasn't a lot of arguments, and they shot him in the head. It doesn't get any more professional than that." The source adds that 'Preme could have had Jay killed by former Supreme Team assassins such as Roy Hale and Harry Hunt, who dispatched the Colombian cocaine distributors in the late eighties. "If I was back in law enforcement looking for the killer of Mizell, I'd be looking at somebody close in with McGriff," the source says, "not McGriff himself. But somebody close in. If he follows patterns, he's got three, four, five bad dudes around him, someone like Roy Hale. If I were looking for the killer, that's where I'd go."

Law enforcement suspected that Jay was murdered by 'Preme because he mentored 50 after 'Preme had warned rappers and hip-hop executives not to work with him in the wake of "Ghetto Qu'ran." Indeed, according to an affidavit filed in 2003 in the federal investigation into The Inc. by Francis Mace, an agent in the IRS's criminal investigations division, agents investigating 'Preme believed that the former Supreme Team CEO was conducting surveillance of 50—with the assistance of Chris and Irv, no less. "50 is in the hood guy r. brewer" read one text message from Chris to 'Preme, according to Mace. "Guy R. Brewer" is, of course, Guy R. Brewer Boulevard in South Jamaica, 'Preme's old stomping grounds. "Yo, this nigga 50 talking shit about you, ja, and bj [the friend of the Lorenzos who introduced them to 'Preme]. It didn't sound pretty," an associate of the Lorenzos complained to 'Preme via two-way pager, according to Mace. To which 'Preme replied, according to Mace, "Yeah, I'm reading it now but it ain't nothing because he's a dry snitcher." 'Preme's scrutiny of 50 did not go unnoticed by 50: When he was interviewed by the feds after Jay was killed he told agents that "he has [a] substantial security team in place guarding him and that he fears for his safety," according to Mace.

Jay's killing and 50 Cent's insistent invocation of his name in rhyme—which began with "Ghetto Qu'ran" and continued all the way into the fall of 2002 with a mixtape track called "Order of Protection" where he claimed that Irv was merely 'Preme's flunky ("You 'Preme's son, nigga")—brought yet more unwanted law enforcement attention to the former Supreme Team CEO. In fact, the feds began to pick up the pace of their investigation into 'Preme after Jay's murder. "When you're doing an investigation and someone very close to it gets murdered, it certainly increases law enforcement interest," explains the former law enforcement source. "Money laundering is one thing; murder is something else." The renewed scrutiny of 'Preme made his fall inevitable and in the fall of 2002, he pled guilty on weapons possession charges related to his 2001 Harlem arrest. With 'Preme freed on $15,000 bail and awaiting a sentencing date in January 2003, Irv sensed that 'Preme would not be on the streets for much longer. So, in November 2002, Irv sent 'Preme on an all-expenses-paid trip to visit his nephew Gerald "Prince" Miller at a Beaumont, Texas, prison. "Whatever you want to say about Prince, he could be the most notorious dude ever, but to 'Preme that's his little nephew," Irv explains, "and at that time 'Preme knew he had to go to jail for the gun charge. Every time he goes in he always feels like it could be his last . . . all that he wanted was to see his nephew again for the last time." 'Preme made the trip in a high style more common to hip-hoppers than to ex-hustlers, staying at the Four Seasons in Houston (under the alias Rick Coleman) and taking a chauffeured limousine to the maximum-security facility at a cost to Irv of $1,200.

It was a fitting last hurrah for 'Preme, made even sweeter by Irv's gift of a $75,000 SUV; but as 'Preme toasted his imprisoned nephew in Texas, U.S. Attorney for the Eastern District of New York Roslynn R. Mauskopf was quietly preparing an indictment of his Picture Perfect Entertainment partner Jon Ragin on credit card fraud charges. She also planned a raid on Murder Inc.'s midtown Manhattan offices. The first hint of what was to come arrived on December 23, 2002, with a New York *Daily News* article headlined ZEROING IN ON RAP'S SEAMY SIDE: GANGSTA DOUGH A MAGNET FOR QUEENS THUGS, which revealed that the feds were looking into "shootings and other crimes potentially motivated by disputes in the rap recording business," with 'Preme emerging as a central figure in the probe. Though the piece did not mention Murder Inc. by name, the accompanying sidebar (which reprinted the lyrics to 50 Cent's "Ghetto Qu'ran" in their entirety) and photos (which pictured an all-star Queens cast of Fat Cat, Pappy, Prince, and 'Preme) made the direction of the federal investigation clear: The hustling and hip-hop eras in southeast Queens would be united at last.

10

Takedown

'Preme had moved carefully since the killing of Jam Master Jay, traveling under aliases and paying for hotel and car bills in cash. By the time the *Daily News* piece came out he was essentially in hiding. "All wiretap activity stopped and he disappeared," an unnamed law enforcement source told the Associated Press. On December 28, 2002, the feds finally caught up with him at the Loews Hotel in Miami Beach where he checked in under the alias Rick Coleman with a $1,000 cash deposit. When the feds burst through his hotel room door, 'Preme was in possession of a Murder Inc.–issued pager as well as Viagra and Ecstasy, a combination in the hip-hop world dubbed "rocking and rolling." (Irv Lorenzo would be caught with the same combination of drugs at an R. Kelly concert one year later.) It was the Baltimore U.S. Attorney's office that had arranged for 'Preme's arrest in Miami, and he was hit with a gun charge relating to a series of visits he made in 2000 to a Maryland shooting range where he performed target practice with machine guns. "With the weapons charge pending, the feds essentially kept 'Preme on ice," explains the former law enforcement source, who had extensive experience working in southeast Queens. "With big issues hanging in the air, especially the killing of a prominent figure like Jam Master Jay, it's nice to know where he is if you have to go look for him."

With 'Preme imprisoned, the feds moved on both Jon Ragin and Murder Inc. Early in the morning of Friday, January 3, 2003, nearly a dozen FBI agents and NYPD officers raided Ragin's home at 175-20 Wexford Terrace in Queens, Murder Inc.'s 29th-floor offices at 825 8th Avenue, and the homes of Lorenzo, his brother Chris, and label accountant Cynthia Brent. "My heart stopped," Irv remembers. "It wasn't just the office, it was my brother's house, it was the accountant's house, it was my house where my kids was at. It was like four different locations hit simultaneously. They was actin' like I was John Gotti. I'm like, 'Yo, I was in the studio last night. I fuck bitches. Guilty as charged. I fuck bitches.' " Even the more street-savvy Chris Lorenzo was taken by surprise by the raid. "We were blindsided," he explains. "There was no lead-up to it to think that was gonna happen. . . . We ain't did nothing. We over here doing what we supposed to do. When we were coming up we weren't doing nothing—why would we do it now?"

The feds, however, believed that Murder Inc. and 'Preme had been crime partners all along. In an affidavit filed with the U.S. Attorney for the Eastern District of New York, IRS special agent Francis Mace claimed that 'Preme was the "true owner of the company," who provided the label with " 'muscle'—threats, violence, and intimidation." The Lorenzo brothers deny the allegation, and executives at the Universal Music Group back them up. "The feds said that McGriff gave the start money for Murder Inc. but that's just not the case," says one source at Universal. "If you look at the history, that would have been improbable. Irv was living in the studio before he got the check from Universal to start the label." The IRS agent's claim that 'Preme and Irv—who are more than ten years apart in age—were childhood friends was particularly absurd. Indeed, in a filing with the U.S. Attorney, Irv's attorney Gerald Lefcourt blasted Mace's investigative work. "It is inconceivable how agent Mace, a United States Treasury agent, could not have learned through reasonable investigative means that a public company such as Universal . . . had openly entered into a contract, through its subsidiary Def Jam, with Mr. Lorenzo." Mace also made several major errors in his affidavit alleging that 'Preme and the Lorenzos were surveilling 50 during the fall of 2002. He claimed that 50 traveled to Canada to record tracks in 2000 (he actually went to upstate New York); he misspelled "Ghetto Qu'ran" as "Ghetto Koran," and he charged that 50 had been "blacklisted" by the music industry after his shooting (in fact, record execs were hesitant to sign 50 because they feared he might be killed). Worst of all, Mace was seemingly unaware of Darryl "Hommo" Baum's involvement in 50's shooting, alleging instead that the incident was part of 'Preme's "plot to kill the rapper '50 Cent.'"

Though the federal investigation into Murder Inc. had been in the works for years, the Lorenzos suspected their archrival 50 Cent was somehow behind the raid on their homes and offices. Indeed, soon after the raid, Irv directed a video for Ja Rule's single "Reign" which depicted an informant handing over information about the label to a prosecutor played by actor Patrick Swayze. The Lorenzos suspected that 50 provided information about the label to cops after he was arrested on weapons possession charges outside Manhattan nightclub Copacabana on December 31, 2002; they also noted that many of the more outrageous allegations made by IRS special agent Mace mirrored the hyperbolic claims that 50 had made about 'Preme and Irv's relationship. (50 claimed that the Lorenzos were being extorted by 'Preme, and he dubbed Irv "'Preme's son.") So, Murder Inc. employed street marketing representatives to hand out flyers near their offices claiming that 50 was a snitch, and they sent dossiers on 50, which included the order of protection documents filed after the violent attack on Jackson by Chris Lorenzo at the Hit Factory in 2000, to hip-hop magazines such as *The Source* and *XXL*.

The label also released a slew of mixtape freestyles attacking 50 including "40 Bars to the Dime Dropper 50 Cent" in which an MC named Young Merc rhymed, "I barely know this coward, half of a dollar, but we'll show him the power of a dollar. . . . Y'all niggas running claiming you gangsta/snitch niggas/Now who the real wanksta?" But the boldest attack on 50 came from the web site Getsmedia.com, which published the order of protection documents in their entirety along with the message: "Real street niggas don't snitch. 50 Cent does not rep the street. He is a coward and a liar. . . . You can't deny court documents!" In interviews, 50 has repeatedly denied that he ever cooperated with law enforcement, and in his autobiography he wrote, "I think that my having a street-based situation and my lyrical content is what made them call me a snitch."

Most upstarts would have crumpled under the weight of such withering attacks from established hip-hop players. But Murder Inc.'s assault on 50 had the unintentional effect of giving him free publicity at the moment he needed it most: His major label debut *Get Rich or Die Tryin'* was set to be released on February 6, 2003. In the weeks before the in-store date of *Get Rich . . .* the street buzz around the record was building to a fever pitch not seen in years. It seemed as though every car cruising the wide boulevards of southeast Queens was blasting music from 50's mixtapes, and the flurry of attacks on 50 from the streets to the Internet only raised his profile. Even so, no one could have predicted the earth-shattering performance of the album: Nearly 900,000 copies were sold its first week in stores. *Get Rich . . .* would become the biggest seller of 2003, besting pop stars like Britney Spears. Sitting in a penthouse suite at the Dylan Hotel in midtown Manhattan just days after the release, 50 seemed more interested in making a case for his stardom on the southeast Queens streets than in the hip-hop scene. "They put me in the newspaper with Pappy," 50 proclaimed, referring to the *Daily News* piece that featured a picture of him along Pappy and 'Preme, "because I wrote a song ["Ghetto Qu'ran"]. They made a comparison. To me, it's like, 'These are the big guys, they're the worst and 50 is a smaller version.' "

50 was also working hard to mythologize the shooting outside his grandmother's house in South Jamaica as well as the murder of his assailant a few weeks after the incident. At the Dylan Hotel that day, 50 dropped tantalizing hints about the identity of his assailant only to pull back when the questioning became too specific:

Do you know who shot you?
I know who shot me.
Who shot you?
I won't say that.
Did this person get arrested?
Nah, he got killed. Freak accident (laughs). He got killed a few

weeks after I got shot. Same situation, somebody waiting on
him.

Why did he shoot you?

He got paid. I had like $100,000 worth of jewelry on. He didn't
come after the jewelry.

50 was similarly coy in interviews with the likes of *Rolling Stone,
Playboy,* MTV, and, most notably, with federal agents investigating
Murder Inc. "When asked specifically who had shot him," IRS agent
Francis Mace wrote of 50 in an affidavit filed in the federal investigation into The Inc., "[he] replied in sum and substance, that he
would not answer the question directly and that agents should read
his music lyrics." His pointed retelling of the attempt on his life was
a strategy ripped from Tupac Shakur's post–Quad shooting playbook, something that didn't go unnoticed by Jimmy "Henchmen"
Rosemond. "'Pac did what 50 does now," Rosemond says, "he makes
a situation to sell records, to become that dude who is that force."
But unlike Shakur, who repeatedly (and publicly) implicated everyone from Rosemond to Puffy, 50 was intentionally vague about the
identity of his assailant.

50 offered street-savvy listeners of *Get Rich . . .* more specific
clues about his shooting than anything he'd provided in magazine
interviews. In an eerie echo of Shakur's accusation that Queens
associate Randy "Stretch" Walker "switched sides" on him, 50
claimed on the track "Many Men" that his former mentor and
'Preme's *Black Gangster* partner Chaz Williams (whom he called
"Slim" on the song) also "switched sides" on him and ordered the
shooting. But unlike Shakur, 50 seemed more sad than angry about
the alleged disloyalty: "Why you want me to die, homie?" he
lamented. When asked about "Many Men" Williams says, "I have no
idea why he said that. You'll have to ask 50." 50 would not respond to
repeated requests for comment.

On "Many Men," 50 also revealed the street name of his
shooter—"Hommo"—and that Hommo himself was killed nearly
three weeks after his own shooting in March 2000. "Hommo"—
short for "homicide"—is one of the most commonplace street names

in the five boroughs. Neighborhoods like Hollis and South Jamaica often boast a handful of "Hommos." But several sources close to the man responsible for the nine gunshots that helped make 50 Cent a hip-hop superstar identify him as a dangerous stick-up kid from the Fort Greene section of Brooklyn named Darryl "Hommo" Baum.

Brooklyn stick-up kids like Baum, who came of age during the crack era, were particularly wild and undisciplined. Indeed, Brooklyn strongmen had such a fearsome reputation that they were often recruited for acts of violence by Queens crews like the Nichols organization. Baum, however, was even ballsier than his peers. On February 23, 1985, he and an accomplice attempted to steal a diamond-encrusted necklace bearing the initials PT from a man named Patrick Truick who was standing in line outside a disco called Love People on Empire Boulevard and Franklin Avenue in Brooklyn. Chain-snatching is a lowest-common-denominator hustle, but this particular act was so bold that it should have gotten Baum and his partner killed. During the eighties, Love People was home to a fearsome crew of drug-dealing Jamaicans dubbed the Shower Posse who executed rivals right on the club's dance floor. Fortunately for Baum, his mark that night was a Navy officer who merely put up a good fistfight instead of pulling a high-powered gun on him.

On June 10, 2000—nearly three weeks after he shot 50 in southeast Queens—Baum's luck ran out but not, as 50 has repeatedly implied in interviews, thanks to his attack on the aspiring rapper. Baum was murdered, federal prosecutors say, because an associate named Rumel Davis had killed hustler Myron "Wise" Hardy. Hardy and his brother Damion (nicknamed "World") allegedly ran a violent Brooklyn crew called the Cash Money Brothers, and just after 1:40 AM that humid June night, as Baum stood on the corner of Quincy Street and Marcy Avenue in Brooklyn, members of the gang came to exact revenge, according to the feds. Cash Money Brothers strongman Eric "E Bay" Moore allegedly pumped a single gunshot into Baum's head and then fled in a getaway car driven by associate Zareh "Puff" Sarkissian.

Baum died a few hours later at Kings County Hospital in Brooklyn; he was just thirty-four years old. 50 would later cheer Baum's demise in interviews, but Baum's longtime friend Mike Tyson was overcome with grief. The pair had grown close in the months before Baum's murder; a friend of Baum's says that he had even stayed at the boxer's home for a few months in late 1999.

So Tyson, who was in Scotland preparing for a bout against Lou Savarese when he got the news of Baum's death, was so upset that he interrupted his training schedule, causing panic among his management who believed that he might lose his will in the ring. In the end, the murder proved to be a distraction; Tyson won the fight in the first round, knocking Savarese out after a mere twelve seconds.

March 25, 2003, should have been one of the happiest days of 'Preme's life: The *Crime Partners* DVD hit video store shelves and the supply rooms of online retailers like Amazon.com. This marked the completion of a project 'Preme had been working on since his release from prison in the mid-nineties, but as thousands of Donald Goines fans snapped up copies around the country, 'Preme sat in a Virginia prison awaiting sentencing on federal weapons possession charges. Worse, with the Murder Inc. raid, any proceeds from *Crime Partners* were to be seized by the feds, and the film's soundtrack, slated to follow the DVD's release, would never see the light of day because its proceeds could also be seized. 'Preme hadn't even had the chance to spend much of the $500,000 advance he had received from Murder Inc. for the *Crime Partners* soundtrack. "He had over $300,000 in the account when the government took it," Chris Lorenzo says. "[Even] if shit goes away they keeping that money."

The Lorenzo brothers had plenty to worry about as well. In addition to the imprisoned 'Preme and the raid on the multimillion-dollar business they had built from the streets of southeast Queens, they had to move from Def Jam's plush midtown headquarters on 8th Avenue to more modest digs downtown on 9th Avenue, and 50 Cent was raining insults and abuse on Ja Rule with such intensity that it threatened to cast the street cred of all of Murder Inc.'s talent into question. On *Get Rich or Die Tryin'*, 50 devoted nearly an entire track to skewering Ja, comparing his gravelly voice to Cookie

Monster's. Then, just before taking the stage at Hot 97's Summer Jam concert at Giants Stadium in June 2003, 50 and his G-Unit crew broadcast a faux public service announcement over the Jumbotron screens dubbed HOW TO RECOGNIZE A BITCH ASS NIGGA. During the PSA, images of Irv Lorenzo and Ja Rule were displayed with the words BITCH ASS NIGGA flashing beneath them. As the 55,000-plus crowd howled with laughter, it seemed 50 had delivered the death blow to Murder Inc. less than one year after Irv had haughtily declared himself the "hottest nigga in the building."

Ja was particularly furious with 50's taunts. After all, the essence of 50's criticism of Murder Inc.—the label was too soft, too indebted to R&B—was most applicable to his music. "He didn't want to respond to this guy," Chris Lorenzo explains, "but all of these things started coming and coming and coming and he just wanted to vent." The minds at Murder Inc. hatched a plan: Record *Blood in My Eye,* an EP with tough street rhymes aimed squarely at 50, and have it released by Death Row's Suge Knight. "Ja and Suge spoke about doing *Blood in My Eye,*" Chris Lorenzo explains. "We was all in the studio, Suge comes in, and him and Rule talk. He was talking about 'Pac and *Makaveli,* which was really an EP; we thought *Blood in My Eye* should be an EP, too." The Lorenzo brothers soon found out than an EP (a shorter version of an LP) would not count as a record on Ja's recording contract, so they abandoned their original plan of making an EP with Knight. "We never intended it as an album," Chris Lorenzo explains, "but Ja wanted to put out and vent because he was silent for so long." Against their better judgment the Lorenzo brothers went ahead with *Blood in My Eye,* intent on stretching out the project into a full album.

As the Lorenzo brothers and Ja were putting in long hours at the recording studio for the expanded *Blood in My Eye,* FBI agents investigating Murder Inc.'s connections to 'Preme were interviewing southeast Queens hustlers on the streets and in the prison system. Former Curtis Scoon associate Derek "Talib" Yancey was on the verge of finishing a 107-month sentence for obstruction of justice related to a robbery and attempted murder case in Virginia when the feds moved him from the White Deer Facility in Allenwood, Pennsylvania, to the federal prison Metropolitan Detention Center (MDC) in Brooklyn for questioning. "They asked if Curtis had any connections to Murder Inc.," Yancey remembers. "I said, 'Not to my knowledge, no.' Then they asked me if Curtis had anything to do with Irv; I said, 'No, they just live in the same neighborhood.'" The FBI agents also questioned Yancey about the murders of Eric "E Money Bags" Smith and Jam Master Jay, cases he knew nothing about as he'd been locked up for several years. As he was led back to his cell after the interview, Yancey noticed that 'Preme's longtime associate Tyran "Tah-Tah" Moore had also been moved to MDC for questioning in the Murder Inc. investigation. Like 'Preme, Moore had been picked up off the streets on a weapons possession charge and was awaiting sentencing. But Yancey says that Moore seemed angrier at 50 Cent than he was at the feds. Moore told Yancey that he was going to sue 50 for implicating him on the track "Fuck You" as the assailant who almost took his life in 2000.

If 50's rhymes were a source of frustration for the imprisoned Moore, they were creating sheer havoc on the streets of southeast Queens. After Karl "Little D" Jordan Jr. yelled 50's slogan "G-G-G-G-Unit" at Murder Inc. rapper Chris Black and Black punched him in the face on Hollis Avenue early in the spring of 2003, Jam Master Jay's nephew Rodney "Boe Skagz" Jones wrote a rhyme mocking Jordan's hubris. On May 14, 2003, Jordan allegedly went looking for revenge, firing several gunshots at Jones, one of which hit him in the leg. A few months later, Jordan was indicted on attempted murder and weapons possession charges. But a spokesperson for the Queens District Attorney's office says that the case has since been dismissed, and as a result the indictment against Jordan has been sealed. The outcome of this straightforward case—Jones had positively identified Jordan as the shooter, there was a clear motive behind the attack, shell casings were found at the scene, and both Jordan and his father had allegedly been seen by Ronald "Tinard" Washington fleeing the murder scene of Jam Master Jay—is puzzling. If 'Preme and Tah-Tah caught weapons possession charges and faced stiff prison sentences, why was Karl "Little D" Jordan, implicated in a high-profile murder *and* a separate shooting, free?

The Queens District Attorney's Office will not comment on the Jordan case, but Karl Jordan Sr.'s status as an informant working for the Queens DA may provide the answer to his son's unusual bit of luck with law enforcement. In addition to testifying in the 1985 murder case of Joseph "Money" Thomas, Jordan had served as a witness in a 1995 case in which his friend and RUN-DMC crew member Darnell "Nellie D" Smith was accused of attacking a southeast Queens street guy named "Spuddy" with a baseball bat. In both trials, Jordan displayed a remarkable capacity for providing lucid recollections of criminal confessions. He provided a spirited defense for his friend, telling the jury that Smith had no choice but to defend himself as he had overheard Spuddy proclaim on Hollis Avenue that "he was looking for Darnell because he was going to fuck him up."

50 was fast becoming not just hip-hop's premier button-pusher but a savvy strategist, conquering rivals like the Lorenzo brothers and 'Preme without so much as engaging in a single act of violence. Unsurprisingly, 50 was also growing aware of his significant skill in vanquishing foes, and he began to turn on even those in his own camp. Early in the evening of September 10, 2003, 50 took to the airwaves at Hot 97, letting loose a nasty freestyle about Lil' Kim, whom he had collaborated with on a track called "Magic Stick." Rappers who collaborate on hit tracks rarely turn around and lob insults at each other. But apparently 50 loved the idea of breaking with this tradition, and he laid into Lil' Kim with relish. "I wrote 'Magic Stick,' I gave Kim a hit," 50 rhymed, "I refused to shoot a video/she threw a little fit/got emotional and shit/now this I don't get/why would I care about your emotions, you're not my bitch." Unfortunately for 50, Kim's live-in boyfriend Damion "World" Hardy, the Brooklyn roughneck whose Cash Money Brothers crew allegedly murdered 50 Cent's shooter Darryl "Hommo" Baum, was listening. Furious, Hardy drove to Hot 97's Lower Manhattan offices and waited outside, according to a source close to G-Unit. 50's security detail left the building first and, spotting the suspicious-

looking vehicle outside, approached it. Undeterred, Hardy rolled the car window down, waved a pistol at 50's crew, and growled menacingly, "What the fuck are you looking at?" Before 50's security detail could respond, Hardy rolled the window back up and drove off.

Believing the confrontation with Hardy had passed, 50 and his entourage piled into their SUVs and headed to the Doubletree Hotel on 455 Washington Boulevard in Jersey City to relax. Just outside the Holland Tunnel, the Jersey City Doubletree is an ideal place for hip-hoppers to unwind; it's minutes from Manhattan, in a quiet neighborhood of new condominium buildings and strip malls. But 50's men were still tense from the confrontation with Hardy, so when the rapper checked into a suite they stood guard downstairs. It was a smart move: Soon after their boss settled in for the night, they spotted a vehicle resembling Hardy's. 50's crew fired warning shots into the air, according to a driver who worked for G-Unit that night, and the car sped off. Another crisis had been averted, but the Doubletree management was none too happy about the incident. Workers at the hotel indicated that the shots came from 50 Cent and his entourage, according to former Jersey City police spokesperson Edgar Martinez. When cops arrived on the scene they found ten shell casings; one of the gunshots had gone so far astray that it shattered the window of a BJ's Tire store separated from the Doubletree by train tracks and a parking lot.

The shooting at the Doubletree should have had legal ramifications only for 50 and his crew, but because Ja Rule happened to be shooting a movie in Jersey City that night with Queen Latifah called *The Cookout,* speculation swirled among law enforcement about his involvement. It was yet another battle in the ongoing war with 50, one that Ja had been reluctantly drawn into. Ja's career seemed to be in a tailspin because of 50, and the Murder Inc. camp was growing increasingly nervous as the November 2003 release date for his album *Blood in My Eye* neared. Even if Ja could survive the negative publicity 50 was creating for him, the Lorenzos were not sure that the star rapper on their roster could withstand the new album flopping.

So, when Nation of Islam leader Louis Farrakhan contacted the Lorenzo brothers with an offer of brokering a truce between Ja and 50, it seemed like a way out. An end to the rivalry with 50 could bring back Ja's career, and the Lorenzo brothers would look good within the black community for uniting with such a storied civil rights leader. "One of the most powerful black men in the country reached out to us," explains Chris Lorenzo. "Who's not gonna sit down with him?" But when the Lorenzos and Ja arrived at Farrakhan's Chicago mansion they quickly realized that the Nation of Islam minister intended to do much more than broker a private, closed-door truce. "We go out there and have a great talk and then it turns out that his son Mustafa wanted to record everything," Lorenzo recalls. "We were caught between a rock and a hard place. . . . You see another motive come out but you're already there and did it [the sit-down]. So what you gonna do? Not do it? You just let it go and basically that's what happened."

At the urging of Russell Simmons and former NAACP leader Ben Chavis's group Hip-Hop Summit Action Network (HSAN), the informal peace talks became a full-blown media event with a promise that 50 would participate and even an air date. The sit-down with Farrakhan would be broadcast on MTV, BET, and nearly a hundred hip-hop and R&B radio stations on November 3, 2003, the eve of the release of *Blood in My Eye*. 50 naturally wanted no part of an event that reeked of hucksterism. "As far as the meeting with Farrakhan, it's not happening," 50 told Washington, DC, radio station WKYS. "I respect [Farrakhan], but it ain't goin' down. Ja put himself in the position he's in." Simmons and Chavis mounted a furious behind-the-scenes effort to change 50's mind, but they were rebuffed by the rapper. Things got worse when the Ja–Farrakhan sit-down was broadcast the night of November 3. It looked amateurish; Ja's face was shot at too close range, the video stock looked cheap, and there were interactions between the Nation of Islam minister and the Murder Inc. MC that had nothing to do with his beef:

FARRAKHAN: And now you're married, have children and you never hit your wife?

JA RULE: Yes, three children—never hit my wife.
FARRAKHAN: That's wonderful, my brother.

In an event that promised reconciliation, Ja seemed remarkably unreflective. "The public makes it so we have to keep assaulting each other," Ja told Farrakhan, "and they're not giving us room to say, 'I'm not thinking about him.' They're not giving us that space." When *Blood in My Eye* hit stores the next day, the Farrakhan sit-down seemed even more ludicrous. Ja insulted 50 on nearly every track, claimed affiliation with Suge Knight's Death Row, and even taunted the feds. Hip-hop fans saw right through the blatant contradictions of Ja's peace brokering and beef mongering, and in its first month in stores the album sold 284,000 copies; his previous album, *The Last Temptation,* sold nearly that many its first week.

The fall of 2003 was a calamitous one for Murder Inc.: The Farrakhan sit-down fell apart, *Blood in My Eye* bombed, a rapper named D.O. Cannon who appeared on Murder Inc. tracks and on Ja's *Blood In My Eye* was gunned down in South Jamaica, and a December 1 *New York* magazine cover story about the label highlighted its connections to 'Preme. The story so infuriated Russell Simmons and Lyor Cohen they called then-editor-in-chief Caroline Miller to complain. Simmons also blasted the piece in a long letter to the editor which ran in the next issue. The pressure on the Lorenzo brothers was so great that on December 3, Irv held a press conference to announce that Murder Inc. was no more; the self-proclaimed world's most dangerous record label would be known simply as The Inc. "Hopefully, everyone will focus on our talent now and not on the word 'murder,' " Irv said at the press conference, flanked by Simmons, Ja Rule, and Ashanti. "Hopefully, people will forget about all the negative energy and give us the kudos we deserve." Simmons took a more confrontational tack at the press conference, characterizing The Inc.'s critics as anti-hip-hop.

Murder Inc.'s name change was a mostly empty gesture: It wasn't going to reverse months of bad PR nor, obviously, was it going to make the federal investigation into the label disappear. Indeed, instead of making The Inc. seem less threatening, the move placed the company in the tradition of Death Row, which changed its name to Tha Row after its profile became too notorious. If the Lorenzos thought The Inc.'s cosmetic changes could turn the label's fortunes around or stave off a federal indictment, they were dreadfully naïve. The Lorenzos' misguided optimism was enhanced after receiving a clean bill of health from a forensic accountant they'd hired to scrutinize their finances for improprieties. The accountant's report supported many of the Lorenzos' primary contentions—namely, that the Universal Music Group, not 'Preme, gave Murder Inc. its seed money—and, as a result, they became convinced that the feds would never indict them. Chris Lorenzo even became combative during his interviews with the FBI that fall. "Why is that you have to become so personal?" Chris remembers telling one FBI agent. "I seen another agent and he's like, 'You gonna go to jail,' and I'm like, 'Wow, I ain't do nothin' and I don't know why you want me in jail.' He says, 'You know what you did!' And I said, 'No, I don't. I better not talk to you anymore. I need a lawyer. Now.' "

With the label's name change and the quickening pace of the federal investigation, 2003 came to a dramatic close for the Lorenzo brothers. As 2004 rolled around, however, there was near-total quiet about the U.S. Attorney's investigation into The Inc. Leaks to the media from the feds were rare, and there were no major events like the killing of Jam Master Jay to turn law enforcement's attentions back toward the label. This quiet period fooled not just the Lorenzo brothers but execs at the Universal Music Group into believing the worst for The Inc. and 'Preme had passed. "Supreme paid his debt to society," Lyor Cohen told the web site allhiphop.com. "He was simply trying to get into business. . . . They have every bit of information and I don't think they will find any wrongdoing. Irv is not a criminal." Irv himself seemed just as sure as Cohen that his indictment would never come. "I can see what they're thinking," Irv says of the feds. "They're thinking, 'Here's 'Preme, who was this criminal figure back in the eighties, and here's Gotti—he's making all of this money in the music industry,' but it's not the case. If you look at my background and my history I've never been convicted of a crime. Why am I going to lose it all now? OK, *now* I'm going to do crime? I'm a talented mother-fucker who makes millions of dollars. What the fuck do I need to sell drugs for? What do I even need to be around a motherfucker who sells drugs for? I don't even need to be around it. For what?" Irv then backpedals on the claim he made in the 2002 *Rolling Stone* profile that he hustled back home in Hollis. "It would be different if you did a background check and it says, 'Irv Gotti was linked to selling drugs in the eighties,' " Irv says. "I was linked to DJing in the park! [laughs] If I was never doing any crime why the fuck am I gonna make millions upon millions of dollars and then say, 'OK, let's move some coke!' It don't make no sense. The government will figure that out."

But the feds weren't looking at cocaine dealing—at least on Irv's part—they were focusing on money laundering. Soon after the forensic accounting in late 2003 that found nothing inappropriate in The Inc.'s books, the feds allegedly found evidence that the Loren-zos were laundering 'Preme's cash through two side companies they'd created, IG ("Irv Gotti") Records, Inc., and MI ("Murder Inc.") Records, Inc. "After the forensic accountant looked at Mur-der Inc., LLC, which is his partner company with Def Jam, we were confident that Irv was not engaged in money laundering," says a source at the Universal Music Group, "but then we were told by the feds about the side companies. Irv was doing something on the side and not telling anybody."

With the evidence about Lorenzo's side companies discovered sometime in 2004, the feds moved quickly, indicting Inc. accoun-tant Cynthia Brent in late November. Brent was roused from her Maplewood, New Jersey, home on charges of laundering more than $1 million of 'Preme's drug money. The case against Brent was similar to the one brought against Thomas "Tony Montana" Mickens: Brent allegedly broke down deposits of cash into amounts of less than $10,000 to avoid filing CTRs with the IRS. An indictment of Ja's manager Ron "Gutta" Robinson—also on money-laundering charges—followed. The noose around The Inc.'s empire tightened even more when, according to a defense attorney working on the case, Robinson and Brent began cooperat-ing with the feds.

It was a relationship that began on the set of a video shoot in southeast Queens, solidified in Manhattan boardrooms, and on January 26, 2005, it would be sealed in a conference room at the U.S. Attorney's office in Brooklyn. Against a backdrop of a massive blowup poster of the *Crime Partners* DVD cover and a flowchart titled "Laundering of Drug Proceeds of the McGriff Enterprise Through Murder Inc.," U.S. Attorney Roslynn R. Mauskopf, joined by agents from FBI, ATF, and IRS as well as New York City Police Commissioner Raymond Kelly, announced the indictment of 'Preme and the Lorenzos on charges including racketeering, drug trafficking, money laundering, and murder. Mauskopf claimed that immediately upon his release from prison in the mid-1990s—"the moment he hit the streets"—'Preme rebuilt his drug distribution network by "selling wholesale quantities of cocaine, crack, and heroin from the streets of New York through a wide corridor on the East Coast down to Baltimore, Maryland, and to North Carolina. 'Preme's new organization—dubbed the McGriff Enterprise by prosecutors—was allegedly assisted in its efforts to hide its illicit proceeds by the Lorenzo brothers. "In Irving and Chris Lorenzo, McGriff's friends and executives in control of the record company Murder Inc., McGriff found two willing allies and a network of businesses at the ready," Mauskopf said. "The Lorenzos and Kenneth McGriff became partners—crime partners—and together they laundered over $1 million in illicit drug proceeds though Murder Inc. and through companies that they owned and controlled."

As insiders at the Universal Music Group expected, Mauskopf alleged that the Lorenzos utilized side companies IG Records, Inc., and MI Records, Inc., to launder 'Preme's cash. She refrained from accusing Murder Inc., LLC, or Def Jam employees of wrongdoing. Indeed, during the press conference announcing the indictment and in the indictment itself Def Jam is referred to as "the other company."

'Preme, for his part, faced the most serious charge of all: murder. "They murdered rap artist E Money Bags—Eric Smith—to seek revenge against their rivals," Mauskopf explained, "and they killed disloyal associates to silence those suspected of cooperating with law enforcement and those who knew too much." The surveillance tape found at the scene of the double murder of Karon Clarrett and Dwayne Thomas in Owings Mills, Maryland, in 2001 revealed crucial clues in charging 'Preme with the killing of Smith, according to New York City Police Commissioner Raymond Kelly. "The videotape at the Baltimore stash house clearly indicated that E Money Bags had been under surveillance," Kelly explained. "On the same block, three shooters surrounded the Lincoln Navigator and fired a total of forty shots. We were able to document that the tape was done moments before the killing." Kelly further noted that the pair alleged to have made the video—southeast Queens couple Dennis "Howabout" Crosby and Nicole "Nicole Love" Brown, also charged in the indictment—might have gotten away with the crime if they had simply turned off the TV while surveilling Smith. He said that Crosby and Brown watched the sitcom *The Hughleys* as they videotaped Smith, and detectives scrutinizing the tape traced the on-air date of this particular episode back to the day that Smith was surveilled.

Such a slipup—foiled by a C-grade sitcom—was all too typical of 'Preme's lack of professionalism, which stretched all the way back to his arrest in 1985 at the sloppy stash house in southeast Queens. Yet these revelations did not lessen the Lorenzo brothers' respect for 'Preme. Nor did the stiff prison sentences they faced—twenty years each—make the Lorenzo brothers doubt that he would be exonerated. As a handcuffed Irv, clad in a white T-shirt and a woolly hooded parka, blue jeans, and hiking boots, was led by cops in front of federal court in downtown Brooklyn on that gray, late-January day, he stared straight into the television cameras swarming around him and proudly proclaimed: "In no way, shape, or form have I ever done anything wrong except make music that the people seem to love."

Irv put on a brave public face but privately it has been hard for him to remain optimistic, particularly because the feds seem intent on grouping all the players in The Inc. indictment as descendants of southeast Queens' eighties heyday. "This investigation traces its roots back as far as the early eighties to the Queens crack organizations of Howard 'Pappy' Mason, Lorenzo 'Fat Cat' Nichols, and Kenneth 'Supreme' McGriff," said FBI Agent Fred Snellings at the Brooklyn press conference. The Lorenzo brothers may have thought such statements would give their street cred a boost, but 50 Cent, who had won nearly every round in his battle against The Inc., saw the indictment for what it was: the tale of two hip-hoppers out of their depth among hardcore hustlers. "It's a sad story actually," 50 told allhiphop.com when asked about the arrest of the Lorenzo brothers. "It's a story about a guy that was blessed with the opportunity to make music and used music to make him appear to be the gangster he's not. [He was] associating himself with gangsters. . . . I guess he's a gangster now."

11

The New Insurgency

The indictment of The Inc. was in many ways the death blow in 50's long battle against the Lorenzos and 'Preme. Not surprisingly, a little more than one month after the arrest of the Lorenzos, 50 kickstarted a brand-new insurgency, this time against Jimmy "Henchmen" Rosemond. In the years following the Shakur shooting at the Quad Studios in late 1994, Rosemond became one of the most respected and feared producers in hip-hop thanks to his hugely popular, Miami-based music industry conference "How Can I Be Down?" and a series of smart signings including chart-topping mid-nineties neo-soul band Groove Theory. When Rosemond was indicted in a massive federal continuing criminal enterprise case in 1996 for allegedly running a crack cocaine operation that stretched from New York to North Carolina, his street credibility skyrocketed. His reputation grew even more when it got out that Randolph Lucas, the southeast Queens strongman who killed parole officer Brian Rooney in 1985 at the behest of Fat Cat, was one of the primary informants for the prosecution. "How the fuck did I get tied up with Fat Cat?" Rosemond remembers thinking upon hearing that the notorious hired gun Lucas would be testifying against him. It turned out that the feds' case against Rosemond was stacked with informants who either barely knew him (like Lucas) or couldn't even pick him out of a lineup. Thanks to the weak case against him, and his high-priced representation, famed Miami divorce lawyer

Roy Black, Rosemond beat all of the most serious charges, serving only a few years in prison on a weapons charge.

When Rosemond came home in 1999, he enjoyed a reputation as a Teflon ex-hustler and was still respected in the music business for his work in the 1990s, so he picked up a succession of great gigs (including executive producing the soundtrack for *Romeo Must Die* in 2000, which featured Aaliyah and Timbaland at their peak). Rosemond's big score came in 2004 when he was approached by Los Angeles rapper Game (né Jayceon Taylor), who had just signed with Dr. Dre's Interscope-distributed label Aftermath, to be his manager. "At first, I would just advise him because the climate that 'Pac had left for me at Interscope was so bad," Rosemond remembers. But after Rosemond began getting Game's tracks exposure on mixtapes from influential New York DJs like Kay Slay, Game implored him to take an official position. Rosemond accepted and began building a savvy marketing campaign for Game that included appearing in a popular commercial for cell phone company Boost Mobile (which featured far better-known hip-hop talent like Kanye West) and a massive billboard for Puffy's clothing company Sean John, which, in turn, brought interest from Joel Silver and Quentin Tarantino, both of whom Rosemond says approached Game about movie roles.

Game also benefited from the mentorship of 50 Cent, who made him part of his G-Unit crew. But as the January 2005 release of Game's debut *The Documentary* neared, Rosemond worried that Game would fall victim to the mediocre record sales of G-Unit members like Young Buck and Lloyd Banks, so he began pulling Game from the crew's commitments. "He wasn't doing the things they expected a G-Unit member to do," Rosemond admits. "That strained things." Separating Game from G-Unit was a gamble but it paid off when *The Documentary* was released on January 28: Nearly 600,000 copies were sold its first week in stores, a number almost impressive as 50 Cent's 2003 debut *Get Rich or Die Tryin'*. Under Rosemond's guidance, Game went from a superstar's protégé to a star in his own right.

Naturally, tensions began to grow between 50 and Game, which were further exacerbated as Rosemond completed production on a straight-to-DVD documentary called *The Original 50 Cent* about Kelvin "50 Cent" Martin, the Brooklyn hustler from whom the rapper took his name. For one of the final shots, Rosemond wanted to shoot 50 purchasing a tombstone for Martin's grave site. "I went to 50 and said, 'I want to tape you putting in the order,' " Rosemond explains. "But he made me chase him for two months for $7,500 so I just bought it. How do you take this dude's name and you won't even invest $7,500?" An attorney representing 50 calls Rosemond's story "specious" and alleges that Rosemond reneged on a promise to donate the DVD's proceeds to Martin's family and to 50's non-profit G-Unity Foundation. "50 Cent is informed that not a dime of the proceeds therefrom has been donated to Mr. Martin's family or to charity," the attorney says. "[He] intends to sue those involved in the distribution and sale of the DVD." Rosemond responds that he never promised to donate money to G-Unity and that Martin's family will receive proceeds from the DVD as soon as they set up a trust.

With 50's beef with Rosemond intensifying and Game's single "How We Do" (which had the tinkling, techno-y orchestrations of Dre's production on *Chronic 2001*) eclipsing 50's new single "Disco Inferno" (a retread of his hit "In Da Club"), 50 phoned into New York radio station Power 105.1 to announce that Game was no longer a member of G-Unit. The timing of the call—made on February 28, 2005, just days before the March 3 release of 50's new album *The Massacre*—seemed suspiciously like a PR stunt. Later that night, 50, joined by G-Unit members Lloyd Banks and Tony Yayo, continued his campaign against his rivals, denouncing Game during an interview with Hot 97, claiming that he had to almost entirely rework *The Documentary* after Game turned in an initially uninspired effort. "Creatively, he got stuck in the mud with it, and I came through and helped the car move," 50 told Hot 97. "I think he has a problem with my position. I think he'd like to be 50 Cent. Like, the head of the situation." As 50 was being interviewed on Hot 97, members of Game's entourage rushed the station's Lower Manhattan studios to confront 50 but were met by his security detail in the hallway.

During the melee, one member of Game's crew—twenty-four-year-old Kevin Reed, who hails from Game's hometown of Compton, California—was shot. Cops found Reed at Hot 97 bloodied and kneeling by the curb along with four spent shell casings. Reed was treated at St. Vincent's Hospital and later released. No arrests were made in the shooting and an anonymous law enforcement source told *The New York Times* on March 2 that those involved in the incident were so uncooperative that they couldn't even piece together the sequence of events that led to the shooting. Rosemond won't comment on the incident as he was not with Game when it occurred. "I was on a plane on my way to Los Angeles," Rosemond says, noting that his presence at Hot 97 could have sparked a Quad-like scandal. "Thank God."

Thanks to a March 9 press conference held at Harlem's Schomburg Center for Research in Black Culture, where Game and 50 publicly pledged to put their differences behind them, mainstream media and even hip-hop magazines characterized the Hot 97 shooting as merely the culmination of a pitched war of words between a mentor and his former protégé. That is undoubtedly true, but there is no question that by forcibly ousting Rosemond's premier artist from G-Unit, 50 meant to send a clear message that, as he had done in the past with 'Preme, he was unafraid to go to war with one of hip-hop's most feared players. It's a scorched-earth style of battle borrowed from the crack era, where the goal isn't simply to outmaneuver rivals but to eliminate them. In an interview with allhiphop.com in early February before his beef with Game began, 50 proudly owned up to his style of handling enemies. "I think Jay-Z is a hustler, and I'm a hustler," 50 explained. "I think the difference is, Jay-Z is OK with hustling around other people while they getting money, as long as he is getting the most money. The difference is the way I came up. . . . We hustle until we get enough finances and manpower and start moving niggas off the strip."

The moves against Game and Rosemond brought mixed results: The publicity surrounding the shooting at Hot 97 helped boost 50's first-week sales to more than one million copies. But Game and Rosemond benefited as well, with *The Documentary* going triple platinum and *The Original 50 Cent* moving more than 100,000 copies. Emboldened by their success, Rosemond and Game responded to 50 by working from 50's playbook against the Lorenzo brothers. Game unleashed an anti-50 onslaught during his performance at Hot 97's Summer Jam in June, shouting "G-G-G-G-U-NOT!" between songs and even staging an onstage beating of a man dressed as a rat, reviving the Lorenzo brothers' accusation that 50 had cooperated with cops. Game's anti-50 crusade, however, seemed like little more than shtick as 50 had staged a similarly confrontational show at Summer Jam just two years earlier. Worse, unlike 50, Game didn't seem like he was relishing the rivalry. "Game looked sad, hurt, lonely," noted music critic Jon Caramanica in his review of the concert in *The Village Voice.*

Game sensed that he needed to devise a smarter strategy to deal with 50, especially after the Lorenzos had been so easily vanquished by him. "I always use what happened to Murder Inc. as the foundation," Game told MTV. "All Murder Inc. did was sit back and let him dismantle them. Me, I can't do it." So Game headed into the recording studio to lay down a blistering tirade against his former mentor called "300 Bars and Runnin'." On the sprawling, nearly fifteen-minute track, released straight to a mixtape called *You Know What It Is Vol. 3,* Game blasted not just 50, but G-Unit members Lloyd Banks and Olivia. Though there were some unoriginal rhymes (Game compared Banks to Cookie Monster, a comparison 50 had made to Ja Rule in 2003), there were also a number of incisively written verses, especially about 50's obsession with the Lorenzos. "All you do is murder. . . ." Game taunted, seemingly trailing off, "Inc.!" Even more impressively, the beats backing Game switched constantly, moving from Mobb Deep's "Shook Ones Pt. II" to Kanye West's "Diamonds from Sierra Leone," an effect that made Game seem as though he could rhyme to just about anything.

When a Los Angeles judge denied 50's motion for an injunction against distribution of *The Original 50 Cent,* Rosemond seemed to have won another round in his fight with the rapper. "We are gratified that the court found that there was nothing improper in the DVD's title or the way in which we are marketing it," Rosemond said. "We remain convinced that there is absolutely no merit to Curtis Jackson's lawsuit and that it should never have been filed. We believe it was filed more as an attempt to further his childish campaign of jealousy against The Game and his management than to vindicate any legitimate legal rights."

That he was able to frustrate 50's campaign against himself and Game was enormously gratifying, but Rosemond seemed unaware that just as 50's "Ghetto Qu'ran" brought law enforcement attention toward 'Preme, the beef with 50 was raising his profile with the feds. In the spring of 2005, a pair of Rosemond's old Brooklyn buddies named Walter "King Tut" Johnson and Jacques "Haitian Jack" Agnant, both suspected but never charged with having a role in the Quad shooting, were moved from state prison to a federal facility. The moves of Agnant and Johnson suggest that the feds may be attempting to connect the Quad ambush to Shakur's murder in Las Vegas in 1996. This theory was seemingly confirmed in early March 2005, when *Newsweek* reported that Rosemond is the subject of a massive federal probe (this time by the U.S. Attorney for the Southern District of New York) into unsolved hip-hop murders such as those of Tupac Shakur and Jam Master Jay. "The U.S. attorney can investigate all they want," Rosemond says. "I'm used to that. I move like I'm being investigated. I never shook that. I just got off federal probation a year ago. I still think I gotta call the probation officer."

Rosemond is less cocky when discussing the possibility that Agnant and Johnson could be cooperating with the feds. "It saddens me to know that Tut and those guys are gonna trade in somebody else for their freedom," Rosemond says. "I hope that's not what he's doing. I love Tut, he grew up with me. But guys like that only remember me one way, so they be like, 'Jimmy's gotta be extorting.' " In a letter from Lee County Penitentiary in Virginia where he is imprisoned on armed robbery charges, Johnson writes: "Jimmy Henchmen knows that I won't destroy other people [sic] lives or trade in somebody else for my freedom." He adds that he was "framed by some very crafty individuals that used their resources to manipulate the government . . . that I was responsible for the attempt [sic] assassination of Tupac Shakur at Quad Studios in New

York and that I was the solution to Tupac Shakur's vicious murder in Las Vegas."

Though the Quad shooting happened more than a decade ago, the memory of it will not fade anytime soon. In late June 2005, a Los Angeles jury heard a lawsuit brought by Biggie's family against the city for allegedly allowing LAPD officers to moonlight as security guards for Death Row's Suge Knight. During the trial—which was halted in early July after the judge ruled that the LAPD had intentionally withheld crucial evidence in the case—several witnesses testified that Knight personally ordered the murder of Biggie in 1997 and even gloated afterward about the way the rapper's overweight body had slowly slumped in his vehicle after he was ambushed by gunmen outside a *Vibe* magazine party in Los Angeles. Nearly every article about the trial noted that the rivalry between Biggie and Shakur began at the Quad.

The specter of the Quad being raised yet again and a frightening incident at a Los Angeles club where a member of Knight's entourage tried to snatch a chain from Game did not chasten Rosemond, who only ratcheted up his increasingly pitched battle with 50 Cent. Just after the Summer Jam concert, Rosemond sent Henchmen Entertainment employees to Hot 97 bearing signs with an image of a rat that read "G-G-G-G-U-NOT!" Rosemond then threatened to send the protesters to every stop of 50 and Eminem's Anger Management tour. But for all of the heat generated by the beef there was nonetheless a cartoonish character to it: Rosemond and his nonstop campaign against 50 had all the subtlety of a WWF match.

During the summer of 2005, Game and Rosemond were inseparable, a partnership of hustling and hip-hop rivaled only by the Lorenzo brothers' relationship with 'Preme. But as the Lorenzos' trial on money-laundering charges grew nearer, they were discovering just how toxic their bond with the former Supreme Team CEO had become. During the late spring of 2005, Irv's attorney Gerald Lefcourt asked Edward Korman, the presiding judge in the case, to have his client's money-laundering charges severed from 'Preme's far more serious murder and racketeering charges. The request was meant to give Irv a much better shot in the courtroom; jurors would be able to consider the money-laundering charges without hearing about the alleged murders committed by 'Preme as well as the Supreme Team's long, violent history in southeast Queens.

A source close to The Inc. says that the Lorenzos believed that the judge would grant the severance motion. But assistant U.S. Attorney Carolyn Pokorny filed court papers opposing the motion and charged that the Lorenzos used their relationship with 'Preme to intimidate rivals. "Indeed, far from being harmed by the McGriff enterprise's murderous reputation, the Lorenzos' alignment with McGriff afforded a level of protection," Pokorny wrote. "Would-be robbers and criminals who extort those in the music industry knew that if they targeted Murder Inc., its employees or executives, they would suffer retribution from the McGriff enterprise." The source close to the label says that Irv was devastated by the feds' tersely worded challenge to the severance motion and, at last, seemed to come to grips with the magnitude of the charges against him and the grave danger of appearing in a courtroom side-by-side with 'Preme.

To the surprise of both federal prosecutors and the Lorenzo brothers' legal team, in July 2005 Judge Edward Korman (the same judge, coincidentally, who presided over Fat Cat's case in the eighties) granted Lefcourt's request to separate the cases; the Lorenzos' trial was then set for October 24. Basking in their good fortune, Irv and Chris headed to Las Vegas to celebrate, and gambling aficionado Chris was feeling lucky enough to enter Harrah's World Series of Poker, where he took in five-figure winnings. 'Preme, meanwhile, was impressing the streets by refusing to roll over on the Lorenzos even as the specter of the death penalty hung over him.

The surge of optimism that the Lorenzos might be acquitted (as well as 'Preme's renewed street cred) inspired others to try to turn a profit from the notoriety of southeast Queens' eighties heyday. Charles Fisher, formerly of the Jam Master Jay tipline, teamed up with Lance Feurtado, one of the Supreme Team's former cocaine suppliers, to make a straight-to-DVD documentary about Fat Cat,

Pappy, Prince, and Tony Montana called *King of Kings*, which was released in the spring of 2005; Prince took a page from his uncle by starting a record label from his prison cell in Leavenworth Penitentiary (Shane "Qasim" Fells, son of crack-era victim Maxine Peterson and the man who gave Irv his first shot on the turntables, is incarcerated with Prince and the pair have become friends); and Curtis Scoon is still shopping *10:13,* his script about the Edward Byrne era.

50 Cent, meanwhile, has transformed the Byrne era into a reference point for hip-hoppers to express power on the streets. The movie poster for his Jim Sheridan–directed biopic *Get Rich or Die Tryin'* features a shot of 50's muscled back, which is adorned with a tattoo that reads SOUTHSIDE, and when G-Unit took over Hot 97 for a weekend of "G-Unit Radio" just before the release of *The Massacre,* the DJ scratched a vocal snippet on a record back and forth until the lyric seemed to hang in the air:

"I've got money like Fat Cat/Heart like Pappy Mason"
"I've got money like Fat Cat/Heart like Pappy Mason"
"I've got money like Fat Cat/Heart like Pappy Mason"

With each spin of the record, the specter of the southeast Queens streets was raised with indelible power and permanence.

The hip-hop generation's memory of southeast Queens bears little resemblance to what actually happened then. The stories told by the Lorenzo brothers and 50—Fat Cat hoarding mountains of cash at Mom's Deli, Mickens cruising in his Bayliner, Prince coolly ordering hits from the Baisley Park Houses—avoid all of the death and pain not only that these kingpins inflicted on others but also that they themselves experienced both on the streets and, later, in the prison system. This is to be expected—nostalgia falsifies history, even more so when practiced by those who never actually experienced the particular historical moment—but it has had a devastating effect on southeast Queens' hip-hop players. Irv Lorenzo's remarkable resuscitation of Def Jam in the mid-nineties will likely be forgotten; even if he is found innocent, he'll probably be remembered as a back-street boy who aroused the ire of the feds just so he could be per-ceived as street credible. While the multiplatinum sales of *The Massacre* prove that 50 is undoubtedly the biggest hip-hop star in the world, the ever-multiplying number of rivalries he has fomented—the Lorenzo brothers, Game, Fat Joe, and Jadakiss among many others—has made much of hip-hop sound like little more than score-settling.

What is particularly depressing is that when a real reminder of the southeast Queens of the eighties emerges—like the murder of Jam Master Jay, in which 'Preme was momentarily a suspect—those who lionize the decade can't run in the opposite direction fast enough. After an initial period of anger and resolve in the wake of Jay's killing, there seems to be little interest among south-east Queens' hip-hop set in solving the case. The huge cast of sus-pects in Jay's murder (which includes a government informant and an aging stick-up kid) as well as the brutal manner in which the crime was committed seems pulled straight from the Edward Byrne era. Jay's death is also difficult to confront because he was a true native son of southeast Queens who never pulled up stakes from the area and suffered financially for helping out so many of his southeast Queens friends. (He was deeply in debt at the time of his death, owing $172,437.90 in unpaid state income taxes and nearly $53,339 in business taxes on his 24/7 recording studio.) Unsurprisingly, many of his friends and business associates are feeling guilty: During the summer of 2005, Joseph "Run" Sim-mons told an interviewer that in the days after Jay's death he was visited by a "ghost" of the RUN-DMC DJ who told him, "You owe me some money." Simmons continued: "I was like, 'Oh God,' because I was in charge of all the money so I offered to give him some right there and then and he was like, 'No no, give it to my wife.'" Simmons told the interviewer that the encounter with Jay's ghost made him realize that he owed Jay $16,000, which he says he then paid to Terri Mizell. Jay's demise—probably at the hands of a friend or a rival from the neighborhood—and its aftermath (when acquaintances tried to steal clothing from his 203rd Street home, according to several of his friends) proves the low regard in which even a hip-hop legend is held in southeast Queens. The streets might be much safer than they were in the eighties, but Jay's death is a reminder that perhaps they haven't changed all that much.

While Jay is memorialized in a touchingly homespun way (in late 2004, members of his family had rappers autograph a van, which they auctioned off on eBay), 'Preme is paid impressive tributes. When Irv Lorenzo speaks about 'Preme he sounds as though he is describing the Batman of the drug game. "People used to hear about him but they never *seen* him," Irv remembers. "Even when I was on the street DJing I never seen him. Funny thing is, my man he used to work for the Supreme Team but *he* ain't never seen Supreme. People worked for the Supreme Team, they would die for the Supreme Team, but didn't know or had never seen Supreme." When Irv was informed that 'Preme was imprisoned for most of the Supreme Team's reign and that this probably explains his status as southeast Queens' invisible man, he just shrugged it off. Hip-hoppers like the Lorenzo brothers refuse to allow reality to impede their mythmaking of 'Preme and Fat Cat, even if it means serving time in prison with the legends themselves.

50 Cent and the Lorenzos have shaped the southeast Queens of the eighties in the outsized image of nineties gangsta rap. But that may soon change as iconic hustlers like Fat Cat are becoming exasperated with both the rappers who are profiting from invoking (or, in some cases, stealing) their legacy and with the hip-hop generation's glorification of the crack era.

In the spring of 2005, Fat Cat was charged with running a multi-million-dollar car theft ring from his prison with Detroit-bred cocaine kingpin turned informant Richard "White Boy Rick" Wershe (a childhood friend of rap rocker Kid Rock, incidentally) and was moved from a cushy Florida penitentiary to solitary confinement in an upstate New York prison. The feds were furious that he squandered their goodwill by rebuilding a new organization from behind bars. The move was not just a punishment but an exile back into a world from which he had long been insulated.

Fat Cat will have a long time to get accustomed to his new surroundings: His projected release date from prison is December 13, 2026, and the new charges related to the car theft ring could bring decades more time behind bars. With hip-hop stars like 50 Cent shaping his story and with little left to lose in solitary confinement, Fat Cat is finally ready to talk. Having come to trust Curtis Scoon since he wrote his screenplay about the Edward Byrne era, Fat Cat chose him as an emissary to deliver a message from his prison cell at the Clinton Correctional Facility in Dannemora, New York, the same place where Tupac Shakur was incarcerated in the mid-nineties:

"My name is Lorenzo Nichols but most simply remember me as Fat Cat. The present glorification of a lifestyle that has cost me the past 20 years of my life, and promises to cost even more with no end in sight is both confusing and amazing to me. My current everyday existence has to be the closest thing to hell on Earth, yet so many young people answer the call of the streets and throw caution to the wind with the consequences being what I now face or worse. In pursuit of the lifestyle commonly referred to as 'balling' I've made choices that have had a devastating effect on many lives, not excluding those of my loved ones and myself. If I could do things over there's much I would change but there seems to be no second chances for me. For those who have options to travel another more positive path, I sincerely hope they make that choice. The cars, jewelry, women and good times have all become a distant faded memory. I would gladly give them all back for a chance to play with my grandchildren and be a father in the true sense to my own children. If nothing else, I hope my predicament serves as a deterrent to all aspiring gangsters or hustlers by reminding them that notoriety comes with a hefty price tag."

EPILOGUE

As Irv and Chris face an uncertain future and a sense that they alone have taken the heat for their relationship with 'Preme, Jam Master Jay's friends and family battle over his legacy in southeast Queens. It's an early summer day, and a crew of Jay's family, friends, and former business associates—including Jeff Fludd, Harold "Lovey" Lawson, Karl "Little D" Jordan Jr., and Jay's brother Marvin and his sister Bonita—is gathered at Jamaica Park at 205th Street and Jamaica Avenue in Hollis for an outdoor concert featuring Jay's nephew Rodney "Boe Skagz" Jones.

Rain has been falling intermittently, but when the DJ begins setting up his turntables near the basketball courts just after 2 PM, the clouds give way to sun. While the DJ seems happy as he dismantles the tarp he'd assembled to protect his turntables from the rain, few others in attendance share his enthusiasm. "I can't even look at some of these people," seethes Lawson. With the third anniversary of Jay's murder approaching, friends like Lawson are growing impatient with the inconsistent stories coming from witnesses as well as the lack of interest in the case from southeast Queens' hip-hop scene. "Man, I wish I was there that night," Lawson continues. "I know that sounds crazy, but I feel like things would have turned out different if I was with Jay."

Jeff Fludd has more mundane worries on his mind. He wants to serve barbeque to the hundreds of kids from Hollis who've turned out to see Boe Skagz, but there is no serving table—nor is there anything to drink. So Fludd enlists Lawson to accompany him on a trip to Long Island to run these errands. The pair climb into Lawson's minivan, which is adorned with SpongeBob SquarePants paraphernalia (Lawson has seven children), and just minutes after leaving Jamaica Park they pass a mural honoring Jay on 205th Street and Hollis Avenue.

The sight of Jay's face should provide a moment for reminiscing and reflection, but Fludd becomes furious when he spots a small camera crew standing in front of the mural. He orders Lawson to turn the car around, and when we pull up right next to the mural, Fludd barks to the crew: "Who are you? What are you doing here? Who do you know in Hollis?" A dreadlocked man holding a microphone explains that he's here to shoot footage for Joseph "Run" Simmons's upcoming MTV reality show and then offers up a few nicknames of Hollis street guys he knows, none of which are recognizable to Fludd and Lawson. "Nah, nah, nah, man," says Fludd disdainfully, "we don't know none of those people. Tell Run he needs to come out here and shoot this himself." Lawson chimes in: "You can't represent Hollis if you can't show your face here." The dreadlocked man grimaces. There is an long, awkward silence and then, satisfied that they'd put a scare into Simmons's crew despite being two middle-aged men in a minivan decorated with a cartoon character suspected of being gay, they drive off to a Home Depot in the nearby Long Island suburb of Valley Stream.

Armed with cases of Sunny Delight purchased at Wal-Mart and a folding table from Home Depot, Fludd and Lawson arrive an hour later in Jamaica Park to find Boe Skagz in a heated argument with two girls. Their shouting is drowned out by the DJ, who has just begun spinning records, but things become so visibly tense that Fludd has to separate the girls from Boe. "It's tough being Jam Master Jay's nephew," Boe says with a shrug. There isn't any sarcasm to Boe's remark and with good reason: Since Jay's murder, Boe has been shot and has watched his hip-hop group with Randy Allen (Rusty Waters) dissolve.

Boe would like to talk about his future and about the interest in him as a solo artist from the likes of 50's manager Chris Lighty, but conversation keeps drifting toward the past, particularly the months before Uncle Jason was murdered. "You know when you got something so good you don't appreciate it every day?" Boe asks, fingering a rolling paper. "That's what that fall was like. I got Jam Master Jay as my uncle: He's a legend and I looked at him like my best friend. Whatever I wanted, like sneakers or whatever, he was my pops. He was like, 'Whatever you gonna do, Boe, *I'm* gonna make sure you good. You got flow? I'm gonna get you signed quickly.'"

Jay made good on his promise, securing Rusty Waters a recording contract with Virgin in the late summer of 2002. But the deal was structured in an unusual way: The record would be handled by Jay and Randy Allen instead of A&R executives at Virgin. Boe says that he approved of the deal but in an interview with allhiphop.com, Boe's grandmother Connie Mizell said that both she and Boe were unhappy with it. "Boe had to go through Randy for everything, even to get his pay," Mizell explained. "I knew it shouldn't be that way. I know Russell [Simmons] didn't hold Jason's money when he first got started."

Boe does admit that the deal with Virgin was meager and that on the morning of Jay's murder he had to borrow money from his uncle simply to eat. "At the time I was broke so I was like, 'Jay, let me have a couple of dollars,'" Boe remembers. "He gave me forty dollars, and I left the studio, and I went to get something to eat with Randy." After lunch, the pair ran errands together around southeast Queens, as they were leaving for a Rusty Waters promotional tour the next morning. Sometime that afternoon, the pair stopped at a popular barbershop at 165th Street and 89th Avenue in South Jamaica, which was featured in Hype Williams's 1998 hip-hop film *Belly*. "When the barber who cuts my hair was ready, Randy told me that he was gonna wait for me but I said, 'Go back to the studio, I'm gonna do my thing here,'" Boe remembers. "Go put your vocals down, and by the time I'm done I'll put my shit down.' We was making a song so it didn't make sense for both of us to be out of the studio while Jay was waiting."

When the barber finished braiding Boe's hair, Boe stepped outside only to run into a friend who seemed stricken with panic. "I look at his face and I can tell something happened," Boe recalls. "He said, 'Yo, somebody was shooting in the studio.' He never said *Jay* got shot in the studio. I expected somebody to be shot but never killed. When I get there Randy's sister Lydia is on the floor and she's crying—the police wasn't there, I got there right before the police came—I see Jay on the floor and I'm hollering at him like, 'Jay, Jay, get up, nigga!' I'm kicking him and shit and he's not responding. I've been shot, too, and sometimes you get shot and you pass right out so I was thinking he was passed out. I was trying to wake him." Boe says that instead of waiting for the cops to arrive he got in his car and drove home, telling his mother (Jay's sister Bonita), "Uncle Jason got shot." Just moments later, Boe says, he heard on the radio that Jay was dead.

Excluding a short interview with MTV where he essentially sat in silence as Randy Allen spoke, this is the first time Boe has spoken publicly about Jay's murder. So he is nervous and stammering as he talks, and he avoids eye contact, instead staring blankly at Jamaica Park's basketball courts where Karl "Little D" Jordan Jr. is playing a pickup game. But there are moments when Boe's story seems both coached and contradictory. He prefaces the anecdote about going to the barbershop on the morning of Jay's murder by saying, "It's not like you go there to get a haircut, you go there to chill. . . . You go to holler at people." Some of Jay's family and friends say they do not believe Boe was at the barbershop, as soon after the murder he claimed to be getting a haircut—not a braiding—when his uncle was killed. Boe's recent recollections, in which he seemed to purposefully mention his braids, seem to take that suspicion into consideration.

Further, Boe's claim that he—not Randy Allen—insisted that Rusty Waters go on their promotional tour in the wake of the murder is contradicted by his grandmother as well several of Jay's friends. "Randy came and told Boe the same night Jay was killed that they had to finish their Rusty Waters record," Connie Mizell told allhiphop.com. "He came and took him to New Jersey or somewhere. He called his mom and told her that he wanted to be with the family after Jason had died, and he couldn't get there because he didn't know where he was and didn't have a way to get back. They asked Randy, and he said they were working, but they were really just in a room. . . . I got tired of waiting and I'm the one who told the guys to call Randy and if Boe wasn't back in two hours, I was going to call the cops for kidnapping. . . . He was being held against his will. Look, what friend is more concerned with that when their friend has died? He thought more of making money than having Boe be with his uncle when his uncle was always there for him."

Boe also offers an unconvincing explanation of his altercation with Karl "Little D" Jordan Jr. in the spring of 2003, which allegedly ended with Jordan shooting him. "Little D is my dude," Boe says. "I made a little song with a couple of lyrics about him he didn't like—but then I got shot. People just put it together that he was the shooter." Boe even offers the information that he and Jordan have grown closer than ever since the shooting. "I'm gonna throw my shorts on and ball with him," Boe says, gesturing at the basketball court. A last question—will Jay's murderer ever be caught?—gets a surprisingly blasé response. "I wouldn't say it's impossible, but it's going to be very hard," Boe says. "I can't spend my whole life trying to figure out who killed Jay." The DJ cues up RUN-DMC's "Sucker MCs," and the crunch of its minimalist drumbeats blaring from towering speakers shakes the pavement below. "If you the dude who killed Jay, you gonna have problems," Boe continues. "Who wants to be that guy?" With that, Boe sprints off to ball with Little D, waving as he makes his way to the court to Jeff Fludd and Harold "Lovey" Lawson, who are cooking hot dogs on the grill. It's a southeast Queens tableau so perfect—Jay's nephew, his closest childhood friend, and his first road manager all enjoying a day in Jamaica Park set to RUN-DMC's music—that it seems almost staged. For a moment at least, the bitterness and rivalries among his friends and family disappear, but then the realization dawns not only that Jay is gone but also that with each passing day the will to find his killer is fading, too.

A few months before my meeting with Boe, I get called in for another interview at The Inc.'s 9th Avenue offices, this time with the other Gotti, Chris Lorenzo. A receptionist brings me to Lorenzo's office, in which several employees are nodding their heads to the growling sub-bass of Houston rapper Slim Thug's "Like a Boss," which is booming through Chris's home entertainment system. Chris shakes my hand and then waves them off, and they immediately leave. As The Inc. employees amble out the door, he says forcefully, "Stay right here, I'm going to find another office for us." This strikes me as strange, as I thought he'd cleared his office for our interview. When Chris returns a few minutes later my suspicions are heightened. "I've found a good place for us to talk, c'mon," he says, and I follow him down a narrow hallway where he opens the door to a tiny, windowless room not much bigger than a coat closet. Faced with Chris's football-player build and the sudden recollection of Chris hunting down 50 Cent in a remote studio in the Hit Factory, I start to panic.

Then Chris eases back into a desk chair, smiles, and pulls out his two-way pager. A message emblazoned on the pager reads: LET JUSTICE BE DONE, THOUGH THE HEAVENS FALL. He explains that this is a quote from the Oliver Stone film *JFK*; he has kept it on his pager since the investigation into The Inc. began a few years ago. "It's in God's hands now," Chris says calmly. "If they wanna trump something up because we helped a friend in a legal fashion so be it." Our conversation is wide-ranging and easygoing, touching on themes like the migration of hustlers to hip-hop in the early nineties ("Everyone back then wanted to be a drug dealer, but no one wants to be a drug dealer now; you wanna be a rapper now") to his satisfaction about the performance of *Crime Partners* ("It's made over $4 million; 'Preme would have made a nice piece of change"). There is no hint of anger or bitterness in Chris's voice during our sit-down, not even when he claims that there are "more agents investigating Murder Inc. than they had on the twin towers. You tell me how much sense that makes."

Chris's tone turns unexpectedly darker when conversation turns to his former Def Jam bosses Lyor Cohen and Russell Simmons. There is residual anger at The Inc., according to sources close to the label, over Simmons's appearance on the Fox News show *Hannity and Colmes* on February 3, 2003 (just one month after the raid on their offices), where Simmons suddenly, without prompting proclaimed, "They don't know who murdered Tupac, who murdered Biggie, who murdered E Money Bags, who murdered Jam Master Jay." These sources say that the Lorenzos were furious with Simmons for bringing up the unsolved murder at a particularly vulnerable time when the feds were hungrily hunting down any and all leads relating to the label (indeed, 'Preme would eventually be charged with Smith's murder). The Lorenzos also feared that they alone—not Def Jam executives—would take the fall for their *Crime Partners* deal with 'Preme (this would also happen).

It is unfair, Chris says, that corporations like the Universal Music Group (of which labels like Def Jam and Interscope, among others, are a part) reap massive financial rewards from hip-hop while only black executives face the consequences of making deals with the street guys like 'Preme who make the music credible. "This is the element that I have to deal with and that Irv has to deal with," Chris says, "so I look at a guy like Jimmy Iovine and get pissed off. Because here's a guy as powerful as he is and he never faces [the streets]. They add fuel to the fires [with high-profile beefs] but they don't have to deal with the street element." It's a familiar charge, and it's one that has been leveled against Interscope's Iovine in the past: When the feds launched an investigation into Death Row in the late nineties Suge Knight's attorney Milton Grimes complained to *The New Yorker* that "their money came from Interscope, and from MCA, and they were hands-on. So if there are going to be indictments, let them take on the industry—not just this one black business." Grimes's point is particularly relevant to The Inc. indictment, which in some sections strains to portray Def Jam as the victims of the Lorenzo brothers' scheming. The feds allege that Irv "induced" the label to fund the *Crime Partners* soundtrack, when in fact it was in its financial interest to do so because Irv had signed on superstars like Jay-Z for the project.

The sense of unfairness is made worse because, according to Chris Lorenzo, both Lyor Cohen and Simmons have maintained a long-term relationship with 'Preme and backed away from him once the federal investigation gained momentum. "Lyor knew 'Preme before we knew 'Preme, from Hollis, from the RUN-DMC days," Chris says. "Russell Simmons knew 'Preme before we knew 'Preme. They used to fuck with 'Preme, you understand? I always tell Lyor and I always tell Russell to this day, 'Stand up with your guy now, he needs you more than ever.' Because they always rubbed it in to me and Irv: 'He's not your friend, I knew him longer than you.' When everything hit, they backed off. That's bullshit. So I always tell Lyor and Russell, 'Stand up, your words might help him right now. Stand up next to your guy. You loved him before, you would always talk about him in high praise. So now in his time of need stand up and say you knew him and he was a good guy.' That's nothing bad. There's nothing wrong with it. They won't do it. Why? That's wack to me, that's bullshit, I ain't with that. They used to always tease Irv and me: 'I knew him longer than you. You didn't know him in this time.' You're right, I didn't. I'm sure they would admit it if you spoke to them but they won't come forward on their own." Lorenzo then says of 'Preme in a whisper, "I'm not sorry that he's my friend, I'm not."

Russell Simmons responds that 'Preme's fate is of little concern to him as he is consumed with working with a number of nonprofits from his Hip-Hop Summit Action Network (HSAN) to the ASPCA. "I'm not standing up for 'Preme," Simmons says, noting that he'd rather fight for animal rights than for a drug kingpin. "I stand up for the chickens. I'm losing millions of dollars with my deal from Pepsi-Cola because I'm fighting KFC. The eight hundred million innocent chickens, I'm standing up for them. I can't stand up for Supreme. I hope he's innocent. I hope he didn't hurt anyone." Of Chris's allegation that Lyor Cohen's relationship with 'Preme stretched back to the eighties when he threw parties with 'Preme, Simmons says, "Lyor didn't know 'Preme like that. I don't even think Lyor was involved with those parties in Queens." Simmons does, however, admit to feeling responsible for the fate of the Lorenzo brothers. "There's a guilt in me for not standing up for Irv and Chris," Simmons says. "I feel like I should have been part of the process. I should have been part of the mentoring. But I wasn't at the office every day. . . . To the extent that somebody could remind them they had such great opportunity, that they were so blessed, that was my job. . . . These are nice kids from Queens. . . . Everybody failed them."

ENDNOTES

Much of the first half of the book is based on hundreds of pages of wiretap and trial transcripts in the cases of Lorenzo "Fat Cat" Nichols, Kenneth "Supreme" McGriff, Gerald "Prince" Miller, and Thomas "Tony Montana" Mickens, all obtained from the U.S. District Court in Brooklyn. Readers interested in examining these documents further can go to www.queensreignssupreme.com.

Prologue

xvii *Let me ask you a question*: Interview with Irv "Gotti" Lorenzo, December 20, 2004.

xviii *Irv taunted Puff Daddy*: Carter Harris, "The J. Lo Effect," *Elle* magazine, June 2002.

xviii *The producer and The Inc. impresario*: Chuck Philips, "Q&A: Irv 'Gotti' of Murder Inc. Breaks His Silence," *The Los Angeles Times,* June 30, 2003.

xx *Two of the allegations against Irv*: Affidavit in support of seizure warrant filed by IRS special agent Francis Mace with the U.S. Attorney for the Eastern District of New York, January 2003.

xx *Though a few eighties-era MCs*: Eric B. and Rakim, "Paid in Full," *Paid in Full* (4th and Broadway).

xxi *When the bottom fell out*: Craig Horowitz, "Jack Stat: Brilliant, Eccentric Jack Maple Rewrote the Book on Fighting Crime—With Maps and Statistics," *New York* magazine, April 7, 2003.

xxi *One of The Inc.'s rappers*: "Ronnie Bumps" appears on *Irv Gotti Presents: The Inc.* (Def Jam) and *Irv Gotti Presents: The Murderers* (Def Jam).

xxii *On 50 Cent's "Ghetto Qu'ran (Forgive Me)"*: 50 Cent, "Ghetto Qu'ran (Forgive Me)," *Power of the Dollar* (unreleased).

xxii *On "Memory Lane (Sittin' in Da Park)"*: Nas, "Memory Lane (Sittin' in Da Park)" and "The World Is Yours," both on *Illmatic* (Columbia).

xxii *'Preme, on the other hand*: Robert Nardoza, press release from the U.S. Attorney for the Eastern District of New York, January 26, 2005: "In 1989, McGriff was convicted, upon his plea of guilty before United States District Judge Thomas C. Platt in the Eastern District of New York, of engaging in a continuing criminal enterprise ('CCE') and was sentenced to twelve years' incarceration."

xxii *Just days after our sit-down*: Murray Weiss, "Club Shoot Twist," *The New York Post,* December 29, 2004.

xxiii *It would be stupid*: John Marzulli, "Club Shooting Eyed in Link to Rap Probe," The New York *Daily News,* December 29, 2004.

xxiii *This theory was given*: Murray Weiss, "Heat on Ja Rule—Eyed by Feds in Midtown Gun Slay," *The New York Post,* July 18, 2005.

xxv *As rap has become drenched*: Juelz Santana, *Back Like Cooked Crack 2: More Crack* (Dipset Mixtapes); Cassidy, "I'm a Hustla," *I'm a Hustla* (Full Surface/ J Records).

1: The Crews Coalesce

4 *Colin Powell's parents bought*: Colin L. Powell and Joseph Persico, *My American Journey* (Ballantine, 1995).

4 *Gangs like Black Rain*: Selwyn Raab, "The Drug Pipeline: From Europe to New York," *The New York Times,* May 21, 1984.

5 *It used to be that drug dealers*: Interview with Mike McGuinness, September 20, 2004.

6 *They paid homage to Ronnie Bumps*: Interview with former Hollis hustler, September 2004.

7 *It became a competition*: Interview with former Corley Family lieutenant, September 2004.

8 *Many claimed affiliation*: Mark Goldblatt, "Hip-Hop's Grim Undertones," *USA Today,* October 28, 2002; Malakiy#17, "5% Nation: The Love That Hate Couldn't Destroy," *F.E.D.S.* Magazine, Vol. 4, Issue 17.

8 *In 1981, 'Preme and a group*: United States of America v. Kenneth McGriff, aka "Supreme."

9 *Though Mickens took*: United States of America v. Thomas Mickens, also known as "Thomas Harris," "Thomas Harries," "James Dean," and "Montana."

10 *After quietly taking*: Interview with former Corley Family lieutenant; interview with Mike McGuinness.

11 *Rivalries had existed*: United States of America v. Lorenzo Nichols, aka "Fat Cat" or "Busy."

11 *My father had a great knuckle game*: Interviews with Raheem Tyler, fall of 2004 and spring of 2005.

11 *If you cry*: Interview with Nichols family member, February 16, 2005.

12 *One late summer night*: Interview with former Corley Family lieutenant.

12 *Fat Cat's organization was all family*: United States of America v. Lorenzo Nichols.

13 *Biz had me counting money*: Interview with Nichols family member.

14 *Fat Cat's grocery store*: Interview with Mike McGuinness.

14 *Cat liked to use guys*: Interview with former Hollis hustler.

14 *Pappy and the Bebos sold cocaine*: United States of America v. Lorenzo Nichols.

15 *Mickens even had business cards*: United States of America v. Thomas Mickens.

15 *In November 1982, the officer*: United States of America v. Thomas Mickens.

15 *Their next meeting took place*: United States of America v. Thomas Mickens.
16 *In December 1984, an undercover cop*: United States of America v. Thomas Mickens.
16 *At the close of 1984*: United States of America v. Thomas Mickens.

2: The Cops Move In

18 *Supreme needs two ounces*: United States of America v. Lorenzo Nichols.
19 *On July 29, 1985*: Interview with Mike McGuinness.
21 *During a phone call*: United States of America v. Lorenzo Nichols.
21 *Just after 5 PM*: Leonard Buder, "Parole Officer Slain in Queens," *The New York Times*, October 12, 1985.
22 *Supreme Team members were issued*: United States of America v. Kenneth McGriff.
22 *When, in September 1985*: United States of America v. Kenneth McGriff.
24 *Just before he went to prison*: United States of America v. Kenneth McGriff.
25 *The party was packed*: United States of America v. Gerald Miller.
25 *'Preme used to book*: Interview with Russell Simmons, March 29, 2005.
25 *The afterglow from the event*: United States of America v. Gerald Miller.
26 *Prince created a business*: United States of America v. Gerald Miller.
27 *At Piniella's request*: United States of America v. Gerald Miller.
28 *A Nichols organization distributor*: United States of America v. Lorenzo Nichols.
28 *Crack started with the Dominicans*: Interview with Mike McGuinness.
29 *Crack was simple and inexpensive*: Crack cocaine preparation from Erowid.org: www.erowid.org/chemicals/cocaine/crack_info1.shtml.
29 *The privates became generals*: Interview with Nichols organization lieutenant, September 2004.
29 *Biz never wanted to sell crack*: Interview with Nichols family member.
29 *We didn't need crack*: Interview with Joseph "Bobo" Rogers, February 2005.
31 *He kicked off 1986 in high style*: United States of America v. Thomas Mickens.
32 *Mickens set up these businesses*: Interview with Mike McGuinness.
33 *On February 3, 1987, Mickens bought*: United States of America v. Thomas Mickens.
33 *On the day of the condo purchase*: United States of America v. Thomas Mickens.
33 *On February 6*: United States of America v. Thomas Mickens.
36 *When a cocaine distributor*: United States of America v. Gerald Miller.
36 *The Supreme Team's direct competition*: United States of America v. Gerald Miller.
37 *Sometimes Prince and 'Preme*: Interview with Nichols family member.
38 *On August 6, 1987*: United States of America v. Gerald Miller.
38 *He established contact*: United States of America v. Thomas Mickens.
39 *One of Young's best girls*: United States of America v. Thomas Mickens.

3: The Game Changes

41   *Glaze played on a weak moment*: Interview with Joseph "Bobo" Rogers.

41   *Horsham's thoughtless treatment*: Leonard Buder, "Drug Boss Tells of Giving Order to Kill 'My Girl,' " *The New York Times,* October 5, 1989.

42   *Before I knew*: Interview with Joseph "Bobo" Rogers.

43   *Just before 'Preme was released*: United States of America v. Kenneth McGriff.

43   *When 'Preme did finally return*: United States of America v. Kenneth McGriff.

44   *The feds were working with Queens Narcotics*: Interview with New York Special Narcotics Prosecutor Bridget G. Brennan, spring of 2003.

44   *In one Supreme Team apartment*: United States of America v. Gerald Miller.

45   *Piniella put himself in charge*: United States of America v. Gerald Miller.

46   *Just after 6 PM on September 2*: Todd S. Purdum, "Shotgun Blast to the Head Kills Witness to a Crime in Queens," *The New York Times,* October 6, 1987; Todd S. Purdum, "Stung by Murder, New York Police Draft Policy on Handling Threats," *The New York Times,* October 9, 1987; Peter Kerr, "Suspect Is Seized in Queens Death of Jury Witness," *The New York Times,* October 11, 1987.

48   *Arjune realized that*: Joseph P. Fried, "2 Convicted in Bombing in Jamaica," *The New York Times,* August 24, 1988.

50   *In any case, no one was surprised*: Richard Esposito and Mike McClary, "If 'We Lose One, They Lose One,' " *Newsday,* March 18, 1988.

51   *On February 25, 1988*: Esposito and McClary, "If 'We Lose One, They Lose One,' " *Newsday,* March 18, 1988.

53   *After a brief dustup*: Interview with former Corley Family lieutenant.

54   *We're all working*: Interview with Mike McGuinness.

55   *In a speech immediately following*: Monte R. Young and Anemona Hartocollis, "A Street Lined with Sorrow; 10,000 Cops Salute Rookie Slain Guarding Drug Witness," *Newsday,* March 1, 1988.

56   *The killing of the cop*: Interview with Joseph "Bobo" Rogers.

4: Downfall

57   *Mayor Koch took out*: Michael Marriott, "Koch Ad Asks Help of Reagan in Drug Battle," *The New York Times,* February 29, 1988.

57   *Following Koch's lead*: Tom Morganthau with Frank Washington, Andrew Murr, Tom Schmitz, and Richard Sandza, "Losing the War?" *Newsweek,* March 14, 1988; Ed Magnuson, "Tears of Rage; Americans Lose Patience with Panama and a Failed Drug Policy," *Time,* March 14, 1988.

58   *On March 7, 1988*: George James, "113 Officers to Fight Drugs at Queens Site," *The New York Times,* March 8, 1988.

58   *They watching all the drug*: United States of America v. Lorenzo Nichols.

58   *We don't even be allowing*: United States of America v. Lorenzo Nichols.

59   *I'm scared*: Interview with Nichols family member.

59   *Not long after purchasing*: United States of America v. Thomas Mickens.

59   *When Tommy is running*: United States of America v. Thomas Mickens.

60   *The feds want him*: United States of America v. Thomas Mickens.

60   *We had lots of buys*: Interview with Mike McGuinness.

61   *Leslie Banks thought she would be*: Interview with former Hollis hustler.

61   *On May 3, 1988*: Beth Holland, "50-Life for Woman in Drug Slaying," *Newsday*, July 13, 1989.

62   *Indeed, just before his arrival*: United States of America v. Thomas Mickens.

62   *The feds quickly traced*: United States of America v. Thomas Mickens.

62   *Everybody knows Thomas*: Carol Polsky, "24-Year-Old Charged with Running Narcotics Empire," *Newsday*, May 11, 1988.

63   *They all grew up together*: Interview with Raheem Tyler.

63   *Just after 12:30 AM*: Sarah Lyall, "Sister of Drug Trafficker Is Killed in Firebombing," *The New York Times*, May 21, 1988.

64   *Dear Momma*: "Jailhouse Letter: Text of Lorenzo Nichols' letter, read yesterday at the funeral of his sister, Mary Nichols," *Newsday*, May 26, 1988.

65   *At around 10:25 that evening*: John T. McQuiston, "Woman Is Slain While Holding Infant in Arms," *The New York Times*, May 30, 1988.

65   *On June 9, 1988*: United States of America v. Lorenzo Nichols.

67   *It was a terrible decision*: United States of America v. Lorenzo Nichols.

67   *So they instructed*: United States of America v. Lorenzo Nichols.

67   *Don't talk like that*: United States of America v. Lorenzo Nichols.

68   *As the dozen or so federal agents*: News services and staff reports, "400 Agents Raid Empire of Drug Czar," *The Washington Post*, August 12, 1988.

69   *Because of his cooperation*: Interview with former law enforcement source, fall of 2004.

69   *All that is known*: Leonard Buder, "Queens Drug Kingpin Reportedly Pleads Guilty," *The New York Times*, September 30, 1989.

69   *Congress passed the Anti-Drug Abuse Act*: U.S. Department of Justice, www.usdoj.gov/dea/pubs/abuse/1-csa.htm. "On November 19, 1988, Congress passed the Anti-Drug Abuse Act of 1988, P. L. 100-690. Two sections of this Act represent the U.S. Government's attempt to reduce drug abuse by dealing not just with the person who sells the illegal drug, but also with the person who buys it. The first new section is titled 'User Accountability' and is codified at 21 U.S.C. § 862 and various sections of Title 42, U.S.C. The second involves 'personal use amounts' of illegal drugs, and is codified at 21 U.S.C. § 844a."

69   *During the signing of the bill*: Excerpt of President Reagan's remarks at the White House upon the signing of the Anti-Drug Abuse Act of 1988 on November 18, 1988, from www.reagan.utexas.edu/archives/speeches/1988/111888c.htm.

70   *Soon after the Anti-Drug Abuse Act*: Almanac of Policy Issues web site, www.policyalmanac.org/crime/archive/crs_federal_crime_policy.shtml.

70   *I couldn't believe he was gonna let*: Interview with Joseph "Bobo" Rogers.

71   *In another courtroom coup*: Murray Kempton, "Fouled by the Company He Keeps," *Newsday*, June 11, 1989.

72   *One juror after another*: United States of America v. Thomas Mickens.

72   *There were no drugs*: Pete Bowles, " 'Tony Montana' Gets 35 Years," *Newsday*, December 15, 1989.

72   *During his cross-examination*: United States of America v. Lorenzo Nichols.

73   *There was no Mickens-like last stand*: United States of America v. Kenneth McGriff.

73   *To celebrate his release*: United States of America v. Gerald Miller.

74   *During a raid*: United States of America v. Gerald Miller.

74   *When cops seized $13,000*: United States of America v. Gerald Miller.

74   *Take the third floor*: United States of America v. Gerald Miller.

75   *Gus would beep Fernando and George*: United States of America v. Gerald Miller.

75   *Do it*: United States of America v. Gerald Miller.

76   *Take the cocaine*: United States of America v. Gerald Miller.

77   *How much do you think you got*: United States of America v. Gerald Miller.

77   *Righteous got all soaked up*: United States of America v. Gerald Miller.

78   *Speaking in Five Percenter code*: United States of America v. Gerald Miller.

78   *So, just after 6 PM*: United States of America v. Gerald Miller.

79   *Why are you doing this*: United States of America v. Gerald Miller.

79   *I could see the plastic*: United States of America v. Gerald Miller.

80   *On August 18, Hernandez and Arroyo*: United States of America v. Gerald Miller.

80   *You tell us*: United States of America v. Gerald Miller.

81   *The four legs of the stool*: Joseph W. Queen and Mitch Gelman, "Cops Fear More Violence," *Newsday*, March 22, 1990.

81   *Like the Supreme Team*: Homicide statistics from the New York State Division of Criminal Justice Services: criminaljustice.state.ny.us/crimnet/ojsa/cja_98/sec1/murder.htm.

81   *By the end of the eighties*: Virginia Byrne, "Random Killings Are Latest Weapon in Crack War," Associated Press, December 28, 1989.

82   *On December 31, 1989*: Curtis Rist, "The Decade When Queens Was King," *Newsday*, December 31, 1989.

82   *The avalanche of "get tough"*: Michael I. Niman, "Incarceration Nation: The US is the World's Leading Jailer," *Buffalo News*, January 4, 2000.

5: The Rap Game

86   *Potential informants were comforted*: Profile of Barnes on Jerry Capeci's "Gang Land News" web site, www.ganglandnews.com/barnes.htm.

86   *Baisley and 40*: Interview with Irv "Gotti" Lorenzo.

87   *Lots of street guys*: Interview with former Hollis hustler.

87   *Daniel held a B.A. in history*: Interview with Russell Simmons, March 29, 2005; Russell Simmons with Nelson George, *Life and Def: Sex, Drugs, Money, and God* (Crown, 2001).

87   *205th Street was the number one*: Interview with Russell Simmons.

88   *He experimented with drugs*: Russell Simmons with Nelson George, *Life and Def: Sex, Drugs, Money, and God* (Crown, 2001).

88   *I walked to school*: Interview with Joseph "Run" Simmons, March 14, 2005.

88 *Russell Simmons was a mediocre hustler*: Russell Simmons with Nelson George, *Life and Def: Sex, Drugs, Money, and God* (Crown, 2001).

89 *At first, I was just the guy*: Interview with Joseph "Run" Simmons.

90 *Here, an aspiring DJ*: Interview with Jeff Fludd, fall of 2004.

91 *I'd say, 'Ya ain't gotta break into people's houses'*: Interview with Jeff Fludd.

91 *The kids from PS 192*: Interview with Darryl "DMC" McDaniels, fall of 2004.

91 *Both parents had jobs*: David E. Thigpen, *Jam Master Jay: The Heart of Hip-Hop* (MTV Books, 2003).

92 *During the late fall of 1982*: Interview with Darryl "DMC" McDaniels.

93 *Nobody wanted to sign*: Interview with Russell Simmons.

94 *Jay could come play*: Interview with Darryl "DMC" McDaniels.

94 *The contract was with me*: Interview with Joseph "Run" Simmons.

94 *Charles Fisher, the former manager*: Interview with Charles Fisher, fall of 2004.

95 *We got three grand*: Interview with Darryl "DMC" McDaniels.

95 *While Joseph Simmons promised*: Interview with Jeff Fludd.

96 *Thanks to corporate sponsorship*: Interview with Jeff Fludd; Russell Simmons with Nelson George, *Life and Def: Sex, Drugs, Money, and God* (Crown, 2001).

97 *Jeff was always troubled*: Interview with Russell Simmons.

98 *When Michael Holman*: Stacy Gueraseva, *Def Jam, Inc.: Russell Simmons, Rick Rubin, and the Extraordinary Story of the World's Most Influential Hip-Hop Label* (One World/Ballantine, 2005).

99 *But Jordan was also a confidential informant*: Documents relating to Jordan's C.I. status obtained from State of New York, Division of Criminal Justice Services; State of New York v. Joseph Thomas.

100 *D was good for a minute*: Interview with Darryl "DMC" McDaniels.

101 *They were growing weary*: Interview with Russell Simmons.

102 *It was a decision made partly*: Bill Adler, *Tougher Than Leather: The Rise of RUN-DMC* (Consafos Press, 2002).

102 *We was fighting*: Interview with Darryl "DMC" McDaniels.

102 *The movie had a ludicrous plot*: Russell Simmons with Nelson George, *Life and Def: Sex, Drugs, Money, and God* (Crown, 2001).

103 RAPPERS' MOVIE DOESN'T DISPEL: Steve Persall, "Rappers' Movie Doesn't Dispel Violent Image," *St. Petersburg Times*, December 13, 1988.

103 *It was a fifty/fifty partnership*: Russell Simmons with Nelson George, *Life and Def: Sex, Drugs, Money, and God* (Crown, 2001).

103 *I was a big star*: Interview with Joseph "Run" Simmons.

104 *Tilton, in turn*: Interview with Jeff Fludd.

104 *As one of Hollis's most well-connected residents*: Interviews with Curtis Scoon, fall of 2004 and spring of 2005.

105 *The vice president of Rush Management*: Interview with Jeff Fludd.

105 *Big D is a family member*: Interview with Russell Simmons.

106 *I was a corny kid*: Interview with Donald Francois, fall of 2004.

107 *Something went bad with Kane*: Interview with Donald Francois.

108 *Kane, naturally, was furious*: Interview with Donald Francois.
110 *He was a corny little cat*: Interview with Jeff Fludd.
110 *I'm from Hollis*: Interview with Chris Lorenzo, January 11, 2005.
110 *But during one summer*: Interview with Chris Lorenzo.
111 *I sold my tapes*: Interview with Irv Lorenzo.

6: Straight Outta Hollis

113 *As far as I'm concerned*: Chuck Philips, "The Violent Art, Violent Reality of Dr. Dre: The Producing Genius Behind Pioneer Rap Group NWA Is No Stranger to the Courtroom," *The Los Angeles Times,* December 15, 1992.
113 *Indeed, the week* The Chronic: Philips, "The Violent Art, Violent Reality of Dr. Dre: The Producing Genius Behind Pioneer Rap Group NWA Is No Stranger to the Courtroom," *The Los Angeles Times,* December 15, 1992.
114 The Chronic *received*: Greg Kot, "Rave Recordings," *The Chicago Tribune,* January 14, 1993; Robert Christgau, "Consumer Guide," *The Village Voice,* March 1, 1994.
114 *The advance of hip-hop*: J. R. Reynolds, "Will Hip-Hop Overwhelm R&B? Rappers Dominated Vets on Album Chart," *Billboard,* December 23, 1993.
115 *You can get fucked*: Jeff Giles and Alison Samuels, "Straight out of Compton," *Newsweek,* October 31, 1994.
115 *They were dancers*: Interviews with Eric "Shake" Smith, fall of 2004 and spring of 2005.
116 *We knew that Randy*: Interview with Donald Francois.
117 *Irv came from a family*: Interview with Tom Sarig, December 2003.
118 *DMX was robbing everybody*: Interview with Chris Lorenzo.
119 *After Giuliani came into office*: Interview with Curtis Scoon.
121 *Eric Smith was particularly impressed*: Interview with Curtis Scoon.
123 *He is the epitome*: Interviews with Jimmy "Henchmen" Rosemond, spring of 2005.
123 *Everyone told him he should stay away*: Connie Bruck, "The Takedown of Tupac," *The New Yorker,* July 7, 1997.
124 *I think that movie changed him*: Malcolm Gladwell, "The Rapper's New Rage; Tupac Shakur Had an Epiphany of Sorts. Now He's Living Up to the Gangsta Rep," *The Washington Post,* December 17, 1993.
124 *I showed him from example*: Interview with Jimmy "Henchmen" Rosemond.
124 *One time, me, 'Pac, Stretch, and Jack*: Interview with Jimmy "Henchmen" Rosemond.
125 *He was trying to get legitimate*: Kevin Powell, "Ready to Live," *Vibe,* April 1995.
127 *The next morning, Shakur appeared*: David Kocieniewski, "Rapped Up; Shakur Guilty of Sexual Abuse," *Newsday,* December 2, 1994.
128 *An EMT who treated*: Wendy Lin, "Hit or a Robbery? Tupac Shakur: They Were Gunning for Me," *Newsday,* December 1, 1994.
129 *The entire case reeked*: Connie Bruck, "The Takedown of Tupac," *The New Yorker,* July 7, 1997.

129   *Weaker than a fuckin' block*: 2Pac/The Outlawz "Hit 'Em Up," *Greatest Hits* (Death Row).

129   *So, in December of 1995*: Interview with Jimmy "Henchmen" Rosemond.

129   *The whole Death Row clique*: Interview with Jimmy "Henchmen" Rosemond.

130   *Isaac, who is serving life*: Interview with Dexter Isaac from U.S.P. Pollock, spring of 2005.

131   *On the album* Don Killuminati: Tupac as "Makaveli," "Against All Odds" from *Don Killuminati: The 7 Day Theory* (Death Row).

132   *This was an unsurprising development*: NWA, "To Kill a Hooker" from *Niggaz4Life* (Ruthless).

7: The Rise of Murder Inc.

134   *The reality of 'Preme's post–Supreme Team life*: Interview with Chaz Williams, November 9, 2004.

135   *For Mic Geronimo's*: Interview with Irv "Gotti" Lorenzo; Cash Money Click, "Get Tha Fortune" (TVT).

135   *'Preme comes out on the block*: Interview with Chris Lorenzo.

136   *I get a call*: Interview with Chris Lorenzo.

136   *Though he'd helped*: Interview with Curtis Scoon.

137   *When Scoon arrived*: Interview with Curtis Scoon.

137   *Nobody gave a fuck*: Interview with Curtis Scoon.

138   *After "gangsta rap" hearings*: J. D. Considine, "Shame, Blame is Critics' Game; Crusaders: Another Round of Protest Against Gangsta Rap is Being Taken to the Doors of Record Companies," *The Baltimore Sun*, December 15, 1995.

138   *He messed it up for guys like me*: Interview with Jimmy "Henchmen" Rosemond, September 2005.

138   *It was a unique time*: Interview with Irv "Gotti" Lorenzo.

138   *We were pretty cold*: Interview with Russell Simmons.

139   *The people who worked there*: Interview with Irv "Gotti" Lorenzo.

139   *Most of Jackson's family*: 50 Cent with Kris Ex, *From Pieces to Weight: Once Upon a Time in Southside Queens* (MTV Books, 2005).

139   *Sabrina was slinging rocks*: Interview with Joseph "Bobo" Rogers.

140   *I looked up to them*: Interview with 50 Cent, February 2003.

140   *Jackson hustled alone*: Such solo hustlers were the product of the NYPD crackdown on southeast Queens in the post–Edward Byrne era. "If the 'hood was cocaine, then the rookie cop's murder was the baking soda," Jackson wrote in his memoir, "and an angry police force was the fire that cooked up new hustlers. Hustlers like me."

140   *Jackson and his sixteen-year-old partner*: The People of the State of New York v. Curtis Jackson and Taiesha Douse.

141   *After I got caught*: Rob Tannenbaum, "50 Cent: The Playboy Interview," *Playboy*, April 2004.

142   *If I was going to take a gangster's*: 50 Cent with Kris Ex, *From Pieces to Weight: Once Upon a Time in Southside Queens* (MTV Books, 2005).

142   *50 the street guy*: Interview with Jimmy "Henchmen" Rosemond.

142   *He said he was developing*: Interview with 50 Cent.

142   *So, eventually 50 turned*: Interview with Chaz Williams.

143   *In the beginning*: Interview with Chris Lorenzo.

143   *Though Williams didn't have*: Interview with Chaz Williams.

144   *That all changed*: MTV News, "DMX Bumps Garth Brooks from Top of Charts," May 27, 1998.

144   *When X came*: Interview with Irv "Gotti" Lorenzo.

144   *Ja celebrated the newfound status*: Ja Rule, "Survival of the Illest Freestyle," from *Survival of the Illest* (Def Jam).

145   *Because* Black Gangster: Interview with Chaz Williams.

145   *It was a paltry deal*: Interview with 50 Cent.

146   *You only get*: Interview with 50 Cent.

146   *For instance, 50 rapped*: 50 Cent, "Life's on the Line" from *Power of the Dollar* (unreleased).

146   *A man whom Ja apparently knew*: Interview with Chris Lorenzo.

146   *Indeed, according to an IRS affidavit*: Affidavit in support of seizure warrant filed by IRS special agent Francis Mace with the U.S. Attorney for the Eastern District of New York, January 2003.

147   *At a lunch meeting*: Interview with Chris Lorenzo.

147   *A source at the Universal Music Group*: Interview with Universal Music Group executive.

147   *Irv slept in the studio*: Interview with Universal Music Group executive, fall of 2003.

147   *Lyor said he couldn't*: Interview with Chris Lorenzo.

148   *Irv Gotti was the best*: Interview with Russell Simmons.

148   *Sensing that Def Jam*: Chuck Philips, "Seagram in Talks to Buy Remaining Stake in Def Jam for $100 million," *The Los Angeles Times*, February 19, 1999.

8: 50's Insurgency

149   *The highlight of the record*: 50 Cent, "How to Rob," from *Power of the Dollar* (unreleased).

149   *I felt I accomplished*: Interview with 50 Cent.

149   *The streets were savoring*: Don Thomas, "Chas [sic] Williams, CEO of Black Hand Entertainment," *The New York Beacon,* January 19, 2000.

150   *At a Murder Inc.–hosted*: Interview with Chris Lorenzo.

150   *Ja's anger at 50 paled*: 50 Cent, "Ghetto Qu'ran (Forgive Me)" from *Power of the Dollar* (unreleased).

151   *I don't like 50 Cent*: Interview with Nichols family member.

151   *50 didn't know*: Interview with Joseph "Bobo" Rogers.

151   *So, according to a former Nichols organization member*: Interview with crew member of Nichols organization, fall of 2004.

151   *Me and 'Preme*: Interview with 50 Cent.

151   *'Preme's attorney Robert Simels*: Interview with Robert Simels, fall of 2003.

152   *That's my man*: Interview with Irv "Gotti" Lorenzo.

152   *I saw Supreme*: Interview with Russell Simmons.

152 *I was basically like*: Interview with Irv "Gotti" Lorenzo.

152 *A source at the Universal Music Group*: Interview with Universal Music Group executive.

153 *'Preme, his sister Barbara McGriff*: United States of America v. Jon Ragin.

153 *His Picture Perfect partner*: United States of America v. the premises known and described as 108-41 159th St., Apartment 1F, Queens, New York.

153 *Things quickly moved*: United States of America v. the premises known and described as 108-41 159th St., Apartment 1F, Queens, New York.

154 *On that December day*: Interview with associate of Eric "E Money Bags" Smith, spring of 2005.

154 *'Preme was wracked*: United States of America v. the premises known and described as 108-41 159th St., Apartment 1F, Queens, New York.

154 *On March 24, 2000*: Interview with Chris Lorenzo.

155 *On May 24, 2000*: Interview with 50 Cent.

156 *After I got shot*: Interview with 50 Cent.

156 *In early 2000*: Interview with Curtis Scoon.

157 *Bentil says that he did*: Interview with Kojo Bentil.

157 *Ja Rule's sophomore album*: Ja Rule, "Put It on Me" from *Rule 3:36* (Def Jam); "Exstasy" also from *Rule 3:36.*

158 *In the spring of 2001*: Interview with associate of Eric "E Money Bags" Smith, fall of 2004.

158 *Smith even confronted Jay-Z*: Profile of Smith in October 2001 issue of *Felon* magazine.

159 *Smith's strong-arm style*: United States of America v. the premises known and described as 108-41 159th St., Apartment 1F, Queens, New York.

159 *The same month that Smith*: Affidavit in support of seizure warrant filed by IRS special agent Francis Mace with the U.S. Attorney for the Eastern District of New York, January 2003.

160 *On August 20, 2001*: United States of America v. the premises known and described as 108-41 159th St., Apartment 1F, Queens, New York.

161 *On October 28, 2001*: Wire services, "A Second Arrest in a Park Shooting," *The New York Times,* September 9, 1995.

162 *On "Fuck You"*: 50 Cent, *Guess Who's Back* (mixtape).

163 *His life story sold me*: 50 Cent cover story, *XXL* magazine, March 2003.

163 *In a July 30, 2002, profile*: Touré, "Hit Man Irv Gotti," *Rolling Stone,* July 30, 2002.

9: Hard Times

164 *Onyx was very successful*: Interview with Russell Simmons.

164 *The one thing we had*: Interview with Darryl "DMC" McDaniels.

164 *Jay was like*: Interview with Donald Francois.

165 *Jay would have been straight*: Interview with Eric "Shake" Smith.

165 *By the mid-nineties*: Interview with source who worked with a Baltimore-based drug trafficker, fall of 2004.

165 *Jay was also working on*: Interview with Eric "Shake" Smith.

166 *Shit was starting to grow again*: Interview with Darryl "DMC" McDaniels.

166 *He ignored phone calls*: Interview with Eric "Shake" Smith.

167 *Don't look at me*: Andy Newman and Al Baker, "Was It a Bad Business Deal or a Music Industry Feud?" *The New York Times*, November 1, 2002.

168 *They said they had*: Interview with 50 Cent.

168 *They didn't want 50*: Newman and Baker, "Was It a Bad Business Deal or a Music Industry Feud?" *The New York Times*, November 1, 2002.

168 *On the night of the murder*: Interview with Curtis Scoon.

169 *That same night*: Interview with Joseph "Run" Simmons.

169 *Russell Simmons received*: Interview with Russell Simmons.

169 *The next morning*: Interview with Eric "Shake" Smith.

170 *As he drove toward Hollis*: Interview with Eric "Shake" Smith.

171 *Smith initially believed*: Interview with Eric "Shake" Smith.

171 *In interviews following*: Michelle McPhee, "Mom's Graveside Vow: Rapper Son's Killer Will Be Smoked Out," The New York *Daily News*, May 5, 2003.

171 *On November 1, 2002*: Newman and Baker, "Was It a Bad Business Deal or a Music Industry Feud?" *The New York Times*, November 1, 2002.

172 *Then I started piecing it*: Interview with Curtis Scoon.

172 *Bentil acknowledges receiving*: Interview with Kojo Bentil.

172 *If you want him*: Murray Weiss, "Rap Session Nixed; Man Tied to Jam Master Jay Won't Talk to Cops," *The New York Post*, November 5, 2002.

173 *Scoon could not*: Alan Feuer and William K. Rashbaum, "Police Study Old Cases in Murder of Rap Star," *The New York Times*, November 2, 2002.

173 *While Allen had named*: Interview with source close to Mizell family, spring of 2005.

173 *Scoon ain't close*: Interview with Russell Simmons.

173 *Jay's mother, Connie*: Interview with source close to Mizell family.

173 *The night of the murder*: Interview with source close to Mizell family.

174 *During an interview*: MTV News, "Rusty Waters Member, Sister Say They're Innocent in Jam Master Jay's Murder," June 25, 2003.

174 *Randy is saying*: Interview with Eric "Shake" Smith.

174 *50 Cent expressed*: DMX, "Shot Down" from *Grand Champ* (Def Jam).

174 *The most pointed criticism*: Michelle McPhee, "Mom's Graveside Vow: Rapper Son's Killer Will be Smoked Out," The New York *Daily News*, May 5, 2003.

175 *A source close to Jay's family*: Interview with source close to Mizell family.

175 *Then, when Washington*: Michelle McPhee, "A New Twist in Jay Slay," The New York *Daily News*, August 20, 2003.

175 *Everybody was a suspect*: Interview with Darryl "DMC" McDaniels.

176 *There were a lot*: Interview with Charles Fisher.

176 *During a star-studded*: Interview with Russell Simmons.

177 *A few people*: Interview with source close to Mizell family.

177 *Russell Simmons admits*: Interview with Russell Simmons.

177 *The feeling was*: Interview with source close to Mizell family.

177 *I don't know if I should*: Alan Feuer, "After Speeches and Gospel at Queens Church, Rap D.J. Is Laid to Rest," *The New York Times*, November 6, 2002.

178 *This would have been easy to dismiss*: Interview with source close to Mizell family.

178 *I had no association with*: Interview with Terri Mizell, fall of 2004.

179 *The Mizell hit was obviously*: Interview with former law enforcement source, fall of 2003.

179 *Law enforcement suspected*: Affidavit in support of application for a search warrant, United States of America v. Premises known and described as business office known as Murder Inc. Records, 825 8th Avenue, 29th Floor, New York, New York, and closed containers and closed items contained therein.

180 *Jay's killing*: 50 Cent, "Order of Protection," *The Future is Now* (mixtape).

180 *The renewed scrutiny of 'Preme*: Patrice O'Shaughnessy, "Zeroing in on Rap's Seamy Side: Gangsta Dough a Magnet for Queens Thugs, Feds Say," The New York *Daily News,* December 23, 2002.

180 *Whatever you want to say*: Interview with Irv "Gotti" Lorenzo.

180 *'Preme made the trip*: Affidavit in support of seizure warrant filed by IRS special agent Francis Mace with the U.S. Attorney for the Eastern District of New York, January 2003.

180 *The first hint*: Patrice O'Shaughnessy, "Zeroing in on Rap's Seamy Side: Gangsta Dough a Magnet for Queens Thugs, Feds Say," The New York *Daily News,* December 23, 2002.

10: Takedown

182 *All wiretap activity*: Tom Hays, "Rap investigation Casts Convict in Familiar Role," Associated Press, February 18, 2003.

182 *With the weapons charge pending*: Interview with former law enforcement source, fall of 2003.

183 *My heart stopped*: Interview with Irv "Gotti" Lorenzo.

183 *In an affidavit*: Affidavit in support of seizure warrant filed by IRS special agent Francis Mace with the U.S. Attorney for the Eastern District of New York, January 2003.

183 *The feds said that*: Interview with Universal Music Group executive.

183 *It is inconceivable*: Gerald Lefcourt and Gerald Shargel, memorandum of law in support of the pretrial motions of defendants Irving Lorenzo, Christopher Lorenzo, MI Records, Inc., and IG Records, Inc., August 31, 2005.

183 *Mace also made several major errors*: Affidavit in support of application for a search warrant, United States of America v. Premises known and described as business office known as Murder Inc. Records, 825 8th Avenue, 29th Floor, New York, New York, and closed containers and closed items contained therein.

184 *The Lorenzos suspected that 50*: Fernando Santos, "Rappers Busted on Way to Gig," The New York *Daily News,* January 1, 2003.

184 *The label also released*: Rich Rock, "Murder Inc. Confirmed Culprits Behind 50 Cent Info Leak," Sohh.com, January 16, 2003.

184 *But the boldest attack*: Ethan Brown, "Hip-Hop Beef: Is It Going Too Far," *New York* magazine, December 1, 2003.

185 *Even so, no one could*: Steve Jones, "50 Cent Brings in Hard Currency," *USA Today*, February 27, 2003.

185 *They put me*: Interview with 50 Cent.

185 *At the Dylan Hotel*: Interview with 50 Cent.

186 *50 was similarly coy*: Affidavit in support of application for a search warrant, United States of America v. Premises known and described as business office known as Murder Inc. Records, 825 8th Avenue, 29th Floor, New York, New York, and closed containers and closed items contained therein.

186 *'Pac did what 50*: Interview with Jimmy "Henchmen" Rosemond.

186 *In an eerie echo*: 50 Cent, "Many Men," from *Get Rich or Die Tryin'* (Aftermath/ Interscope).

186 *50 would not respond*: Friends of Chaz Williams say that 50 naïvely believed that Williams (who had mentored 'Preme) was an all-powerful force on the streets of southeast Queens who should have prevented his shooting.

187 *Brooklyn stick-up kids*: The People of the State of New York v. Darryl Baum.

187 *Baum, however, was even ballsier than his peers*: According to Jimmy "Henchmen" Rosemond, who knew Baum from the streets of Brooklyn, Baum was a kleptomaniac addicted to chain-snatching and pickpocketing.

187 *On June 10, 2000*: United States of America v. Damion Hardy, also known as "World."

187 *50 would later cheer*: Interview with associate of Darryl Baum, fall of 2004.

188 *In the end*: Spencer Cobb-Adams, "Tyson Crushes Savarese in 38 Seconds," *The Boxing Times*, June 24, 2000.

188 *He had over $300,000*: Interview with Chris Lorenzo.

189 *Then, just before taking*: Ethan Brown, "Hip-Hop Beef: Is It Going Too Far," *New York* magazine, December 1, 2003.

189 *He didn't want to respond*: Interview with Chris Lorenzo.

189 *Former Curtis Scoon associate*: Interview with Derek Yancey, fall of 2004.

190 *After Karl "Little D" Jordan Jr.*: Michelle McPhee, "A New Twist in Jay Slay," The New York *Daily News*, August 20, 2003.

191 *In addition to testifying*: The People of the State of New York v. Darnell Smith.

191 *Unfortunately for 50*: Interview with source close to G-Unit, fall of 2003.

192 *Workers at the hotel*: Interview with former Jersey City Police spokesperson Edgar Martinez, fall of 2003.

193 *One of the most powerful*: Interview with Chris Lorenzo.

193 *At the urging of*: Ethan Brown, "Hip-Hop Beef: Is It Going Too Far," *New York* magazine, December 1, 2003.

194 *The fall of 2003*: Ethan Brown, "Hip-Hop Beef: Is It Going Too Far," *New York* magazine, December 1, 2003.

194 *The pressure on the Lorenzo brothers*: Lola Ogunnaike, "Record Label Drops Murder, Keeps Inc.," *The New York Times*, December 4, 2003.

195 *The Lorenzos' misguided optimism*: Interview with Chris Lorenzo.

195 *Supreme paid his debt*: Nolan Strong, "Lyor Cohen Speaks on Gotti, Feds, JMJ," allhiphop.com, March 22, 2003.

195 *I can see*: Interview with Irv "Gotti" Lorenzo.

196   *After the forensic accountant*: Interview with Universal Music Group executive, February 2005.

196   *With the evidence*: United States of America v. Cynthia Brent, also known as "Cynthia Carr."

197   *Against a backdrop*: United States of America v. Kenneth McGriff, also known as "Supreme."

198   *As a handcuffed Irv*: Jeff Leeds, "Hip-Hop Producer Surrenders in Money Laundering Case," *The New York Times*, January 27, 2005.

199   *It's a sad story*: Nolan Strong, "Irv Gotti and Brother Chris Plead Not Guilty, 50 Cent Speaks on Situation," allhiphop.com, January 27, 2005.

11: The New Insurgency

200   *When Rosemond was indicted*: United States of America v. James J. Rosemond, aka "Jimmy Ace."

201   *At first, I would just advise*: Interview with Jimmy "Henchmen" Rosemond.

202   *I went to 50*: Interview with Jimmy "Henchmen" Rosemond.

202   *An attorney representing 50*: Statement from 50 Cent Attorney Miles M. Cooley, May 21, 2005.

202   *Creatively, he got stuck*: Michael Wilson and William K. Rashbaum, "Rapper's Potshots on the Air, and Gunshots at a Radio Studio," *The New York Times*, March 2, 2005.

203   *No arrests were made*: Michael Wilson and William K. Rashbaum, "Rapper's Potshots on the Air, and Gunshots at a Radio Studio," *The New York Times*, March 2, 2005.

203   *I think Jay-Z*: Amanda Diva, "50 Cent: Unforgivable Gangsta," allhiphop.com, March 2005.

204   *Game looked sad*: Jon Caramanica, "The Sound of the City," *The Village Voice*, June 13, 2005.

204   *I always use*: MTV News, "Game Calls Attacks on 50, G-Unit Self-Defense: 'I Feel Like It's Five Against One,' " June 22, 2005.

204   *So Game headed*: Game, "300 Bars and Runnin'," *You Know What It Is Vol. 3* (mixtape).

204   *We are gratified*: Statement from Czar Entertainment, July 21, 2005.

205   *In the spring of 2005*: Greg Sargent, "King Tut's Back: Will Tupac Trial Resurrection Follow?" *New York* magazine, January 10–17, 2005.

205   *This theory was seemingly confirmed*: Johnnie L. Roberts, "Hip-Hop Probe: The U.S. Attorney Has Launched a Quiet Probe into the Hip-Hop Business," *Newsweek*, March 4, 2005.

205   *In a letter*: Letter from Walter "Tut" Johnson dated May 22, 2005.

206   *Though the Quad shooting*: Michelle Caruso, "Informant Said 'Suge' Knight Had Rapper Killed," Knight-Ridder, June 24, 2005.

206   *Just after the Summer Jam*: Interview with Jimmy "Henchmen" Rosemond.

206   *During the late spring*: Anthony M. DeStefano, "Rap's 'Gotti' to Request Separate Trial," *Newsday*, March 19, 2005.

207   *Indeed, far from being harmed*: Anthony M. DeStefano, "Rap's 'Gotti' to Request Separate Trial," *Newsday*, March 19, 2005.

207   *To the surprise*: Interview with spokesperson for the U.S. Attorney for the Eastern District of New York, July 2005.

209   *Jay's death is also difficult*: New York State Probate Court documents.

209   *Unsurprisingly, many of his friends*: Contact Music News, "Reverend Run: Jam Master Jay Visited Me After His Death," contactmusic.com, July 29, 2005.

210   *People used to hear*: Interview with Irv "Gotti" Lorenzo.

210   *In the spring of 2005*: "Florida Attorney General Crist Announces Arrest of Six in Multimillion-dollar Interstate Auto-theft Ring," *Fed News*, March 24, 2005.

211   *Fat Cat will have a long*: Bureau of Prisons records, www.bop.gov.

211   *My name is Lorenzo Nichols*: Message from Lorenzo Nichols, June 2005.

Epilogue

213   *It's an early summer day*: Interviews with Jeff Fludd, Rodney "Boe Skagz" Jones, Harold "Lovey" Lawson, May 15, 2005.

215   *Boe had to go through Randy*: Nolan Strong, "Connie Mizell-Perry: Open, Honest, Part 1–2," allhiphop.com feature.

216   *Randy came and told Boe*: Nolan Strong, "Connie Mizell-Perry: Open, Honest, Part 1–2," allhiphop.com feature.

218   *Stay right here*: Interview with Chris Lorenzo.

218   *There is residual anger*: Interview with Inc. employees, spring of 2005; Russell Simmons appearance on *Hannity and Colmes*, February 3, 2003.

219   *This is the element*: Interview with Chris Lorenzo.

219   *It's a familiar charge*: Connie Bruck, "The Takedown of Tupac," *The New Yorker*, July 7, 1997.

219   *The feds allege*: United States of America v. Kenneth McGriff.

220   *I'm not standing up*: Interview with Russell Simmons.

ACKNOWLEDGMENTS

THANKS TO: my wife Kristen, my parents Susan and Stanley Brown, and my brother Josh for their support and tolerance; all of my friends, Joe, Josh, Dave, Derek, Adam, Kate, Kira, Andy, Jason L., Jon B., BMG, Juan Carlos, Seth, and Ana for their friendship and sense of humor; Jud Laghi at ICM for taking on this project and believing in me during a very dark time in my life; Andrew Miller at Random House for being the first to step up to the plate; Shane "Qasim" Fells and all of my contacts on the streets of southeast Queens and in the federal and state prison systems, too numerous to mention here, for their honesty, openness, and trust; the family of Lorenzo Nichols (particularly Raheem Tyler) for their trust, cooperation, and permission to use family photos; my law enforcement contacts, particularly Bridget Brennan and Mike McGuinness, for their expertise and insight; Sean Kennedy for his reporting and research assistance; Grouchy Greg at allhiphop.com for the conversation, insight, and his willingness to share contacts; Robert Levine for his friendship and longtime guidance; Michael Mayer and Juelz Santana for the incredible music; Logan Hill and Boris Kachka for their friendship and encouragement; and a special thank-you to the clerks at the U.S. District Court in Brooklyn for their assistance in locating case files.

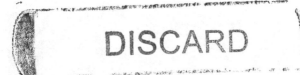